An
Industrialist
in the
Treasury

An
Industrialist
in the
Treasury
The Post-War Years

Edwin Plowden

ANDRE DEUTSCH

First published 1989 by
André Deutsch Limited
105–106 Great Russell Street
London WC1B 3LJ

British Library Cataloguing in Publication Data

Plowden, Edwin
  An industrialist in the treasury: the post-war years
  1. Great Britain. Economic policies, 1945–1953
  I. Title
  330.941′0854

ISBN 0 233 98364 3

Printed in Great Britain by
WBC Print Bristol & Maesteg

Contents

Foreword

The book can be best described as 'a fragment of autobiography'. That is a title last used, to the best of my belief, by Arthur James Balfour, but it is no worse for that. Edwin Plowden's book is certainly not a full autobiography, mainly because it covers only six years of his life, but also because it eschews for himself the permanent centre-stage role which is the essence of the *genre*.

Nor, fortunately for its readability, which in my view is great, is it merely an objective and analytical account of the issues with which H.M. Treasury had to deal during the latter years of the Attlee government and the first years of the second Churchill administration. Lord Plowden, as it happens, is a master of analysis and judgement. But to this book he does not merely bring these qualities, which he has demonstrated in many a government report. He also brings an acute and quizzical personal observation to the time when Britain, governed by the Butskellite consensus, was key to the creation of the institutions of the Western world.

For these events Lord Plowden's position, while not spotlighted in the centre of the stage, was more involved than that of an occupant of even the most over-hanging box. It was more like a trusted second in a boxing ring. All three of his Chancellors, Cripps, Gaitskell and Butler, were substantially dependent upon him and his relationship with each of them was based on an affection which, while it was impartial, was in no way impersonal.

From this vantage point he has been able to give us pen portraits, etched with an unusual combination of precision and sympathy, of all three (and of a number of other participants as well). The picture of Cripps as an essentially rather convivial man, whose contrary habits were forced on him only by a combination of a bad digestion and of a belief in the salvation of the economy through the excessive work of the Chancellor, is particularly enjoyable.

There are also some special insights to the changing habits of British governments. In 1949 the whole Cabinet considered the issue of devaluation and took a decision of principle in favour on 29th July. It was not implemented until 18th September. There were no leaks in the interval. It would in my view be quite impossible twenty or thirty or nearly forty years later to imagine such a secret being shared with such a large number of people and yet preserved over such a large number of weeks.

Again, and along the same lines, we have the story of the great 'Robot' dispute of 1952. Butler, in his first six months as Chancellor, had been persuaded by a combination of the Bank of England and a peculiarly dynamic Treasury official (R. W. B. Clarke) that the only escape from Britain's balance of payments constraints lay in floating the exchange rate and making the pound nominally convertible although blocking all the then very large sterling balances. He had the support of the Prime Minister and of most of the informed members of the Cabinet for this course.

It was violently opposed by Lord Cherwell (the 'extra lobe' of Churchill's brain) who was then Paymaster-General and in the Cabinet, by Butler's Minister of State at the Treasury (Sir Arthur Salter) and by the Whitehall 'irregulars', Plowden himself, Robert Hall (the Chief Economic Adviser) and Lionel Robbins. A lot of things were remarkable about this struggle. First, it engaged passions and not just intellects. The opponents, in particular, rapidly worked up an almost tribal internal loyalty. Second, these *francs-tireurs* won. They stopped the Chancellor and the Bank and what had looked like a majority of the Cabinet dead in their tracks.

Third, Edwin Plowden managed successfully to oppose his Chancellor without seriously impairing relations with him. Butler was still anxious for him to stay on for another eighteen months. Furthermore, his opposition had been not merely intellectual but highly operative. The shift of position which most scuppered Butler was that of Anthony Eden. Plowden was with Eden in Lisbon – as one of the three 'Wise

Men' of NATO who were presenting their report to the NATO Council of Ministers – when this shift occurred. It was a notable example of his ability to take strong positions without arousing rancour.

Fourth, it once again illustrates the incredibly high standards of secrecy which were observed in British government in those days compared with anything which we have since seen under Lord Wilson or Mr Heath or Mrs Thatcher. At the time of the Robot argument Hugh Gaitskell, only six months out of the Treasury himself, was shadow Chancellor and I was one of his two or three closest parliamentary collaborators. I knew nothing about Robot, and I believe that he knew very little. It was like living next door to the Borgias and being surprised subsequently to discover that the diet there was not exclusively made up of health foods. Today such a dispute would reverberate from Whitehall to Threadneedle Street to Wapping and back to Westminster within a few days.

What has been the particular quality of Edwin Plowden which made him so sought after by three very different and considerable Chancellors and, at the same time, so well-regarded by the Treasury officials alongside whom he worked, but compared with whom he was paid much more, given a rank much more than commensurate with his age (then barely 40) and whose advice he sometimes controverted? This latter point is important, for in theory I suppose he could have acquired his cancellarian popularity by being a sort of teacher's pet or trusty familiar of the Chancellor who could speak to him in a more relaxed manner than more hierarchical officials. Lord Plowden tells us that he did perform something of this function, although as the Treasury in my experience was, within the confines of its own eliteness, an irreverent and even equal society, it was less necessary than in many other departments.

But there was a great deal more to his role than this. When I became a minister for the first time in 1964 one of the first things that I did was to get Edwin Plowden to chair a small but major inquiry into the future of the aircraft industry. At the end of my second period as Home Secretary, twelve years later, one of my last acts as a minister was to get him to undertake the chairmanship of the newly established Police Complaints Board. Apart from the fact that he was the natural chairman in both cases, the tasks could hardly have been more disparate.

Why did I want him to perform two such different roles? In the first

case my primary interest was that he should shine a searchlight of sceptical judgement upon a somewhat cushioned industry. In the second
case as well I wanted his judgement, but I also wanted the authority of
his reputation and experience to launch a necessary but controversial
scheme. This retrospective analysis of motives brings one close to an
appreciation of Edwin Plowden's peculiar qualities, although to the two
that I have stressed there have to be added a devotion to public duty and
a faith that rational discussion *could* solve nearly all problems – but not
an equal faith that it *will*, owing to the inherent irrationality of others,
politicians certainly included, but not exclusively so.

These qualities of mind and outlook made a strong appeal to his
three Chancellors, as they subsequently did to me, although they are
perhaps less fashionable today. This is despite the fact that Edwin
Plowden liked to stress that he was a businessman in Whitehall. There
was an element of throw-away conceit about this, rather in the way that
Ralph Partridge, although perfectly at home in the bosom of
Bloomsbury, would have described himself as a farmer, or that Joseph
Alsop, when writing the most successful column in Washington, always
referred to himself in print as 'this reporter'. But there was also truth:
Plowden had worked most of the pre-war decade for C. Tennant Sons
and Co., in the slightly improbable role of selling Dead Sea potash all
over Europe at undercutting prices in order to secure an invitation to
join the cartel which they were undercutting. I do not think that he had
anything to do with MI6, but it sounds an almost perfect cover.

Then he had six wartime Whitehall years and twelve months back
with Tennant's before his six years as Chief Planner which were
followed by another six as chairman of the Atomic Energy Authority. In
1960 he started his major private-sector spell, of which thirteen years
were spent as chairman (and after that as president) of the engineering
conglomerate Tube Investments. During this period he ranked as one
of the seven or eight most princely of the captains of British industry.

But he was never my idea of a British – or even an American –
businessman in public life, bringing the urgent but limited perspectives
of the boardroom to government. It is as impossible to imagine him
paraphrasing Secretary of Defense Charles E. Wilson of General
Motors and saying 'what is good for Tube Investments is good for Britain'.

What Edwin Plowden is more like is a great French administrator, a product in the old days of one or other of the *Grandes Ecoles*, more recently almost inevitably of the Ecole Nationale d'Administration, who can turn his hand with versatility but without amateurism from the private to the public sector, from high policy to the profit-and-loss account. The greatest of them of this century was Jean Monnet, whose pre-1939 career was not entirely unlike Plowden's. Monnet, however, had an *idée fixe*, which is not something to which Plowden either could or would wish to lay claim, and as a result played a major part in casting half a continent in a new mould. So the comparison does not wholly run. Robert Marjolin or even André Giraud, former Defence Minister, are other French figures who come to mind.

Yet when Edwin Plowden found himself in the autumn of 1951, at the age of 44 and partly by accident, with Monnet and Averell Harriman, as one of the three 'Wise Men' of the Western world who were to soothe away the strains of rearmament by the fairness of the burden-sharing, there was no bathos about his participation even if there was not complete success in the enterprise. Lord Plowden was a major figure at what Dean Acheson half self-mockingly called 'the creation', and his book matches the importance and insight of his contribution to it.

ROY JENKINS

Acknowledgements

The origin of this book lies in the pressure from my children over the years to write something about my time in the Treasury from 1947 to 1953. It could not have been written without the help of the Economic and Social Research Council and of the Royal Institute of Public Administration. The RIPA applied for (and subsequently administered) the grant made by the ESRC which allowed Russell Jones to work with me from October 1984 to August 1986. He has done nearly all the research and much of the drafting. He has moreover performed the much more difficult task of helping me to remember why we did certain things and what were our perceptions of the economic and political issues of the time. I have retained few papers and unlike some of my contemporaries have never kept a diary. The book therefore is in effect a joint effort, although the views expressed and the reasons given for the actions taken in those fateful years are entirely my responsibility.

His immense industry, skill and patience in researching at the Public Record Office and elsewhere has given him a knowledge of the period and of the people which often deluded me into believing that he had lived through the period. In fact he was not born until some time after. It has been a real pleasure to work with him.

I am greatly indebted to many people who gave us so much of their time to read our early drafts, who agreed to see us and discuss the past or who wrote to us. They include Sir Alec Cairncross, Lord Croham, Lord Franks, Dr Lincoln Gordon, Lord Home, Sir Donald Mac-Dougall, Dr Richard Mayne, Lord Roberthall, Sir Austin Robinson, Lord Roll, Lord Sherfield, the late Earl of Stockton, the late Lord

Trend, Sir Tobias Weaver and Lord Zuckerman.

Besides the ESRC and the RIPA, we thank the Public Record Office, the United States National Archives, the British Library of Political and Economic Science, the Treasury, the Cabinet Office and the universities of Oxford, Cambridge and Bristol.

We are especially grateful to my son William, without whose support, enthusiasm and determination the project would neither have started nor been completed.

We owe a special debt to Roy Jenkins for writing such an understanding and generous foreword. His comparisons of the changing habits of British governments written with his experience of holding the offices of Chancellor of the Exchequer and Home Secretary are particularly valuable.

Finally, I would like to express our special thanks to Ann King, who deciphered our handwriting and typed the whole book in many drafts, and to my wife who had to put up with my grumbling about having undertaken in my old age a task of a kind I had never done before.

INTRODUCTION

Returning to Whitehall

The newspaper headlines of 27th March 1947 read: 'SIR EDWIN PLOWDEN TO BE CHIEF PLANNER.'

If I had had time for reflection I might have thought how strange it was that someone who ten years before had been working in a junior capacity in the private sector should in peacetime have become a senior civil servant working for a Labour government. I had never contemplated working in Whitehall. As it turned out, including the war years, I was to spend nearly twenty years there working full-time until 1960. From then to the present day I have been chairman of four government committees of inquiry and deputy chairman of another, as well as chairman of four governmental standing committees.

Chance inevitably plays a great part in influencing everyone's life. I came down from Cambridge in 1929. I had been offered and accepted a job with an international company which wished me to start at the end of the summer. When I duly appeared, they said the international business situation looked so menacing that they were taking on no new staff. I was then forced to spend the best part of a year looking for another job.

As the slump following the Wall Street Crash gathered strength, companies were not taking on people but sacking them by the hundred. It was the period of my life most filled with frustration, depression and disillusionment. Prospective employers would not see one, did not answer letters and sometimes if they did see one, said come back in one, two or three years' time. Inevitably, depression and then despair took hold and it was easy to become convinced that one's own failings were to blame. The fact that people could see no reason to interview one was the worst aspect. Since that time whenever people have approached me about a job I have always tried to see them or at least get someone else to do so.

Eventually, I got a job with the International Standard Electric Corporation, a subsidiary of the American multinational company IT & T. After a short time they started sacking people. Perhaps because I was cheap – £3 per week – I was given the choice of being made redundant or joining Standard Telephone & Cables, their main manufacturing company in England. Of course I accepted. After some time on the shop floor, I was sent out to sell internal telephone equipment, making several unsolicited calls a day on companies building or modernising factories.

One day, while working at Standard Telephones, a Cambridge friend of mine asked me to join him after work for a swim at the Chelsea Baths and to have supper afterwards. There were two others present: one was a young man called Denis Wrangham who was then working for the city merchant firm, C. Tennant Sons & Co., dealing in commodities, metals and chemicals. He asked me if I liked my job. When I said 'no' he told me that in about two years' time his firm would have a vacancy for someone like me, who knew the Continent and could speak French and German, a result from having been to school in Switzerland and having spent a short time at Hamburg University. Whether having worked for a year as a farm labourer and for several months as a general handyman at one of the hospitals of the Grenfell Medical Mission in Labrador was an advantage or not I do not know. He asked if I would like to meet his chairman, Lord Glenconner. When I met him he confirmed that they would have a job for me in two years' time. I suggested that I would be much more useful in two years' time if I joined them at once. He agreed and a few months later I joined Tennant's.

After a time, because the manager of my department was ill, I was put in charge of the sales of potash fertilizer from the Dead Sea. There existed at that time a potash cartel in Europe whose contracts with buyers stated that if reasonable quantities of potash were offered by reputable sellers at lower prices than those of the cartel, it would meet the competition. The objective of Palestine Potash, for whom my company acted as sales agent, was to join the cartel. The output of the cartel was many hundreds of thousands of tons, while that of Palestine Potash was 10,000 tons a year. I used to travel all over Europe offering quantities of potash to large buyers at prices lower than the cartel price, thereby causing the cartel losses, but what was undoubtedly more important, disturbance to their customer relations. Eventually the policy succeeded and we were invited to join the cartel.

At the time of Munich it was clear to me that there was going to be a war. I asked one of my brothers, once a regular soldier and at the time in one of the intelligence organisations, how to go about joining the Territorials. He suggested I should first see Desmond Morton, who was making plans for a Ministry of Economic Warfare. Desmond Morton, who in the war was to become personal assistant to Churchill, said the war, when it came, would be won by blockade. If I liked, I could have some initial training now and join the Ministry of Economic Warfare (MEW) on the outbreak of war. The training was a few hours a week at the Industrial Intelligence Centre at 70 Victoria Street learning how details of enemy exports and imports were to be collected and compiled. I accepted, and on the outbreak of the war reported for work at London School of Economics. I was assigned to enemy export intelligence under Lord Justice du Parcq.

After Dunkirk it became obvious that the war was not going to be won by blockade. I felt I was wasting my time at MEW. I asked to join the army but was told they had no use for elderly subalterns – I was 33 – they had plenty of young ones. I did not know what to do. Denis Wrangham, who had also left Tennant's for a wartime post in the civil service, was at this time in that part of the Air Ministry out of which Lord Beaverbrook was forming the Ministry of Aircraft Production (MAP). I asked him if there were any vacancies – there were. I applied and was taken on in a finance branch then based in Harrogate. I went to Harrogate where I stayed three weeks and was then told to come to London because there was a man called Hennessy, recruited by Beaverbrook from the Ford Motor Co., who was spending money like water. I arrived in London with instructions to see that Hennessy did not spend money without the proper financial authority. On three successive days I called to see him and each day I was told he was too busy to see me. On the fourth day, he sent a message saying he did not need any bloody civil servant to tell him how to spend money; he knew how to do that on his own. On the afternoon of the sixth day, Saturday, he sent for me. He had with him the aluminium controller, Geoffrey

Cunliffe, whose control was about to be transferred from the Ministry of Supply to MAP. Hennessy said to me: 'You say you know how to get money. Here is Cunliffe who has been trying for the best part of a month to get authority to spend £100,000 to buy all the aluminium pots and pans in the shops to be melted down and turned into aircraft. What can you do?'

I returned to my room and rang up the Treasury. It being Saturday afternoon, they had all gone home. The man I wanted to speak to was Bernard Gilbert, an established civil servant who subsequently became the senior Second Secretary in the Treasury and succeeded me as Chairman of the Economic Planning Board. When I rang him at his home Mrs Gilbert said, 'He is not home yet' and then added, 'no, stop – he is just coming through the garden gate.' I spoke to him on the telephone and told him the story to which he quite reasonably asked, 'Why do you want it on Saturday afternoon?' to which I replied, somewhat untruthfully, 'Lord Beaverbrook wants it personally.' It was true that the idea originally had been Beaverbrook's, who had thought it would make people feel that they were making a personal contribution to the defence of the country. 'Oh, very well,' he said, 'you can have it.'

I returned to Hennessy and told him that we had the necessary authority. He turned to Cunliffe and said, 'You have been trying unsuccessfully for a month, but you see we can do it in twenty minutes.'

After that I got on extremely well with Hennessy. I was eventually transferred from the finance side to the supply side and over the period of the war I was put in charge of various departments, and in this way got to know Stafford Cripps when he was Minister of Aircraft Production. In 1945 he made me Chief Executive, in which post I stayed until March 1946 when MAP and the Ministry of Supply were amalgamated. Then after three months' holiday I returned to C. Tennant & Sons Co.

If I had not gone swimming that summer afternoon I would not have met Denis Wrangham. I doubt that I would ever have thought of joining MAP had I not known him. If Gilbert had caught a later train and if I had not got authority for £100,000 to spend on aluminium pots and pans, I do not think I would have been transferred from a finance division to the production or supply side where the action was. And had I not been transferred, I doubt if I could have met Stafford Cripps, in which case I certainly would not have become Chief Planner and spent so much time in Whitehall.

I have emphasised the importance of chance in my life. Chance can neither be foreseen nor planned for. There is always a tendency for people looking back at the past to wish that they or their forebears had planned and acted differently. They seem to believe, retrospectively, in freedom of choice. One of the themes of this book is that this belief is often an illusion. People forget the enormous influence that past events and experiences have on popular expectations and feelings. Our regrets about what we think we might have done or could have done are usually illusory.

Most of us tend to judge past events in the light of what we know now, not by what we knew then and that, I believe, leads to the greatest illusions.

CHAPTER ONE

The Situation in 1947

The war and its immediate aftermath were periods of great austerity. In 1945 rationing was extensive, with food, clothing, furniture, petrol and coal particularly hard hit. Taxation rates were punitive by today's standards, and luxury items were frequently deliberately priced (or rather taxed) out of the range of most consumers. Licences to produce or distribute a wide spectrum of items were required, while often the volume of production was limited by the availability of raw-material supplies. The quality of goods was strictly monitored, in some cases to keep items functional and to ensure there was no wastage of essential supplies. Perhaps the most obvious examples are provided by the utility schemes for clothes and furniture. In the mass-consumer society of today it is hard to imagine the hardships, the boredom and the inconvenience caused by these austerity measures.

Besides the obvious sacrifices and dislocations which the war brought in its wake, it also rendered Britain all but bankrupt. After an initial period in which imports had to be paid for in hard cash, the problem of the balance of payments had been eased by the Americans' 'Lend-Lease' arrangement, amounting to $27,000 million, the Canadians' gifts and loans totalling to $2,450 million, and the Commonwealth and other allied and neutral nations' acquiescence in exchange controls, stringent import limitations and the running up of more than £3,000 million of sterling balances. The problem was that while these flows allowed wartime economic planning to evolve without excessive reference to the external account, they represented massive post-war obligations. But this was not all: Britain had also sold off, or disposed of,

1

foreign investments amounting to £1,000 million. Moreover, potential invisible earnings were further depleted by the enormous losses suffered by the merchant fleet.

On the visible side of the balance of payments, although imports, which had been strictly controlled, had fallen to a little over 60 per cent of their 1938 volume by the end of the war, exports had been deliberately run down to less than one-third of their 1938 volume in order to release resources for the war effort. Britain ended the war with an enormous current account deficit amounting to 10 per cent of GNP and the biggest external debt in her history. As a victor, Britain was expected to play a leading role in the policing and rebuilding process that was necessary throughout the world. Overseas government expenditure was running at £700 million in 1943–4, and a slightly higher level in 1945. The need for garrisons in Germany and the stationing of troops in every corner of the globe to keep the peace meant that this outlay could not be run down too rapidly, nor was Britain keen to do so. We still considered ourselves to be one of the three great world powers. Britain was also obliged to make significant contributions to international organisations such as United Nations Relief and Rehabilitation Administration (UNRRA), the International Monetary Fund (IMF) and the International Bank for Reconstruction and Development (IBRD).

It had been assumed in Whitehall that after the ending of the European war, fighting in the Pacific would go on for a further two years at least, thus allowing us to rebuild our exports while continuing to receive US aid. However, the dropping of the two atomic bombs on Japan changed all this. Under US law 'Lend-Lease' had to end immediately on the cessation of hostilities and, indeed, one week after VJ Day, President Truman announced an immediate stop to 'Lend-Lease' payments. The British Government was forced to re-examine its approach to the post-war world. Unless new funds could be found to tide the country over until recovery was well under way, Britain would have to make some hard choices. These were, in short, a sudden withdrawal from our overseas responsibilities with consequent loss of prestige and power; or the prospect of austerity above and beyond anything experienced in wartime and the indefinite postponement of wartime plans for extensive social reform; or a combination of aspects of both of these options.

Britain was eventually saved, at least in the short term, by the negotiation of loans amounting to $5 billion from North America. $3.75 billion was made available by the Americans and $1.25 billion from Canada, but there were strings attached. While the monetary terms of the loans, at an interest rate of 2 per cent and a repayment period of fifty years from 1951, do not with hindsight appear onerous, the government had hoped for, and was led by Keynes to expect, a grant or, at least, an interest-free loan as compensation for our efforts on behalf of the Allied cause. After all, Britain alone had fought from the first day of the war until the last. However, the real problem with the loan centred on the additional conditions related to the basic constitution of British external economic policy. Britain was expected to adhere strictly to the multilateral principles of the Bretton Woods IMF international trade and payments system and to abandon the restrictions on the convertibility of sterling into dollars for current transactions by July 1947.

It was not made clear in the Anglo-American Loan Agreement how the sterling-dollar exchange rate would be held once sterling was convertible, unless world trade was such that the demand for dollars did not lead to a greater conversion of sterling into dollars than Britain's small gold and dollar reserves could withstand. Moreover, the demand for dollars could not be reduced by discriminating against American imports by increasing tariffs or reducing quotas. While Britain could still count on the Imperial Preference system of discriminating tariffs, neither the size of the tariffs nor the range of goods which the Dominions and Colonies could supply made this a decisive factor in Anglo-American trade. In effect, therefore, the Anglo-American Loan Agreement was workable only if the world shortage of dollars prevalent at the end of the war rapidly evaporated. This was not to be the case and, as the post-war hopes for freer trade failed to materialise, the IMF proved ineffective and the terms of trade moved sharply against manufactured goods. A near bankrupt and impoverished Britain was left bereft of financial defences in an extremely harsh and inhospitable environment in which she was also playing a major military and political role.

Unfortunately, despite these frightening facts and figures, the major part played by this country in the victory of the Allies tended to deflect attention from the underlying weaknesses of the British economy both at home and abroad. Initially, few were willing to accept the fact that Britain was much closer to our European neighbours than our North

American allies, both in terms of economic strength and international influence.

In the 1945 general election, Labour came to power with a massive overall majority of 146 seats in a Parliament of 640. Despite Britain's immense problems, Labour were determined to maintain Britain as a world power. They added to these problems when they committed themselves to honouring the objectives of both the 1944 White Paper on *Employment Policy* and the Beveridge Report on the Social Services. All this was to be realised by a rather nebulous economic policy which they referred to as 'democratic planning'. It can best be described as a mixture of physical controls, nationalisation and exhortation, laced with a dash of Keynesianism and a liberal dose of wishful thinking.

This is not to deny that initially the government's plans appeared to be working satisfactorily. In 1946 the British economy boomed: by the end of the year the volume of exports was, with the help of a seller's market, already 111 per cent of the 1938 level, while imports had been kept to around the wartime level thanks to the government's strict restrictions and the difficulties involved in obtaining most of what was needed. At the same time, despite the rapid pace of demobilisation, unemployment remained negligible by pre-war standards and production soared. This success led to optimism, not to say self-satisfaction, on the part of ministers. In October of that year the Chancellor of the Exchequer, Hugh Dalton, was content to say:

> I have been able, as Chancellor, to meet all the demands on the public purse literally with a song in my heart. If we keep going together as we have since VJ day, the shortages and frustrations which still afflict us will disappear like the snows of winter, and give place to the full promise of springtime.[1]

Unfortunately, however, this recovery was built on shaky foundations. Too many of Britain's exports were going to 'soft' and inconvertible currency areas, while we were increasingly being forced to buy food and raw materials from the United States as the world's main supplier and at prices that rose sharply as controls were removed and almost every war-damaged country queued up to buy. Imports into Britain from the Western Hemisphere rose from 30 per cent of the total before the war to 45 per cent in 1946. On the other hand, exports to the Western Hemisphere fell from 17 per cent of the total before the war to 13.5

per cent in 1946. In short, Britain was running up a massive and increasing deficit with hard currency areas. As a result, the dollar drain on the reserves accelerated from a monthly average of $65 million in the first nine months of 1946 to a monthly average of $135 million in the last quarter. $600 million of the $3.75 billion lent by the United States was used up in the first five and a half months it was available.

During the dreadful winter of 1947, to make matters worse, what has been described by one commentator as 'a striking example of incompetence in industrial planning by a government dedicated to economic planning'[2] resulted in a serious fuel shortage, with disastrous consequences for industry and exports. As coal stocks declined in late 1946, the Ministry of Fuel and Power, under the guidance of Emmanuel Shinwell, was slow to grasp the real extent of the problem, and when it did its reaction was to build up stocks at the power stations rather than to supply industry. In fact the margin of shortfall in coal output and distribution was not great, and timely cuts in consumption and a more urgent recruitment policy for miners might have stopped industry grinding to halt in many areas. As it turned out, substantial exports to the dollar area were lost and unemployment temporarily rose to some 2.5 million at the end of February.

In March 1947 the outflow of dollars escalated to over $300 million, while in the meantime the terms of trade continued to deteriorate. Between 1946 and 1947 they worsened by 7 per cent. In the second quarter the picture degenerated still further and by the end of June $1,890 million had been lost in six months – more than half of the US loan. As this crisis took shape there was a marked drift in economic policy. Although the economists in the Economic Section of the Cabinet Office had been warning ministers for some time that the economy was overstretched, the Cabinet, given little lead by the Chancellor, found it hard to agree on any specific deflationary action. They appeared largely oblivious of the link between the domestic pressure of demand and the external account and were anxious neither to destroy incentives nor to check recovery. Moreover, the Foreign Secretary, Bevin, and the Minister of Defence, Alexander, who feared a return to American isolationism, strongly resisted cuts in military commitments overseas and a more rapid timetable for demobilisation. Ministers contented themselves with efforts to 'talk-up' production and a general agreement not to make the imbalance in the economy worse. In Dalton's words, they were convinced that the 'risk of inflation now is less than the risk of deflation later'.[3]

As spring turned into summer and criticism of the government mounted in the press, there was still little coherent thought at ministerial level on how to deal directly with the escalating dollar crisis. The Prime Minister, Attlee, was preoccupied with India and Palestine and gave no lead. Bevin was also distracted by foreign affairs, while the Lord President, Herbert Morrison, was laid low by a thrombosis for much of the first half of the year. When he did return to work at the end of May he soon became embroiled in the debate over steel nationalisation. For all the statements which Stafford Cripps made as President of the Board of Trade on the need for more efficient planning, Dalton was eventually the only minister truly to grasp the seriousness of the immediate situation and to offer positive advice. However, even he seemed to accept the crisis with a growing sense of reservation and impotence.[4]

In May, on the advice of the Treasury, which had by this time come to the conclusion that their previous current account deficit and dollar drain estimates were far too low, Dalton sought cuts in the hard currency import programme of £200 million, of which £150 million were to be in food imports.[5] He was, however, given little or no support by his colleagues who were frightened by the uproar such measures would create in the Parliamentary Labour Party and amongst the public, and he saw the food cuts whittled away in Cabinet to a mere £50 million.

At the official level, while the Overseas Finance Division of the Treasury had managed to form a fairly clear picture of the factors at work on the balance of payments, their ability to keep up with the development of events was hampered by a lack of relevant and up-to-date statistics: the Statistics Section of the Treasury Overseas Finance Division was not set up until later in the year. At the same time, Sir Wilfred Eady, the man in charge of this part of the Treasury, appeared rather out of his depth in such matters. For its part, the Bank of England gave advice to the Chancellor which, even allowing for hindsight, appears over-optimistic and unrealistic.

It was at last clear that in most of the Western world there was a dollar problem – one that was to be our most serious problem for the next five years.

This was the scene at the time I returned to Whitehall.

CHAPTER TWO

The Setting Up
of the CEPS and the
Economic Planning Board

It would be wrong to assume that there was no machinery in Whitehall for executing plans for converting the economy from a war footing to that of peace. The trouble was that such machinery as did exist was co-ordinated ineffectually and was incapable of meeting the necessities of Britain's desperate plight.

The idea that a 'central planning staff' was needed to organise Labour's positive control of the economy had been bandied about in Whitehall since the end of the war. Stafford Cripps, President of the Board of Trade, had also made reference to the requirement for such a body in the introduction he drafted for the first published *Economic Survey* released in February 1947. In early March, after a discussion and exchange of notes with Max Nicholson, the head of Herbert Morrison's office[1], the Permanent Secretary to the Treasury, Edward Bridges, minuted the Prime Minister on the need for the appointment of a full-time Chief Planning Officer in the Cabinet Office, together with departmental planning officers under his direction in six of the main departments. He also suggested that each of these departmental planning officers should have a staff of his own, and that there should be a small hand-picked staff in the Cabinet Office under the Chief Planning Officer which would report to ministers through the official Steering Committee on Economic Development[2]. Attlee accepted Bridges' proposals, and an announcement to this effect was made in Parliament on 18th March.

Soon after the announcement, I was asked by John Henry Woods, the Permanent Secretary to the Board of Trade, whether I would be interested in heading the new planning staff as 'Chief Planner'. I told him I was reluctant to leave the private sector and return so soon to Whitehall and declined the offer. But when soon after he made a second approach, I agreed to take on the job for a year on certain conditions, of which I remember the following: (a) that I should suffer no drop in salary, (b) that I should have the use of a car and driver, (c) that I should have a really good private secretary who could turn my uneducated thoughts into limpid prose, (d) that George Turner, then a Second Secretary in the Ministry of Supply, should be my deputy and, finally, (e) that a statement should be made reducing to reasonable proportions the exaggerated expectations that had been built up in Parliament and the press about the importance and, in particular, the powers of the job. These conditions were accepted, except for (d) and a not very satisfactory interpretation of (e).

My appointment was made public on 27th March 1947 at the same time as the intention to form a tripartite Economic Planning Board was announced. My salary of £6,500 per annum was almost twice that earned by Edward Bridges and caused considerable consternation amongst the press and Labour Backbenchers. Because of a bout of flu which developed into jaundice, it was not until the beginning of May that I started work. In fact when I found that I could not start work for several weeks all my doubts about the wisdom of taking the job returned. I wrote to Edward Bridges and suggested that they should find someone else. He came down to our house in Essex and with his usual charm told me not to be silly and persuaded me that I should come to London and start work as soon as I was well enough.

Stafford Cripps subsequently told me that when he put forward my name his colleagues thought I was too young. I was 40. He said that Rab Sinclair, who had been Chief Executive of the Ministry of Production in the war, was asked first but refused on the grounds that he had just become Chairman of the Imperial Tobacco Company. The next to be considered was Ronald Weeks, a businessman who had been Vice-Chief of the Imperial General Staff during the war, but he had just become chairman-designate of Vickers and was not available either.

Initially, Rab Sinclair came two days a week for a period of three months as my industrial consultant. His standing in Whitehall and in industry gave me enormous moral support in tackling a job which was regarded with some scepticism in Whitehall and by both sides of industry, but which the press had built up to greatly exaggerated importance and power. Rab Sinclair was a charming and most helpful person. When I became Chief Executive of the Ministry of Aircraft Production in 1945 he sent me a long hand-written letter telling me of some of the problems and difficulties I should face as Chief Executive of a major wartime production department. He also gave me much useful advice on how to deal with those problems and, what was even more important, an offer of help whenever I needed it – an offer of which I readily availed myself.

My wartime experience in Whitehall convinced me that the planning staff must be small. Also that it should see its job as quite distinct from that of other departments, who were there to carry out policies in areas for which they were responsible, while our task was to advise and to co-ordinate. The most successful members of the staff were those who understood this distinction and acted on it. Some found it hard to grasp that they were not supposed to be executives; they were consequently often frustrated and less effective than their colleagues.

Edward Bridges, who had advised ministers to set up the planning staff, gave us his full support. A major contribution was his choice of people best able to pursue this policy. We were fortunate that most of those who first joined understood this.

The Central Economic Planning Staff or the CEPS, as the group became known, was manned by people seconded to it from various departments for periods of about two years. Although it never grew at any one time to much over forty people, the number who served in it during the six and a half years I was there was many more than this. A large number who worked in the CEPS went on to senior jobs in Whitehall and no less than six became Permanent Secretaries.

Hugh Weeks, who had been head of the Programmes and Planning Division of the Ministry of Production for the last few years of the war, came to us from industry, to which he returned after a year.

Douglas Allen, later Lord Croham, a Principal in the Board of Trade, was seconded as my Private Secretary. At a time when no one knew quite what we were expected to do, when we were deluged with paper on all sorts of subjects which could not possibly concern us, he remained calm and wise, and showed outstanding common sense together with a capacity for working infinitely long hours. His advice and support were crucial in preventing mistakes and in initiating such success as we did have.

He remained with the CEPS until the middle of 1953, two years as my Private Secretary and then as a member of the staff. I am, and shall always be, deeply grateful to him. His subsequent career, which led him to be Permanent Secretary of the Treasury and Head of the Civil Service followed by distinguished posts in the City and industry, is public knowledge.

In June 1947 Austin Robinson joined us from Cambridge. He had been a close friend and colleague of Maynard Keynes. During the war he had served in the Economic Section of the War Cabinet Office and then as Economic Adviser and head of the Programmes Division at the Ministry of Production. For an academic economist he held refreshingly practical views and kept his feet on the ground at all times.

He took a leading part in the preparation of the UK four-year plan for the European Recovery Programme and was of enormous help in setting up the CEPS during the eighteen months he stayed with us. To my great regret he decided to return to academic life at the end of 1948. He told me he liked living as a don but working as a civil servant. When Sir Denis Robertson, Professor of Economics at Cambridge, told him that he must choose one career or the other he decided to return to academic life. He was a great loss.

Austin Robinson brought with him Kenneth Berrill, Patricia Brown and Robin Marris. Kenneth Berrill, after a distinguished academic career, became head of the Government Economic Service in the years 1972–4 and then head of the Central Policy Review Staff in the Cabinet Office. Later he entered the City and became the first chairman of the Securities and Investment Board. Patricia Brown went on to join the Treasury where she remained. Robin Marris returned to pursue an equally distinguished academic life in England and the United States. Their contributions were indispensable in the early days of the CEPS.

Alan Hitchman and Bill Strath also joined the CEPS in 1947. Alan Hitchman, who had been Ernest Bevin's Private Secretary during the war, became my deputy in 1948. His wide knowledge of the Civil Service and its workings combined with his great common sense made him a most formidable operator. It was he as much as anybody else who fitted the CEPS into the co-ordinating role the economic policy-making machinery had lacked since the war. He left us in 1949 to become a Third Secretary in the Treasury but continued to work closely with the CEPS. In 1951 he became Permanent Secretary of the Ministry of Materials, in 1952 Permanent Secretary of the Ministry of Agriculture, and in 1964 deputy chairman of the Atomic Energy Authority. He was a great friend and I owe him much.

Bill Strath succeeded Alan Hitchman as my deputy in 1949. He stayed until 1955. He then became successively Permanent Secretary of the Ministry of Supply and the Ministry of Aviation. Later he went on to join me at the Atomic Energy Authority, and then at Tube Investments. All in all we worked together for the best part of over thirty years. He had a penetrating, analytical mind which quickly cut to the heart of any problem. His advice was always sound and fearless. He was perhaps the first to see the potential advantages to this country of association with the European Coal and Steel Community. During his time with the CEPS he worked more closely and continuously than anyone with the economists in Economic Section. His contribution to the harmonious and constructive co-operation of the CEPS, Economic Section and the relevant branches of the Treasury was a major influence in the evolution of a coherent economic policy.

I mention these colleagues by name because, although some stayed only a relatively short time, they set the pattern on which we were to work for the next six years.

The departmental planning staffs which Cripps had talked of in his initial announcement to the House of Commons never, in fact, came into existence. A number of planning liaison officers attached to the CEPS were initially installed in the Trade, Fuel and Power, and Food ministries but, as it turned out, our contacts with them were minimal and their exact role remained obscure. The posts were soon abolished.

The Economic Planning Board (EPB) of which I was to be chairman was not appointed until July. There were divisions among officials as to how many representatives of the unions and employers should attend, and what relationship the Board should have with the other quasi-corporate bodies advising the government on economic policy at the time: the National Joint Advisory Council (NJAC) and the National Production Advisory Council on Industry (NPACI). Edward Bridges wanted a consistency of membership among the three bodies, while others wanted to knock the three bodies into one Economic Planning Board and extend its terms of reference. In the end, all three bodies remained in existence and their memberships often overlapped. The

NJAC dealt with labour questions, the NPACI with production problems and the new EPB with planning.

The EPB's terms of reference were to provide the government with advice on the framing of remedial measures to solve our immediate economic problems and to assist in the preparation of a long-term plan for the economy. The EPB was also seen as a means by which government policy could be better communicated and explained to industry and to the public. A small Economic Information Unit was set up in the Treasury to assist in this latter task, and in particular to help to stimulate production. It was headed by Clem Leslie, who had been Director of Public Relations at the Ministry of Supply and the Home Office during the war.[3]

At first the TUC were not at all eager to be represented on the EPB. They feared it might limit their freedom of expression and handicap them in making direct approaches to ministers. Eventually, however, they were convinced of the EPB's potential value and their misgivings were allayed. Three trade union members sat on the Board, together with a similar number of employers, three Permanent Secretaries, the Director of the Economic Section, and several representatives of the CEPS.[4]

At the beginning of July 1947 Morrison, who as Lord President was ministerial 'economic overlord', proposed that the EPB and CEPS should be under his own direct departmental jurisdiction rather than in the Cabinet Office. He believed that the initial arrangement isolated his small personal staff and so weakened his bargaining power. His efforts were firmly resisted by Edward Bridges and the issue was finally settled by the Prime Minister: we stayed where we were.[5] The first meeting of the EPB took place on 21st July 1947, just after sterling had been made convertible and as the currency crisis which had been threatening since the end of the war erupted.

With the summer upon us, the date agreed with the Americans in 1945 for convertibility was fast approaching. The Bank of England remained confident that the act itself would not exacerbate the dollar drain. Dalton accepted this conclusion and on 8th July informed the House of Commons that 'in large measure 15th July has already been discounted and the additional burden of assuming these obligations under the Anglo-American Loan Agreement will be noticeably less than people suppose.'[6] No effort was made to try and postpone convertibility.

At the beginning of July, Britain's dollar deficit was running at some $500 million a month and, soon after sterling became convertible, a massive run on the pound developed. On 29th July Dalton warned the Cabinet that the US dollar credits were likely to be exhausted by the end of October at the latest. In the six weeks to 14th August the drain of dollars averaged $115 million a week, compared with an average weekly figure of $77 million for the second quarter as a whole.

During these weeks neither Attlee nor Morrison as 'economic overlord' gave any lead to their colleagues and the Cabinet fell into disharmony and disarray, its confidence shattered. No effort was made to keep the United States informed of developments nor to ask for her advice. While an austerity package was hastily cobbled together in early August, it produced resignation threats from Dalton, Cripps and Bevan and did little to allay fears in the City of imminent financial disaster.[7] The whole exercise amounted to little more than an exhortation for greater production and effort and for voluntary wage restraint.

The crisis continued to deepen. On 17th August, Dalton told the Cabinet that the government had little alternative but to abandon convertibility or see sterling 'free fall' within a few weeks. On 20th August the 'emergency and temporary' suspension of convertibility was announced. A mere $400 million of the US loan remained, and even this was temporarily frozen by the Americans. In fact the suspension of convertibility did not arrest the dollar drain. Even in the last quarter of 1947 some $700 million was paid out, and indeed it has been stated that in some ways the crisis actually became more acute after the suspension of the formal obligation than before it.[8]

On 23rd August the government announced further cuts in rations and the suspension of foreign travel for pleasure purposes. In mid-October, Dalton and Cripps circulated a joint paper on the crisis to Cabinet. In it they stated that they expected the dollar drain to continue at the rate of $2 billion a year in 1948, implying a reduction in the reserves to £90 million by the end of that year unless funds could be drawn from the IMF and the United States released the $400 million they had frozen. The Americans did so in December 1947. Dalton and Cripps proposed to reduce the drain in 1948 by £175 million or $700 million, so as to leave at least a minimum of reserves at the end of that year and to reduce the prospective gold and dollar deficit in 1949 to more manageable proportions. Import economies amounting to £120 million were to bear the brunt of the strain, including food cuts of £75 million.[9] Once again the debate in Cabinet was heated over measures which would reduce the average calorie intake to below the wartime level and which implied the breaking of several large long-term contracts. Eventually, however, after a hard struggle, cuts in food imports of £66 million were accepted.[10]

Up to this point neither I nor the CEPS were directly involved, as responsibility for the Treasury and financial policy rested with the Chancellor, Hugh Dalton, and not with the Lord President, Herbert Morrison, to whom we were responsible. I now became more involved as the cuts in the dollar import programme were to be reinforced by a reduction of the domestic investment programme, modest reductions in military expenditure, higher export targets and a deflationary Budget. In 1947 investment was running at a level that was putting excessive demands on manpower and resources. The Cabinet agreed on 1st August that the scale of investment should be reduced, particularly where it was making no contribution to the export drive or import saving. The task of reviewing the investment programme was allocated to the CEPS in consultation with other departments.[11] After more than two months' painstaking work we in the CEPS produced a report which put forward a reduction of 18 per cent in the forecast for fixed investment in 1948, with construction being cut by 17 per cent and plant, machinery and vehicles by 22.5 per cent. When Dalton saw the report he welcomed it as 'a real start to central planning'.[12] Other ministers also approved our recommendations and, with slight amendments, they were made public in a White Paper on *Capital Investment in 1948* (Cmd. 7268) before the end of the year.

In actual fact, in order to ease the external position, I myself and my colleagues in the CEPS and the Economic Section wanted to go much further in our pruning of investment than the report suggested. However, the number of large-scale projects which could be postponed without widespread dislocation was remarkably few.[13] As Robert Hall, the Director of the Economic Section put it, the cuts proposed were 'as heavy a contribution as we dare[d] to make'.[14]

In November, Dalton's last Budget ushered in higher rates of purchase and profits tax and the freezing of food subsidies at £329 million per annum. This was the first post-war Budget specifically to be used to reduce inflationary pressure through fiscal policy. The fact the Dalton had taken action to freeze food subsidies rather than increase them in response to inflationary pressure can be viewed as an indication of a move to Keynesianism. Indeed, Treasury officials fought long and hard to get the subsidies cut in half and Edward Bridges even went so far as to talk of their drastic reduction as 'the pivot' of the whole Budget exercise. In the end, however, Dalton, while he was convinced they should not be increased, thought the reduction of the subsidies too great a political risk, as it would undoubtedly hit the poorest hardest, and could lead to a further upsurge in wage demands at a time when the government was already considering more active intervention in the labour market to suppress wage inflation.[15]

One other policy measure was introduced in response to the external crisis; this was the initiation of a major agricultural expansion programme. In July 1947 the Ministry of Agriculture submitted a plan for the agricultural sector which sought to increase the net value of total agricultural production by £40 million by 1950–1.[16] This represented less than 5 per cent of our food imports and some officials, including myself and Austin Robinson, thought that this was inadequate. The Lord President's Committee, which presided over major issues of domestic policy, was convinced that a larger agricultural expansion programme would be of greater use to our balance of payments, and the ailing dollar balance in particular, than any comparable capital investment programme in another sector.[17] Representatives of the CEPS, Economic Section, Treasury, Ministry of Food and Ministry of Agriculture met and, with the scientific advice of Sir Solly Zuckerman and of Professor Engledow, Professor of Agriculture at Cambridge, produced an alternative plan for agriculture. We raised the target for an increase in agricultural production to £100 million by 1950–1, some 20 per cent above the 1946–7 level, or 50 per cent above the pre-war average (calculated on the basis of 1945–6 prices).[18]

The plan was accepted in August and an Agriculture Act was subsequently passed which introduced a series of supporting measures, including a system of assured markets, subsidies and guaranteed prices. In point of fact the expansion programme was revised on several occasions over the next few years to meet the demands of various external shocks to the economy, and its time horizon extended to 1952–3. However, the thrust of the programme remained much the same. The major effort throughout was directed towards the expansion of livestock and livestock products to reduce our dependence on dollar sources of meat, bacon and eggs. Much of this expansion depended on increased supplies of imported feeding-stuffs, but great emphasis was also placed on the development of indigenous resources by a vigorous campaign of grassland improvement and conservation, and by an expansion of the acreages devoted to coarse grains and other crops. Through the use of much more intensive fertilization it was hoped to provide far greater amounts of high protein feeding-stuffs.

Solly Zuckerman was forever impressing upon me his belief that with enough nitrogen fertilizers we could achieve almost anything.[19] It was not until many years later when I was chairman of a House of Lords Select Committee dealing with the EEC Common Agricultural Policy (CAP) that I realised how clearly he and others had forseen the agricultural revolution that was to take place over the next forty years. At the time, the Malthusian view that the world population would outstrip its ability to feed itself still prevailed. Today it has given way to the excesses of the CAP and the agricultural programmes of the United States and other countries.

Half of the programmed increase in output was intended to come from using additional labour and raw materials, such as feeding-stuffs, and the other half from improvements in efficiency, such as better use of land, labour and capital resources, particularly to achieve higher yields of eggs, milk and meat per head of livestock. For increased efficiency we put our reliance on further mechanisation and the ingenuity of farmers and farm workers.[20]

Despite rapid initial growth the 1947 target of a 20 per cent expansion in agricultural production was not realised by 1951. By 1949–50 output was 13 per cent up on the 1947 level but there was scarcely any improvement during 1950–1. Moreover, the net dollar savings were minimal except in terms of wheat production. The Agriculture White Paper of 1952 diagnosed the problem as a lack of financial resources in the agricultural sector, particularly amongst the smallholders. In the 1952 and 1953 annual price reviews substantial grants were paid out to small farmers and those cultivating difficult land. As a result the target was reached by 1952–3.[21]

The strain on sterling was relaxed towards the end of 1947 and in 1948 and, although the fall in fixed capital investment programmed for 1948 never took place, inflationary pressure fell off perceptibly. Control of investment was quite simply not effective. The convertibility crisis marked the end of the respite offered by the American loan. It forced the government to accept that there really was a dollar problem and the need for action to cope with it. It also proved a significant step in the transition to Keynesian economic management with which I was to become deeply involved during the rest of my time in Whitehall. Even allowing for the difficulties created by a lack of relevant and up-to-date statistics, ministers, unrestrained by their official advisers in the Treasury and the Bank of England, were indecisive and willing to trust to luck throughout. They began with an optimistic import programme and a domestic financial stance that was far too lax. Then they delayed the necessary cutbacks until after the suspension of convertibility and, in effect, closed the door long after the horse had bolted. Had action been taken even as late as May the catastrophe could have been greatly reduced. They were also unwise in neglecting either to seek the advice of the Americans as the crisis deepened or indeed to inform the British public of the full gravity of the situation until August. The official Whitehall machine can hardly be said to have covered itself in glory in 1947.

CHAPTER THREE

Changes in
Ministerial Responsibilities
and the Machinery of Government

By the autumn of 1947 I was feeling increasingly disillusioned with my job. During the summer the CEPS had played little part in attempts to deal with the convertibility crisis; no one seemed to know what our role was in the Whitehall machine. The main reason for this lay in Morrison's performance as overall 'economic co-ordinator'. A wartime Minister of Supply and Home Secretary, he had been given the job by Attlee more as a tribute to his position in the party after the war than anything else. In addition, he was also Leader of the House, Deputy Prime Minister and the minister responsible for nationalisation. Morrison was a politician of great experience and judgement, a fixer and organiser rather than a man with any firm grasp of economics or public finance. He was often bewildered by the complexities of economic policy-making. Moreover, he had no professional economists in his own small staff, and found the ideas of the economists in the Economic Section of the Cabinet Office obscure and unconvincing. The Economic Section had strong views that economic planning should be conducted in terms of Keynesian demand-management, but these were not the views of Morrison, at least in the years 1945–7.

In September I was sufficiently frustrated and upset with developments to tell Cripps of my anxieties and warn him that, although it might be an embarrassment to the government, I was thinking of resignation. As usual he listened sympathetically to my case but then urged me to be patient for a while as 'things are going to change'.[1] There had been tensions in the Labour Cabinet since its inception and,

18

in retrospect, I think Cripps must have been referring to his own dis-illusionment and his plan to replace Attlee with Bevin and install him-self as 'economic overlord'. But Cripps's attempt to unseat the Prime Minister failed, largely because Bevin was unwilling to plot against his old friend and ally and because Morrison would not do anything to put his rival Bevin into No. 10. In the event, Attlee offered Cripps the job of economic overlord instead of Morrison, and he accepted.

Cripps took over his new post at the end of September with the title of Minister of Economic Affairs. While the Treasury remained the domain of the Chancellor, Cripps was given overall control of both the home economic front and trade policy, with authority over the five pro-duction ministries – Labour, Supply, the Board of Trade, Fuel and Power, and Works – together with the CEPS, Economic Section and Economic Information Unit. As it turned out, this arrangement lasted for only six weeks before Dalton resigned following his budget in-discretion. Cripps then acquired the Treasury portfolio to become the first of the modern chancellors. In this short period, however, there were already signs that confusion was developing between the Ministry of Economic Affairs and the Treasury about the responsibility of each department. It was clear that the demarcation disputes that had existed under the previous system of organisation would re-emerge, throwing policy-making into turmoil again.

Much has been written of Cripps's stern and severe image. He was, in fact, a tremendously kind and generous man, not without a pleasant sense of humour. Moreover, until he became seriously ill, he enjoyed a glass of wine and was a heavy smoker. He was always willing to listen to the most junior official and used to send round handwritten notes of thanks to many of his civil servants at Christmas. His kindness, his generosity and his disciplined devotion to duty were inseparable from his strongly held religious beliefs.

Cripps brought with him to the job tremendous energy, enthusiasm and national pride. He had the clearest and most incisive mind that I have ever dealt with. Before the war and his movement into full-time politics, Cripps was a brilliant barrister, becoming a King's Counsel at the age of 37. Thereafter he remained the lawyer *par excellence*. He would show the most remarkable mastery of facts and clarity of exposi-tion even when he might not actually fully understand a subject. When he did understand a subject, he was quite simply impossible to defeat

19

in an argument. I can remember saying to him in exasperation on many occasions, 'I can't fault your argument Chancellor, I can't see where you are wrong, but I know you are.'

He once said to me, 'If you gave me the papers of any case I have fought in the last twenty years for one hour, I could go into court and fight it again.' Then he paused for a moment and corrected himself, 'No, I would not need the papers.' He said this was no tribute to him, he just had a mind like that. He could put away the facts about a case in a drawer, pointing to his head, and draw it out when needed and it was all there. His memory must have been like that of Macaulay, as illustrated by an extract from his journal, 16th August 1849.*

He told me that before going into court on an important case he never took any food and not even a sip of water because 'it detracts from the clarity of thought'. It was a belief shared by Sherlock Holmes, who said that 'the faculties become refined when you starve them'. This practice may also have reflected the ill health from which he had suffered all his life.

One could not write about Cripps without mentioning his passion for punctuality which was almost an obsession. To be one minute late for a meeting was pardonable, five minutes was not. Senior civil servants were sometimes to be seen running down Great George Street to avoid the sarcastic greeting that often met latecomers. Several years of working for him in the Ministry of Aircraft Production and in the Treasury has, I must admit, had some effect on my own behaviour, but not I hope the harsh reception for latecomers.

It is easy to see the value to the Treasury of having its case argued in Cabinet and Parliament by a man of Cripps's intellect and ability. In this way, he was the perfect minister. He was also a great communicator. He would regularly address hundreds of Treasury officials in mass meetings at Caxton Hall to explain what he was trying to do and to build

---

* 'The Express train reached Holyhead about seven in the evening. We sailed as soon as we got on board. The breeze was fresh and adverse, and the sea rough. The sun set in glory, and then the starlight was like the starlight of the Trades. I put on my great-coat and sat on the deck during the whole voyage. As I could not read, I used an excellent substitute for reading. I went through Paradise Lost in my head. I could still repeat half of it, and that the best half. I really never enjoyed it so much.'

up their confidence. He was equally at home with trade union leaders, employers' representatives and the general public. He always tried to be scrupulously honest and would go out of his way to make clear in speeches the full facts of the situation as he saw them. To my mind he was second only to Bevin in commanding the support of the man in the street and, together with the Foreign Secretary, one of the Labour Party's greatest assests.

Cripps also never forgot that people needed to be led rather than directed. He once said to me, and with good reason, 'I consider myself to be one of the best draftsmen in the country, and I itch to re-write almost every paper which crosses my desk. However, I refrain from doing so because if I did I should never get the best out of my officials – they would become disillusioned and say, "Why try, he alters everything anyway." Thus, unless a paper is truly bad, I content myself with comments and the odd amendment.' Cripps, however, did undertake extensive rewriting of his speeches.

Many people have criticised his political judgement. I cannot speak of his time in politics before the war, but during the time I worked with him he made, in my opinion, two important errors of political judgement. First, there is no doubt that his attempt in 1947 to unseat Attlee and replace him with Bevin with the aid of Morrison, who cordially disliked Bevin, showed little grasp of the realities of the situation. Second, it was unwise in his broadcast announcing the devaluation of sterling in 1949 not to start, as Robert Hall and I wanted him to do, by expressing regret that he had been forced by circumstances to agree to something he had wished to avoid. His judgement of individuals could sometimes be, in my opinion and that of other officials like Edward Bridges, quite misguided.

I have been asked whether he found it easy or difficult to persuade his colleagues to adopt policies which were bound to seem harsh to the electorate. I think the answer must be that he found it easier than his predecessor. This was not only because he was a most persuasive man but also, and perhaps more important, because his colleagues had been so frightened by the apparently insoluble problems that had confronted them that they welcomed the proposals of someone who so clearly knew what he wanted to do.

He was a wonderful man to work for, and I had a great affection for him. I owe him much both for my time under him in the Ministry of

Aircraft Production and for his strong support when I was in the Treasury during the time he was Chancellor.

As supreme co-ordinator of economic policy and Chancellor, Cripps was in a much more powerful position than Morrison had ever been. Unlike Morrison, he had full responsibility over economic and financial policy, but he was also lucky enough to have various political protégés in key departments who were alive to the need for firm action: Harold Wilson who took over from him as President of the Board of Trade, Nye Bevan at the Ministry of Health, Hugh Gaitskell at the Ministry of Fuel and Power, and Douglas Jay as Economic Secretary in the Treasury. Cripps kept these protégés fully informed of his thinking on important issues. For example, I would regularly see Nye Bevan on his behalf.

The ministerial moves which took place in the autumn of 1947 were accompanied by a number of changes in the committee structure. For example, at ministerial level a new Economic Policy Committee chaired by the Prime Minister became the main focus of economic co-ordination, with the Production and Priorities Committees acting as clearing houses for more day-to-day matters. The upshot of these modifications to the policy-making process was that the Treasury came to re-establish its position at the centre of economic decision-making which it had lost during the war, but with a much expanded role. At first, apart from Bridges, there seemed to be few among the senior Treasury officials who appreciated the difference between looking after candle ends and making economic policy.

After my disillusionment in the summer I welcomed these changes. I was convinced that with Cripps in charge Britain's economic performance would improve and that the advice of the CEPS and the Economic Section would not be ignored or lost in the machine. My wartime experiences had convinced me from the outset that only by keeping the CEPS small and integrating it into the Treasury, which I always believed would recover its natural pre-eminence in Whitehall, could we exert a worthwhile influence on policy. We had to work with the machine and avoid doing things which other departments considered were their responsibility, and where better to make sure this happened than in the machine's control room? From this time on I felt that the CEPS could contribute something to Britain's post-war recovery.

Subsequently the work of the CEPS fell into two broad categories.

First, there were problems of co-ordination associated with the broader aspects of economic policy: questions affecting the general level of economic activity; the size and raw material requirements of the major industries; the total size of the investment programme and investment in the Commonwealth and elsewhere overseas; general questions affecting manpower, and general questions affecting national income and savings in relation to fiscal policy, the level of consumption, and so on. Second, there were more detailed aspects of certain major economic questions: the division of the investment programme bet- ween individual sectors; the general balance of colonial development; special problems in raw materials' allocation; and the resolution of con- flicting claims on scarce productive capacity and manpower which arose in the special circumstances of the transition to peace. In 1950 the CEPS also took on a special task in analysing the economic prob- lems created by the Korean rearmament programme.

Most CEPS advice was provided via the official and ministerial com- mittee structure or in the form of internal memoranda and minutes to the Chancellor. The Chancellor would more often than not discuss CEPS advice with me, and on each day I would have a number of opportunities to put to him my own personal opinion on matters of pol- icy. From time to time I was also asked to brief the Prime Minister directly.

In contrast to the CEPS, apart from the period just after its incep- tion, the Economic Planning Board (EPB) never became much more than an adjunct to the policy-making process. In its early days the EPB was a support to ministers in getting difficult and unpopular policies accepted. From the beginning ministers never came to meetings and later showed little interest in it. These meetings, in turn, became less frequent and more sparsely attended. It developed into a talking shop which rubber-stamped the conclusions and recommendations set out in papers drafted by departments, the CEPS, or Economic Section. It was rarely, if ever, a prime mover for policy changes. The major de- cisions were taken in the ministerial Economic Policy Committee or the Official Steering Committee on Economic Development and its suc- cessors.

Robert Hall is convinced that the reason why the EPB had such a limited impact on policy was the fact that ministers would not directly involve themselves in its meetings. Because of this the trade unionists and employers' representatives could not be sure that their opinions were reaching the Cabinet in the form which they desired. Douglas Allen (Lord Croham), however, is convinced that the addition of a ministerial chairman would actually have reduced the Board's effectiveness still further. He believes it would have reproduced the position at meetings of the more recent National Economic Development Council. At these, he suggests, if there is a Conservative government, the CBI tends to side with it and the TUC to be in opposition, while if there is a Labour government the reverse is true.

November 1947 saw the beginning of a close and productive relationship between Robert Hall and myself which was to last until my departure from the Treasury in October 1953. He had taken over from James Meade as Director of the Economic Section of the Cabinet Office or *de facto* Chief Economic Adviser at the same time as the CEPS was set up. He was an Australian who in the twenties had come to England as a Rhodes Scholar and continued in Oxford as a don. During the war and early post-war period he had worked in the Raw Materials Section of the Ministry of Supply as a civil servant. When he came to the Economic Section it was in a state of some disarray. James Meade had been ill for some time. Furthermore, many of the well-known economists who worked there in the war, such as Lionel Robbins, had decided to return to academic life. The Section lacked an accumulated body of experience and was finding it hard to get its opinions across to Dalton and Morrison. As the CEPS had been at first, it was rather in limbo. Robert Hall changed all this and built up morale among his juniors. He was a remarkably practical and cautious man who thought everything through thoroughly. He was also an extremely hard and conscientious worker who in the early years of his appointment had a bed installed in his room in the Cabinet Office. During the week he would literally live on the job. He quickly won the respect and confidence of Cripps and re-established the Economic Section as a vital link in the policy-making chain. Although until 1953 it nominally remained in the Cabinet Office, under his guidance it became, in effect, part of the Treasury, and was treated as such.

Robert Hall and I quickly established a rapport and became the close friends we have remained until this day. With the return of Austin Robinson to Cambridge and the departure soon afterwards of Kenneth Berrill and Robin Marris, it was Robert Hall and his fellow economists who from 1949 came to provide the CEPS with any specialist economic analysis and information required. But before this date we had begun to tender advice in tandem much of the time. Robert Hall would most often provide an idea or a piece of analysis, we would discuss it, and then I would present it to the relevant committee or to the Chancellor as best I could. As such, he loaded the gun and I fired the bullets or, as 'Rab' Butler put it, I was 'the *vulgarisateur* or publicist for his ideas'.[2] To a considerable extent this followed from my position in Whitehall. Throughout my time as Chief Planning Officer I insisted on being employed on a yearly basis and, as such, could maintain an independence of action not open to permanent officials.

Robert Hall remained as Chief Economic Adviser for thirteen years and won the admiration of no less than seven different chancellors with views as diverse as those of Cripps and Thorneycroft. Moreover, he presided over what in retrospect was to become a golden age for the British economy, with low inflation, consistently full employment and sustained growth. More than anyone else in Whitehall he was responsible for the development and implementation of the economic techniques which underpinned this golden age.

Edward Bridges, Fellow of All Souls and the son of the poet laureate, was the Permanent Secretary to the Treasury and senior Whitehall official throughout my years as Chief Planning Officer. After progressing through the Treasury ranks he had been appointed Secretary to the Cabinet in 1938 and held this position throughout the war. He became Permanent Secretary to the Treasury in 1945 and, remarkably, was for a brief period both Cabinet Secretary and Permanent Secretary to the Treasury. He was a superb administrator with a tremendous capacity for work and was responsible for much of the machinery of government then in operation. Furthermore, even though he would never have classified himself as an economist, his many years of experience in the Treasury meant that he had a strong feel for matters of public finance and political economy. In general, like Robert Hall, he thought in Keynesian terms although he was more sceptical and cautious about what financial policy could achieve. As official guardian of the government's purse strings he was ever wary of higher public expenditure.

Edward Bridges was also an extremely nice and modest man. For example, on my joining the Treasury he asked me how I wished to work. Did I wish to work over him, alongside him, or under him? My answer was that of course I would work under him and for the next six years this is how we worked. He ensured that ideas worked out by the Economic Section, the CEPS, or other parts of the Treasury, in particular Overseas Finance, were properly considered and co-ordinated. If they were important enough they would be discussed and considered by the Economic Steering Committee, the most senior committee of officials of which he was chairman. Robert Hall and I were both members and I took the chair in Edward Bridges' absence.

Most economic policies have some impact on foreign affairs. It was essential, therefore, that we in the Treasury should know the Foreign Office view while policies were being planned. During most of the time I was in the Treasury, Roger Makins (later Lord Sherfield) as Assistant Under-Secretary and Deputy Under-Secretary of State, was in charge of the Economic departments at the Foreign Office. Like Edward Bridges, he was a Fellow of All Souls. He had an acute mind and a robust view of where British interests lay. His experience as Economic Minister in Washington and, before that, as assistant to the resident minister at Allied Forces Headquarters, Mediterranean, strengthened his conviction that it was essential to keep the United States in Europe if Europe was to recover economically and be defended in the long run. He made us all especially conscious of the danger of a retreat into Fortress America.

Roger Makins subsequently went on to become Ambassador in Washington, Joint Permanent Secretary of the Treasury, where he took over from Edward Bridges, and succeeded me as chairman of the Atomic Energy Authority. He has since had a wide and extended career in the financial world both in this country and the United States.

CHAPTER FOUR

Marshall Aid

The year 1947 also saw the beginning of one of the most important episodes in economic co-operation that the world has seen, when the Marshall Aid Programme, technically the European Recovery Programme (ERP), was born. Marshall Aid was to have enormous implications for the British economy and British economic policy over the following four years. It gave us a breathing space which we badly needed, despite the doubts expressed by some latter-day historians about its necessity. It is quite certain that without the prospect of the ERP, we would have had to impose yet more stringent controls and restrictions on food and raw-material imports, domestic consumption and production in the aftermath of the convertibility crisis.[1] One of our first exercises on the setting up of the CEPS was to make an analysis of what the basic food ration would have to be in the event of the reserves running out in the near future. The conclusions we reached were horrendous. The average daily calorific intake per person would, we estimated, have had to be reduced to something like 1,700–2,000, far less than in the war years.

There was also a possibility that without Marshall Aid Britain would have had to turn increasingly to barter, to abandon many of our overseas obligations, and shelve some of the plans for the Welfare State. Politically, the implications of such action would have been enormous both at home and abroad. Domestic stability would have been threatened, while in Europe communist governments might have come to power in France and Italy. In both countries there were powerful communist parties. There is no doubt in my mind that Marshall Aid brought Britain and

Europe the help we needed when we were in a desperate situation.

After the severe winter of 1946–7 senior members of the Truman administration became convinced, no doubt in part because of Britain's request that we be relieved of our military obligations in the Eastern Mediterranean, that 'without further prompt and substantial aid from the USA, economic, social and political disintegration will overwhelm Europe'.[2] Thus US thinking in the spring of 1947 began to emphasise the need for an integrated European recovery plan, as distinct from piecemeal aid. This view found expression in General Marshall's famous speech at Harvard on 5th June 1947. On 9th June, Ernest Bevin, who saw this as an opportunity it was vital to seize, enlisted the support of Georges Bidault, the French Foreign Minister, for a positive response to Marshall's stipulation that 'the initiative ... must come from Europe'.[3] After an abortive conference with the Russians, who refused to participate in a European recovery plan because it would infringe upon national sovereignty, the British and French decided to go ahead on their own. In July 1947 they called a second conference in Paris at which representatives of sixteen European nations attended.

The conference set up a Committee for European Economic Co-operation (CEEC). Oliver Franks, the head of the British delegation, was made chairman, and instructed to produce a report on what Europe needed to do to get back on its feet and obtain overall dollar 'viability' by 1951. Questionnaires were immediately sent out to member countries calling for four-year production programmes for basic industries and services and balance of payments projections, both overall and with the Dollar Area. By the fourth week in September, after a period of frenzied activity, a provisional report was completed and signed by the foreign ministers of the sixteen countries. It consisted of an 86-page general volume and a 355-page second volume containing the reports of four technical committees: Food and Agriculture, Fuel and Power, Iron and Steel, and Transport. The total claim for assistance amounted to $22.4 billion, of which $19 billion was to be financed by the United States. Further discussions on the report took place in Washington between CEEC officials, led by Franks, and the US government to try to reconcile it more with what American officials believed Congress would accept. In the meantime, and not without a struggle, Congress approved special interim aid of $597 million for France, Austria and Italy, to tide them over until the main programme could be launched.

By mid-December 1947 the joint efforts of the Franks' mission to Washington and US officials had produced the draft of a European Recovery Plan in the form of an Economic Co-operation Bill proposing to set up a European Recovery Programme (ERP) with an Economic Co-operation Administration (ECA) to run it. The Bill was presented to Congress by President Truman. It put the total amount of aid for the first fifteen months of ERP at $6,800 million, and for four and a quarter years at $17,000 million, considerably less than had originally been requested but, nevertheless, a lifeline for the shell-shocked economies of Europe. Bevin rightly described the US administration's report to Congress as 'an outstanding document showing great vision and courage'.[4]

Oliver Franks' contribution to the success of the CEEC was enormous. In my time at the Ministry of Aircraft Production during the war I formed the view that of those recruited temporarily into the administrative side of the Civil Service, the people who adapted themselves best to the new environment were under 40 and were dons, lawyers and businessmen, in that order. Of course, there were many able businessmen who held senior posts with notable success: Rab Sinclair, Charles Craven, Graham Cunningham, to mention only three. Businessmen were markedly successful in allocation controls where expertise in a particular product was most important.

Of those who came into Whitehall from the universities, Oliver Franks was quite the most outstanding in ability. I first worked with him at the end of the war when in 1945 he was made Permanent Secretary of both the Ministry of Supply and the Ministry of Aircraft Production, of which I was Chief Executive. Our task was to amalgamate the two departments. This was done by 31st March 1946 when I left Whitehall, I thought for ever.

We next met when he was appointed chairman of the CEEC. There is no doubt that the successful conclusion of the report owes much to the way he was able to secure agreement on such a difficult subject from governments holding such divergent views.

Some time later, after he had returned to Oxford as Provost of Queen's College, I was asked to find out if he would be willing to go to Washington as Ambassador. Both he and his wife were dismayed at the prospect of giving up working with and guiding young people. Barbara

Franks laid particular stress on this. Fortunately for the country and the Western world, they eventually decided to accept. For four years he did the job with outstanding success. Over those years, on various occasions, I went with him to the US Treasury or State Department to negotiate some difficult point. After hearing him open the discussion it often struck me that we had a much better case than I had feared – so lucid and so persuasive was his presentation of it.

The British contribution to the CEEC and the briefing of our representatives in Paris was co-ordinated at an official level by the London Committee, chaired by R. W. B. 'Otto' Clarke of the Treasury. By this time the CEPS and the Economic Section were getting a better understanding of the economic problems facing the country and were able to make a considerable contribution to this briefing.

'Otto' Clarke was an Under-Secretary in the Treasury's Overseas Finance Division. He was one of the most colourful figures in Whitehall at the time. He had a most fertile and stimulating mind, and was forever circulating minutes detailing his latest idea or scheme. Before the war he had worked as a journalist on the *Financial News*. He became renowned in Whitehall for his ability to produce a perfectly presented, lucid and well-argued document at short notice. His capacity for work was phenomenal. He was often brought in to draft reports or papers on which it was proving hard to secure inter-departmental agreement. While I did not always agree with him and indeed, as we shall see, had some major disputes with him over matters of policy, he certainly made the Treasury a brighter and more interesting place. Between 1959 and 1961 we were to work closely on the *Report on Control of Public Expenditure* which was produced by a committee of which I was chairman.

Parallel to the quantitive recovery programme the CEEC considered European integration, the furtherance of which was a major American objective. Many American officials and politicians, particularly those with a strictly limited knowledge of European history, saw the creation of a United States of Europe as an essential means of setting the Continent back on its feet and ensuring its salvation from communism. Only by following the example of the new world could the old world be saved.

On 7th August 1947 Edward Bridges held a meeting of senior officials to discuss with Oliver Franks the position in Paris with regard to

European integration. Oliver Franks explained that in his contacts with the Americans there had been one constant element: the CEEC report must contain a new idea about Europe in order to ensure a satisfactory response from Congress. The Americans were not yet exactly sure what they wanted, but he noted that there had been a steady emphasis on a European customs union, the need for financial stability and satisfactory currency arrangements. In his opinion, Britain's position at the CEEC was such that we could rally the other nations to recommend the type of European project that we favoured. Against this background, officials discussed the instructions to be given to our delegation in Paris.

On the matter of a customs union, ministers had already considered a paper by officials. They had concluded that a general European customs union was not really practicable at any stage in the foreseeable future, and that our attitude towards any smaller grouping of countries in a customs union must be one of great caution. The difficulties with a customs union were great, apart from the technical problems of negotiation. Officials could not see how a customs union with Western Europe could be reconciled with Imperial Preference and our trade with the Empire which, at that stage, was twice as important as our trade with Europe; only a quarter of Britain's trade was with the Continent. It might be theoretically possible to develop a system which would include both Europe and the Commonwealth, but it was highly unlikely that such an arrangement would be acceptable to the Americans. We felt it would be dangerous if the CEEC conference made an optimistic report on the prospects of a customs union unless we were fairly certain that it could be followed through successfully. Congress would presumably vote aid on an annual basis, and it would be disastrous if rosy hopes of European integration were followed by disillusionment.

It was decided, therefore, that the British delegation should make clear in Paris that the United Kingdom would find it especially difficult to enter any European customs union because of its links, both economic and political, outside Europe, and particularly with the Commonwealth. Furthermore, there were the most formidable practicable difficulties in the formation at any foreseeable date of a customs union of the highly developed economies of Europe. The ultimate advantages would have to be weighed against the severe dislocation which would be caused by its formation. Nevertheless, if it appeared to the conference that a customs union was one of the forms of co-operation that would best promote European recovery we would, notwithstanding our special difficulties, be willing to join with others in a study group to examine the problems, and to consult with the Dominions.

Ministers had already considered the question of the integration of European steel production. They had decided that the United Kingdom should support a proposal for special consideration to be given to the expansion of production of certain 'bottleneck' steel products, and should agree to join a study group to consider the long-term European production/requirements positions. We should, however, make no commitments either to submit our production to international allocation or to modify our own steel development programme according to the recommendations of the study group. Consequently, the study group should confine itself to the establishment of facts. It was decided that these instructions relating to steel should also be applied to discussions about other commodities.

Two other areas of European co-operation were discussed by officials: monetary co-operation and trade co-operation. On the former subject it was hoped that a special fund of US dollars would be made available to the participating countries, preferably through the IMF, to help them settle balances as between themselves, and ultimately to make their currencies convertible. On the latter subject it was noted that proposals had been made by some participants that all import restrictions in Europe should be abolished. Officials would not support such a scheme, on the grounds that even if it were possible, which they doubted, it would not be desirable as it would divert potential exports from Europe to hard currency areas into European consumption. However, it was thought that import restrictions might be eliminated for some less essential goods and that we should support the administration of import restrictions on a non-discriminatory basis between the participating countries, preferably by global quotas open to all of them. This was believed to have the advantage of helping to break up bilateral barter agreements. The discussions were carried out by officials who were familiar with ministerial fears and thinking, but naturally final decisions were made by ministers.

In short, in 1947 there seemed to be strong economic as well as political arguments for a cautious attitude by Britain to more integration with Europe. Economic perceptions strengthened political arguments in favour of Commonwealth links. Besides such factors as the desire to keep a strong and long-term American presence in Europe, the indifference of the British public to the European ideal, and the prestige derived from a colonial empire, attitudes were conditioned by the world shortages of food and raw materials. Economists in Whitehall believed at the time, wrongly as it turned out, that primary products were, for the foreseeable future, in general likely to remain much scarcer than they had been in the 1930s. This led them to advise close ties with the Commonwealth, which had ample natural resources and which could both supply us and earn dollars for the Sterling Area. European integration would lead to specialisation in manufactures for the European market and reduce our dollar-saving/earning potential. The concomitant of this was that any future links with Western Europe must not weaken Commonwealth links.[5]

A customs union study group was set up in Brussels in the autumn in 1947. To the satisfaction of our Paris delegation, in the event, the CEEC Report contained no spectacular commitment to European integration. Each signatory of the Report merely undertook

(1)   To co-operate with one another and with like-minded countries in all possible steps to reduce the tariffs and the barriers to the expansion of trade, both between themselves and the rest of the world.

(2)   To remove progressively the obstacles to the free movement of persons within Europe.

(3)   To organise together the means by which current resources can be developed in partnership.[6]

This was, however, by no means the end of the story as far as European integration was concerned. Once the extent and form of Marshall Aid had been decided upon by Congress, American pressure for European integration was to become a fact of daily life.

In all these discussions ministers and officials were at one in believing that our priorities were to keep the United States in Europe and to maintain close links with the Commonwealth and the Sterling Area.

Closer relationship with Europe, while desirable, must not be allowed to damage those priorities.

Although 1947 was certainly not an easy year, by the end of it I was beginning to feel that, with Cripps as economic co-ordinator, the probability that Marshall Aid would soon come on stream, a new and more coherent machinery for economic policy formulation, and with the chastening experiences of the last twelve months fresh in our minds, there was a light at the end of the tunnel. There seemed to be reasonable prospects that Britain could be steered back to more robust economic health within the foreseeable future.

CHAPTER FIVE

1948:
The Sky Clears a Little

In its review of the previous twelve months, the *Economic Survey for 1949* described 1948 as a 'year of great and steady progress' by comparison with the trials and tribulations of 1947.[1] In 1948 production rose rapidly, exports expanded even more swiftly and the balance of payments moved back into overall surplus, although a large dollar deficit remained. As a result, ministerial confidence returned and the atmosphere of crisis dissipated somewhat. By the end of the year the number of shortages had declined and the government could allow some reduction in the number of limitations and restraints on private business.

The current account surplus for 1948 is today estimated at £26 million, implying a swing of some £400 million over the previous year. At the heart of this considerable improvement in Britain's external account is the fact that while exports grew in volume terms by 25 per cent in 1948 to reach their highest level since 1929, import growth was restricted by the government's strict purchasing policies to a mere 4 per cent.

The tougher fiscal policy introduced by Dalton in the previous autumn had much to do with Britain's success in 1948, especially as, in April, Cripps consolidated the restrictive measures of November 1947 with a 'no change' Budget aimed at securing a 'true overall surplus' of £300 million. Fiscal rectitude, supported by an allocation of raw materials designed to give priority to the export industries, allowed Britain to take advantage of the sellers' market for goods in 1948, and kept domestic spending down.

1948 marked the onset of the 'Crippsian Age' in which Britain was repeatedly told to tighten her belt, and the austere and morally incorruptible figure of the Chancellor was held up as an example for all to follow. As Cripps himself made clear on numerous occasions, Britain's consumption requirements were at this stage 'the last in the list of priorities. First [were] exports; second [was] capital investment in industry; and last [were] the needs, comforts and amenities of the family.'[2] Total personal consumption fell by 0.6 per cent in 1948, having risen by 10 per cent in 1946 and 3.3 per cent in 1947. Personal taxation rates were still punitive, the standard rate of income tax remained as high as 9s (45p) in the pound, and rationing was at its most severe in this year. The points system for certain items was still in operation,* there were limitations on bread purchasing, and each week the average citizen was expected to make do with 13 oz of meat, 1.5 oz of cheese, 6 oz of butter or margarine, 2 pints of milk and 1 egg. By modern standards of consumption these rations were adequate but austere. Furthermore, this was also the time when some extremely odd items appeared on shop shelves in an effort to offer consumers a wider choice and reduce dollar expenditure. A corner shop in 1948 might well be offering whalemeat, reindeer and snoek, a fish which the Ministry of Food insisted was an appetising and satisfactory alternative to cod, haddock and plaice but which the average person considered virtually inedible.

A further factor in the restriction of personal consumption at this time was the introduction of the first post-war incomes policy in February 1948. Wage or incomes restraint was even at this early stage nothing new. Regular exhortations for moderation in wage bargaining had been made by ministers since the war ended. Several inter-departmental working parties had already drafted reports on the subject by the time I returned to Whitehall.[3] Furthermore, *A Statement on the Economic Considerations Affecting Relations between Workers and Employers*, approved by both the TUC and employers' representatives, which emphasised the need for British industry to keep its costs competitive, had been released in January 1947.[4] The convertibility crisis, however, forced the government to think seriously about a more formal attack on wages which had been rising at a rate of 8–10 per cent per

---

* The method whereby miscellaneous groceries, clothing and footwear were rationed.

annum since the beginning of 1946.

In the midst of the run on sterling the Prime Minister had made a strong 'appeal to workers in all industries and employments not to press ... for increases in wages, or changes in conditions which would have a similar effect'[5] and authorised the setting-up of another official working party to make suggestions on what further measures should be taken to restrict wage inflation. This group of senior officials, of which I was a member, issued an interim report to ministers in September 1947, but the debate as to what represented the optimum statement to make on wages policy continued at all levels for four more months. Numerous radical proposals for checking wage inflation were put forward for consideration, including the imposition of a public sector wage freeze, the announcement of a universal and statutory wage freeze, the allocation of a government representative to all major wage negotiations, and Cripps's own preference for the creation of a 'Central Appeal Tribunal' to which claims considered against the national interest could be referred. All of these were, however, rejected by ministers as too interventionist and too politically contentious for a Labour government.[6]

In the end, a White Paper entitled the *Statement on Personal Incomes, Costs and Prices* was issued. This followed the Ministry of Labour's more conciliatory line, and accepted the undesirability of direct interference by the government in wage negotiations. Instead it called for a voluntary freeze of wage rates and of 'incomes from profit, rent or other like sources', except where an undermanned industry could not attract labour in any other way, and where productivity had increased. The document also underlined that collective agreements should be strictly adhered to, and that wage increases would not necessarily be taken into account in the control of prices and margins.[7]

Thereafter, at the meetings that ministers and officials such as myself had with the TUC to discuss the White Paper, trade union leaders made clear their resentment about the lack of consultation immediately before the document's release, but nevertheless decided to call a special executive conference in March to discuss the wages policy. The conference backed the policy with two provisos. It insisted that workers 'below a reasonable standard of living', and those who sought to maintain established differentials, be able to apply for wage increases also.[8] The latter was a reason specifically rejected in the

White Paper.[9] Subsequently, the government persuaded the Federation of British Industries to accept voluntary dividend limitation and further extended its policies of price subsidy and control. Furthermore, in his first Budget speech Stafford Cripps announced a 'once and for all' capital levy on investment income in the previous year for those earning in excess of £2,000 per annum, thus indicating to the public that all sections of society would be expected to make sacrifices for the sake of Britain's economic recovery.

In fact the 'special contribution', as the levy was called, had excited considerable controversy in Whitehall. Though it was strongly urged on Cripps by Labour backbenchers, we in the Treasury were worried that it might be seen by the public as an annual Budget device. This, we believed, might serve to undermine industrial confidence and have a disincentive effect on production at a time when exactly the opposite was required.[10] Cripps was not convinced by the Treasury's arguments. Because of my close association with him, I was asked by my Treasury colleagues to see if I could persuade the Chancellor to change his mind. Just before the Budget I managed to convince him that he should strongly emphasise the contribution's 'once and for all' nature and scale down his proposals to a level more acceptable to City and industrial opinion.[11]

Allowing for the fact that the four exceptions to the general rule laid down in the White Paper could potentially have exempted every single trade union, by the spring of 1948 the Labour movement had committed itself for the first time to a policy that was in many ways contrary to its *raison d'être*. The policy was monitored closely at an official level, not least by myself and Robert Hall. Its progress was also followed with interest by ministers. It was widely regarded as successful. Over the eighteen months between the release of the White Paper and devaluation, even though unemployment never went much above 300,000 and considerable excess demand remained in the economy, wage inflation fell to an average of around 3 per cent per annum. This paved the way for similar downward movement in retail price inflation, which averaged about 4 per cent over the same period. Even though a good deal of suppressed inflation remained hidden by controls and rationing, by the standards of the 1970s and 1980s these figures are remarkable. They owed a lot to the fact that, at that time, the trade union leadership exerted much firmer control over the rank and file than was the case in the 1960s and 1970s and also reflected the fact that workers still retained a fear of unemployment from the inter-war years. During this period I was able to have regular, informal discussions of these problems with Vincent Tewson, General Secretary of the TUC, and other senior trade union leaders as well as with Norman Kipping, Director General of the Federation of British Industries, and other industrialists.

The only major cloud on the horizon in 1948 was the current account deficit with the Dollar Area. Although this was reduced by 50 per cent over the year, and the dollar drain declined in each of the first three quarters, the picture would have been considerably worse had it not been for what Cripps was to describe as an 'unexpectedly satisfactory' allocation of $1,293 million of Marshall Aid for the year 1948–9.[12]

In early 1948, as Congress debated the European Co-operation Bill, there remained a good deal of uncertainty as to whether or not Marshall Aid would be forthcoming. Ministers and officials were hopeful, but lived throughout this period with the fear that Congress might shatter all our hopes. We had to make projections and contingency plans on the assumption that no additional dollar aid would be received. The implications of such a scenario were frightening. In February 1948 it was calculated that on existing policies the dollar drain would exhaust all our reserves by the end of 1949. The Chancellor warned his Cabinet colleagues that circumstances might necessitate 'an operation as grave and as difficult as that needed on the outbreak of war' and a complete reorientation of Britain's foreign and defence policies.[13]

It was also logical at this stage for us to try to define the principles which should govern our policies if aid were forthcoming, and the sort of conditions we would be prepared to accept from the United States in return for aid. Ministers were agreed that two inter-related principles should guide our planning in respect of the European Recovery Programme. First, they declared that 'Marshall Aid should be used in such a way as to free us as soon as possible from outside economic support' and, second, in achieving this they believed that 'Britain must take the lead among, and co-operate to the fullest possible extent with, the other participating European countries.' It was accepted that this second principle would lead to closer ties with Europe, although never was it envisaged that Europe would take pride of place in our foreign relations above those with the United States and the Commonwealth. As far as the conditions of aid were concerned, ministers deemed it 'undesirable that any opening should be given for excessive interference by United States representatives in our domestic affairs'.[14]

April 3rd saw Congress finally approve the Economic Co-operation Bill and the provision of $17 billion of aid for a four-year period. Two weeks later the CEEC was recalled to assemble a European organisation to supervise the working of the European Recovery Programme, distribute aid, foster co-operation and work in tandem with the US Economic Co-operation Administration (ECA) which Truman had set up under the guidance of the industrialist Paul Hoffman. Soon afterwards, the Organisation for European Economic Co-operation (OEEC) was established. It was based in Paris.

The first chairman of the OEEC was Paul-Henri Spaak, the Belgian Prime Minister. Spaak was very much the American choice for the job because of his pro-integration sentiments. Robert Marjolin, the French economist and deputy to Jean Monnet at the Commissariat du Plan, was made Secretary-General. The Americans would have preferred Jean Monnet, who was then General Commissioner for the French modernisation plan and was later to be a key figure in the plans for the reconstruction of Europe. They were further disappointed when it was decided that the Secretary-General's powers should be limited to carrying out the decisions of the Council and a seven-man Executive Committee. The Executive Committee was to become the most powerful entity in the OEEC hierarchy. It was chaired by a British delegate, Edmund Hall-Patch. Hall-Patch was a remarkable man who before being seconded to the Foreign Office from the Treasury had been at different periods in his life a saxophonist, a novelist and a financial adviser to the Siamese government. He was not a great favourite with the Americans. They saw him as the resolute personification of the conservative, official British view on European co-operation and integration. Moreover, they had wanted the Executive Committee to be composed of finance ministers, with Cripps in the chair or, failing this, had hoped Oliver Franks would have been chosen by Britain in his place. Franks, however, was about this time made our Ambassador in Washington, an appointment which indicates in no uncertain terms that the United States was more important in British foreign policy than Europe.

Overall, both ministers and officials were happy with the constitutional make-up of the OEEC. It seemed to offer Britain some protection at least from American pressure for a rapid movement towards European integration. We were convinced this pressure would not be long in coming.

Following the creation of the OEEC, each member country had to negotiate a bilateral treaty with the United States government embodying certain principles laid down in the Economic Co-operation Act to ensure the continuity of assistance after July 1948. The first drafts of these treaties produced angry reactions in all OEEC countries because of both their substance and their tone. We in Britain were no exception. Negotiations between the US government and OEEC countries took place in Washington, and with less than two weeks to go before final signatures were required, we retained serious objections to a number of clauses which ran contrary to the ground rules we had laid down for American ERP aid early in the year. By this time all the other OEEC members had completed their negotiations and, according to Oliver Franks, we could expect no assistance from other European countries in securing an acceptable draft.[15]

At this stage, the provisions of the treaty which were still causing consternation in the Cabinet were:

(1) That Britain would be required to use materials bought with aid under the programme only for purposes specified in the submissions put forward in support of our requests for aid.

(2) That the British government would be required to 'stabilise its currency', maintain a 'valid' rate of exchange, and balance its Budget.

(3) That Britain would have to consult with the Americans about exchange rate policy.

(4) That the United States wanted a twelve-month period of notice for termination of the agreement.

(5) That most-favoured-nation treatment should be extended to our trade with Japan.

There was quite simply not a chance that any British government would sign an agreement containing obligations such as these. Cripps's response to the deadlock over the bilateral treaty was to circulate a memorandum to the Cabinet drafted three months earlier by the Economic Section. It had been written at a time when we were still not assured of Marshall Aid and when a very heavy balance of payments deficit for the year was forecast. It outlined in some detail the economic consequences for the nation if indeed the United Kingdom received no ERP aid. If aid was refused and the balance of payments deficit was financed out of reserves in 1948–9, the reserves would be reduced to £270 million by the end of the year, or half the level to which they had fallen during the convertibility crisis. We in the Treasury thought the lowest acceptable level for the reserves should be £500 million. Only drastic action could prevent the reserves' falling below that level. More strenuous efforts to expand exports to the Dollar Area would be needed, gold and dollar payments to non-dollar countries would have to be all but curtailed, and draconian import cuts imposed. It was estimated that only some £215 million would remain to finance dollar imports. This would imply no more food and tobacco from the Dollar Zone except for Canadian wheat, a sharp reduction in oil imports and a 12 per cent cut in raw-material imports as a whole.

The implications of all this for the home economy would be enormous. It would be necessary to reduce the rations of tea, sugar, butter, bacon, cheese, eggs and meat. The average calorific intake would be about 10 per cent below the pre-war average. No standard petrol allowance would be provided. The Agricultural Expansion Programme would have to be abandoned in so far as it depended on imported feeding-stuffs, there would be more widespread restrictions on consumer goods, and unemployment might escalate to 1.5 million or more. Cripps summed up the political situation in a paper to the Cabinet:

> These adjustments to the balance of payments would administer a number of violent shocks to the home economy at a number of separate points. The results to the structure of output, exports, investment, consumption and employment are extremely difficult to assess. We could be faced with an abrupt transition from a partially suppressed inflation to something not unlike a slump.[16]

After discussion of this memorandum in Cabinet, Cripps and Attlee hastily arranged a meeting with Lew Douglas, the US Ambassador in London. In no uncertain terms, they made clear to him the British objections to US interference in internal economic policy or trade and payments policy. Douglas transmitted these representations to Washington and, within two days, wordings for the various outstanding clauses were agreed which ministers believed would protect the British government's integrity and sovereignty. On 25th June the Cabinet authorised our negotiators in Washington to sign the Agreement on Economic Co-operation between the United Kingdom and the United States.[17]

In fact, most senior officials always believed that providing we kept our heads the Agreement would be signed on time and the drastic measures outlined to the Cabinet by Cripps would prove unnecessary. In our view, it really was absurd to think that the governments of the two most powerful nations in the Western world could allow themselves to reach the position of scrapping the whole Marshall initiative at such a late stage, and thereby hand over to Moscow a diplomatic, strategic and economic windfall beyond the Kremlin's wildest dreams.

The US government was anxious that the OEEC itself should perform the task of dividing up ERP funds amongst its members; they saw this as a step towards the European integration they were seeking to encourage. Opinion in Whitehall was set against this idea, as a constitutionally powerful OEEC threatened to push us closer to Europe and farther away from the United States and the Commonwealth than we wished to go. We preferred that Washington undertook the role of aid allocation. However, the Americans forced the issue and we had to acquiesce in their demands, at least in the short term.

To allow the OEEC to play its prescribed role, member states had to submit detailed annual requests for aid. It was also required by the European Co-operation Administration (ECA) in July 1948 that OEEC countries should provide a 'Long-Term Programme' for the balance of payments and production to illustrate in general terms the means by which they proposed to achieve viability in 1952–3 at a satisfactory level of economic activity. The individual Long-Term Programmes could then be pieced together by the OEEC to provide a general statement on Western European viability for the ECA.[18]

The bilateral treaty we had signed with the Americans did not make the preparation of a Long-Term Programme mandatory but, although we were under no obligation, officials on the European Co-operation Committee decided that such a move would prove, on balance, to be 'in our own interests', provided it was 'kept as general as possible' and did not represent a series of formal commitments.[19] When ministers came to discuss the subject they were initially by no means convinced. There were worries that it would lead to political embarrassment for the government. The point was made at a meeting of the Economic Policy Committee that: 'As shown by our experience with the two *Economic Surveys* published in this country, any subsequent curtailment of published plans was inevitably represented by political opponents as failure on the part of the Government.' The questions were also raised of how much realism other governments would be prepared to show in their plans, and whether or not it was sensible to put forward a European plan 'when several of the Governments concerned had no effective control over their economy'.[20]

On the other hand, however, it was suggested that 'the preparation of the original proposals for European co-operation which had been undertaken in Paris in 1947 had exercised a helpful influence in bringing other European Governments to face the realities of the situation; and ... that even greater benefits would flow from the work of a long-term programme.' It was never proposed by the ECA that the plan should be detailed and contain annual targets. It was to be drawn up in the broadest terms. Finally, there were fears that without such a plan for viability, the US government would find it difficult to persuade Congress to provide the much-needed dollars in subsequent years.[21] It was these fears, that although $17 billion had been promised by the US government, Congress might veto or scale down future payments if they were unconvinced of a commitment to viability among OEEC nations, which more than anything else convinced ministers that they should back the idea of a Long-Term Programme. On 12th July 1948 I recommended to senior officials that the work on this project should be completed by October so as to be ready in time for the Conference of Dominion Prime Ministers scheduled for that month.[22]

In point of fact the Long-Term Programme had a long pedigree. For example, several attempts had been made in the war to foresee the future of international trade and the likely course for the British balance of payments after hostilities had ceased; the Board of Trade had carried out a massive survey of Britain's long-term export prospects in 1945–6; two annual *Economic Surveys* had already been published and there were also two unpublished yearly 'Economic Surveys'. Furthermore, since our establishment in the spring of 1947, we in the

CEPS had been working in conjunction with the Economic Section and other departments on two 'Long-Term Economic Surveys' to provide a background of economic fact and forecast for the preparation of economic plans.[23] These 'Long-Term Economic Surveys' were to have vital implications for the make-up of the Long-Term Programme and must therefore be discussed here.

A first draft of a survey for the years 1948–51 was circulated in May 1947.[24] The essence of this document was that by 1951 exports must have increased in volume terms to 175 per cent of the 1938 level and that this would consequently allow imports to be some 90 per cent of their 1938 level, bearing in mind the loss of invisible income during the war and changes in the terms of trade. General consumption was assumed to be 20 per cent above the 1947 level and productivity was expected to increase by 2.5 per cent per annum. To achieve the balance of payments targets, the engineering, vehicle and chemical industries would have to increase their exports two and a half times over pre-war levels, and another wide range of industries would have to achieve an increase of one and a half times the pre-war level. The crucial problem was seen as bringing manpower into the agriculture, mining and textile industries.

In June 1947 Austin Robinson, who was fulfilling his final obligations in Cambridge before joining the CEPS, was asked to comment on this survey. He wrote a stinging criticism which was circulated at official level. He thought that the external problem was considerably more difficult than the survey made out. The export estimate for 1951 of 175 per cent of the 1938 volume was unrealistic. A year previously it had been calculated in Whitehall that world exports of manufactures might be about 35 per cent above the pre-war level by 1951, but since then the prospects for lowering trade barriers had deteriorated. Moreover, the previous estimates assumed a poor export performance by West Germany and Japan, leaving an increase of about 155 per cent in world exports of manufacturers to be divided among Britain, the United States and other exporters. These assumptions now appeared to be much less certain. The prospects for Britain's exports being substituted for other countries' exports depended on their elasticity of demand. His estimate of this ruled out a large increase. He also thought that the survey had underestimated the raw-material imports we would require by £50 million, and that more import-saving ought to be possible from a large expansion of the agricultural sector.

Austin Robinson also made the general point that the main objective of planning should be to make planning unnecessary, that is to say to 'organise the productive economy of the British Isles which will meet the requirements of the British population without rationing and controls and with the minimum of discriminatory taxation designed to steer consumption away from forms which the public would prefer'. He saw a plan as a means to adjust the available resources to the desiderata of the nation.[25] I heartily agreed with these views. To me the idea of planning and control for its own sake was unrealistic, both politically and economically. It was our job to plan so that we might return the economy to a more normal state of affairs where consumer sovereignty would be re-established. Planning was a means whereby we could overcome the enormous effects of the war on our nation, just as it had been a method whereby we could achieve the maximum mobilisation of resources in the war. I was also convinced that fiscal and monetary policy, which had been largely ignored in the survey, would become increasingly important in the management of the economy as time went on. Accordingly, I sought and received in qualified form an assurance from Edward Bridges that the Treasury would be prepared to execute any fiscal policy which was agreed to be desirable in the future.

A draft of the 1948–51 Survey was discussed by the EPB on 7th August 1948. The Board agreed with a covering note supplied by the CEPS that there should be three broad stages in planning for recovery. In stage one, we should improve basic supplies and services to industry and step up export production and import saving. In stage two, we should seek to improve the equipment of manufacturing industry with the main emphasis on export and import-saving industries. In stage three, we should seek further to expand output and the equipment of industry in order to meet the full demand of the home market in addition to exports, and undertake non-industrial investment to improve amenities and the standard of living.[26]

By the time the '1948–51 Economic Survey' was presented to the EPB the convertibility crisis had rendered much of its detail out of date. It was never shown to ministers. In the autumn we began work in the CEPS on another Long-Term Survey to cover the years 1948–52 which was to occupy us for much of the next year. On this occasion, Austin Robinson was put in charge of the project. We also received the co-operation of the Economic Section, Central Statistical Office and other economic departments in this task.

During the early summer of 1948 a 'Draft Long-Term Economic Survey for 1948–52' was circulated. To my mind, this was a marked advance on the previous year's effort. The latter had attempted to give a general view of the economy but it did not make a serious study of the future of exports. It merely took 175 per cent of the 1938 volume as a basis for planning and considered the plausibility of the figure only by reference to home production possibilities. Moreover, it made no attempt to provide a schedule of labour requirements by industry, or of required levels of industrial output, though there were discussions on a few major industries.

The main changes in the 1948–52 Survey were derived from the view that we could not rely on an export volume greater than 145 per cent of the 1938 level. This, in turn, implied that we could not afford more than 75–80 per cent of the 1938 import volume; that we must expand home agriculture by at least 50 per cent above the pre-war level; that growth in gross investment would have to be limited to 10 per cent over the period to 1952 with the scale of social investment remaining static; and that by 1952 consumption per head would only be marginally above that of 1938, with a relatively smaller proportion of consumers' expenditure going on food and clothing. The Survey also set out 'four broad objectives' for the following years:

(1)   To secure a balance of payments by means that will permit us to achieve the highest possible national income.

(2)   To restore the nation's capital equipment and raise it to a state in which it can afford a firm foundation for future development.

(3)   To bring consumption standards back towards the pre-war levels as rapidly as is permitted by increases of productivity and is consistent with the first two objectives.

(4)   To establish an efficient and smoothly working economic system in which the incentives to produce and consume will operate with no more control and compulsion than is absolutely necessary.[27]

The 1948–52 Survey was comprehensive and persuasive, not to say courageous. It sought to make clear to ministers what we saw at the time as the unpalatable truths confronting the nation, so that they might summon the country to greater efforts and prepare them for prolonged shortages. This was not easy. After all, the government had a strong interest in social reform and in the establishment of a Welfare State. The idea of restricting current expenditure on social policy, and of telling people that food would be short and rationed for four years ahead was bound to be disagreeable. Nevertheless, ministers, albeit grudgingly, accepted these conclusions.[28]

With hindsight, the Survey's focal point – the prospects for the balance of payments and overseas trade – proved overly pessimistic and was based largely on irrelevant pre-war trends and concepts. The Survey had concluded that it would be difficult to export because of secular world trends. This view led to the conclusion that we should endeavour to increase our self-sufficiency as much as we could in the context of the multilateral international trade and payments agreements to which we were party. Although the Survey went sadly astray in its appraisal of the prospects for world trade and Britain's share in it, it is only fair to say that the remarkable forces that led to the great post-war expansion of world trade were not, at that stage, easy to detect. Those who were taking a more optimistic view found it hard to back up their arguments with convincing evidence. Indeed, officials felt at the time that it was morally wrong to rely upon optimism and to hope that it would all come right in the end. We had to face up to grim realities and prepare for the worst. It was not our job to provide figures and projections which were politically convenient but economically fanciful.

Ministers originally intended to publish a version of the 'Long-Term Economic Survey 1948–52' but, with the decision to submit a Long-Term Programme to the OEEC and publish it, this idea was dropped and the Survey pushed to one side. By the middle of July the CEPS and Economic Section were working hard on the Long-Term Programme. It was accepted at an early stage by ministers and officials that the assumptions in the balance of payments section of the Long-Term Survey should be used as the basis for the Long-Term Programme,[29] and indeed much of the work done over the previous ten months or so was to prove invaluable to us in drawing up our OEEC submission. For example, the Long-Term Programme also utilised the Survey's estimates of productivity growth per annum (2.5 per cent) and growth in consumption per head over the next four years (3 per cent).

The UK Long-Term Programme was never intended as a rigid blueprint for future action. We believed that planning over a long period must be flexible. As Austin Robinson put it, it would be 'a mistake to attempt to create detailed straitjackets in an operational plan'.[30] Moreover, the Long-Term Programme was always meant to be a provisional document, having been prepared in ignorance of the programmes of other countries. It was assumed that the United Kingdom, in common with other participating countries, would need to adjust its own programme as the joint studies in Paris proceeded. Furthermore, the Long-Term Programme was never designed to be a truly comprehensive study of the nation's economic prospects in all areas. Its general framework was one prescribed by the OEEC for its own purposes; it was neither exhaustive nor what we ourselves would have preferred had we had the choice. Finally, no statistical forecast in it could be taken very seriously. Predicting future events in economics will always be an inexact science at which, as Robert Hall frequently used to say to me, 'nobody is very good'. For example, the movements of external payments and receipts four years hence depended on so many factors completely out of our control that estimates could never be described as more than intelligent guesses based on certain arbitrary assumptions. The same qualifications also applied, although to a lesser degree, to predictions of home production and investment.

The Long-Term Programme was, therefore, merely a signpost to the future. It pointed the direction in which we felt we had to go and gave some measure of the efforts needed to reach our objective. The figures included were primarily there for purposes of illustration.

The Programme aimed at closing a balance of payments gap estimated at £630 million in 1947, and leaving a surplus of around £100 million by 1952–3. Total overseas earnings were assumed to rise over that period by more than a quarter, from £1,650 million in 1948–9 to £2,090 million in 1952–3. Although imports from the Western Hemisphere were assumed to be cut by about 20 per cent and exports to the Western Hemisphere increased by 55 per cent, the Programme envisaged a continuing shortage of dollars in 1952–3. The prospective deficit with the Western Hemisphere was put at over £70 million. To cover it Britain would have to rely on the gold production and dollar earnings of the rest of the Sterling Area, with which Britain was expected to have a substantial surplus put in the Programme at over £200 million.

To build this surplus on current account while still offering a slight improvement in the standard of living Britain had to expand home production considerably. The Programme assumed that expansion would be sufficient to provide for an increase in the volume of exports to 50 per cent above 1938, rather more than 10 per cent above the 1948 level; capital investment at a rate of about £2,000 million a year; a 15–20 per cent rise in the supply of manufactured goods and a substantial increase in home-produced supplies of food to replace imports. The farmers' contribution was viewed as especially important, and the Programme assumed that the Agricultural Expansion Programme would be successful. The growth in manufacturing output was targeted at a level 13 per cent above the 1948 figure. It was hoped to raise coal output by nearly a quarter, electricity generating capacity by a half, and steel output by a sixth.

Investment resources were to be concentrated on developments contributing directly to the country's economic strength. More than two-thirds were to be devoted to industrial and agricultural investment and under a quarter to housing and social services. It was also proposed to undertake a substantial net increase in investment in the Colonies over the four years, particularly in the provision of basic services.

The achievements envisaged in the UK Long-Term Programme depended on full co-operation with other countries in Western Europe and the Commonwealth, and on financial stability at home. It was made clear in the document that it was the objective of the government's budgetary policy to maintain full employment, while ensuring that sufficient purchasing power was withheld to finance the large investment programme without inflation. It was also emphasised that continuing restraint with regard to personal incomes would be needed from all sections of the community if an upward spiral of costs and prices was to be avoided. Indeed, the wholehearted collaboration of the public was seen as vital if the objective of viability was to be attained.[31]

The Long-Term Programme was submitted on 1st October to the OEEC in Paris, together with our programme for 1949–50, and was presented there by Austin Robinson and Donald MacDougall. It received a favourable response. In December it was published, and by the new year it had been integrated into an OEEC 'Interim Report' together with the other nations' programmes. It was the first and only long-term economic plan to be issued by a British government before

Labour's National Plan of 1965. With the completion of the Long-Term Programme, interest in long-term planning waned in Whitehall. Thereafter, economic planning was increasingly seen in terms of measures to maintain full employment, restrain inflation and preserve the external balance. As I had predicted, we turned more and more to demand-management rather than direct intervention in the allocation of resources. Controls that were no longer seen as helpful in the management of demand were dropped as over the next five years or so the shortages that gave rise to them were overcome. Increasingly, it was the Budget and credit control which we used to guide the economy, although for the next few years at least, import control and investment programming also retained a vital importance.

Any comparison of the forecasts of the Long-Term Programme with the actual out-turn must allow for numerous changes in statistical definitions. A detailed study made in 1955 shows, however, that the aims of the Programme were achieved by 1952–3, both in broad outline and considerable detail. Of course, over the four years after 1948 the British economy was greatly affected by a major devaluation and a large increase in armaments expenditure throughout the Western world. These events rendered the original assumptions of the Programme largely inappropriate; nevertheless, industrial production was about one-third above the pre-war level, as the Programme had supposed. The allocation of output was also much as set forth in the Programme. Investment increased more than expected, though as a result of construction rather than productive investment. By 1952–3 the volume of exports had, in fact, reached the programmed figure of 50 per cent above 1938 and the balance of payments, if revalued at 'programmed prices' to eliminate the worsening of the terms of trade, showed at least as great an improvement as had been hoped for. The same was also more or less true of both the increase in dollar earnings and the fall in dollar expenditure.[32]

It would be a mistake to attach too much importance to the now almost forgotten Long-Term Programme and the four-year Economic Survey which underlay it. At the time, however, these documents did help to clarify the minds of officials and ministers alike, and brought home to us the full extent of the task facing us in the aftermath of the convertibility crisis. As such, they were a significant step on the road to our post-war recovery and deserve more attention than they have previously received.

CHAPTER SIX

1949:
Sterling Devalued

From a casual glance at the economic indicators for 1949, it appears to have been a year of continued recovery and progress. Full employment was maintained; price and wage inflation, thanks to a second Crippsian austerity Budget and the success of the 1948 White Paper on Incomes, Costs and Prices (Cmnd. 7321, February 1948), remained minimal; industrial production, gross investment and exports all continued to rise. However, by comparison with the relative calm of 1948, 1949 was to prove a year of crises. Once again, it was the external account and the dollar balance, in particular, which turned out to be at the heart of our problems. The result was that arguments over the merits of a devaluation of sterling and various measures to accompany such a step were to dominate the lives of officials in the Treasury for much of the year.

While the possibility of using devaluation as a means to balance Britain's post-war external account had been discussed on numerous occasions during the war, the subject received scant attention in the early post-war years when Britain sought to finance an unavoidable deficit by borrowing, principally from the United States and Canada.[1] It was only when the current account began to move back into surplus in 1948 that a move from the existing exchange rate of £1 = \$4.03 began to appear to some officials as a possible option. The movement towards an overall surplus hid the fact that a large gold and dollar deficit with hard currency nations remained, while the expanding sales to countries with soft currencies yielded an inconvertible surplus of 'unrequited exports'. Devaluation, it was asserted, would make hard currencies softer and soft currencies harder, and thus reduce the problem.

Between February and September 1948 devaluation and indeed the possibility of allowing the pound to float for a time were discussed in an informal manner by Treasury, Bank of England and Economic Section officials, but their conclusion was that the case for such action was not proven at that time.[2] Robert Hall, for one, was 'mainly influenced' in reaching this decision by the fact that 'most of our dollar exports were in short supply and by the inflation then going on in the USA which might well have made their costs rise at some stage above ours'.[3] I myself was not directly involved in these discussions, nor to my knowledge was the subject ever raised with ministers.

Early in 1949 the Economic Section advised the CEPS that the US economy seemed to be moving into recession, casting a shadow over the optimism we had felt at the end of 1948. During the following months industrial production and stockbuilding in the United States fell off rapidly and had a major effect on Sterling Area exports, with the result that our balance of payments on current account again moved into deficit. Devaluation quickly became a favourite topic of debate among informed outside opinion. At about the same time, Robert Hall raised with me the case for an official inquiry into the subject. His personal opinion, and also that of his deputy Marcus Fleming, was that now 'all the advantages are in favour of devaluation'. Furthermore, as deflation, the traditional cure for a payments deficit, had been abandoned, he believed that 'the onus is certainly on those who say that devaluation will not be a remedy to prove their case'.[4]

I was soon convinced not only that there should be an inquiry but that devaluation was inevitable, and we set about the task of trying to persuade other officials and ministers at least to consider the proposal. This was to prove a long and arduous process. Senior Treasury officials only gradually changed their views. The Bank of England, not unreasonably fearful that ministers would be most reluctant to accompany devaluation with the necessary deflationary measures, remained opposed. The Chancellor never wavered from his conviction that such a policy was morally wrong when other countries held their reserves in sterling.

Cripps retained, moreover, an emotional hankering for direct controls, including severe limitations on imports and measures to discriminate against purchases from the United States. Indeed, at one time he wanted to forbid all imports of American tobacco. As taxes on tobacco raised some £800 million each year and there was in the short term no alternative source of Virginian tobacco, we in the Treasury were horrified at the prospect of raising a comparable sum from other taxes. It was only when we emphasised to the Chancellor that tobacco duty was the only tax which the average Englishman would stand in a queue to pay that he was persuaded to drop this idea.

From the late spring sterling came under increasing speculative pressure. Much of this emanated from the United States. Senior American officials – such as Snyder, Secretary of the Treasury, and Hoffman and Harriman at the ECA – encouraged by press and financial opinion, became convinced of the need for a wholesale realignment of currencies, including a sterling devaluation, if European recovery was to continue beyond the end of Marshall Aid. Towards the end of March it became clear that the Americans were keen to push a resolution through the IMF calling for a major inquiry into European exchange rates. Despite the horror of UK officials and ministers at the destabilising potential of such a move, and the strong protests voiced by Oliver Franks in Washington, the Americans were not to be dissuaded and the resolution was passed.[5] Speculation was further encouraged in May by the conclusion of the Report of the Economic Commission for Europe that 'European currencies in general are over-valued in respect to the dollar '.[6]

At the beginning of June, at the suggestion of Oliver Franks, two senior officials, Robert Hall and Henry Wilson-Smith (head of the Treasury's Overseas Finance Division), were sent to Washington to talk to the Americans about Britain's economic position and to try to persuade them to behave with greater discretion. During their discussions it became obvious to Hall and Wilson-Smith that US officials were concerned lest we had abandoned the objectives of convertibility and non-discrimination agreed when the IMF was set up in 1944 and during the loan discussions in the following year. It appeared to the Americans that in the face of a worsening dollar shortage, our policy was actually to move in the opposite direction. They argued that now supplies were becoming more plentiful, the pull of prices was in favour of American goods. Only if British and Sterling Area goods were made cheaper in comparison with American ones, would market forces begin to move in a direction which would reduce the dollar shortage. Sterling devaluation was therefore a necessity.[7]

Henry Wilson-Smith, who previously had been opposed to devaluation, was so influenced by the Americans' arguments that within a month he had reluctantly joined those of us who believed devaluation was both necessary and inevitable. His influence in the Treasury, particularly with Edward Bridges, was important.

By this time the balance of payments was deteriorating rapidly, with the dollar balance leading the way. At the same time our reserves were declining with increasing speed. The loss escalated from £82 million in the first quarter of 1949 to £157 million in the second. In early June, Cripps warned his colleagues that within a year all the reserves would be gone and that sterling might collapse completely, while Attlee drew comparisons with the calamitous events of 1931.[8] Despite this atmosphere of escalating crisis, however, nobody in the Cabinet was, at that stage, prepared seriously to contemplate devaluation. Instead, ministers were content to agree to a series of stop-gap proposals put forward by Cripps to stem the immediate outflow. These included a cut of 25 per cent in dollar expenditures over the coming year, the suspension of fresh dollar commitments until the end of September other than in exceptional circumstances, and a Commonwealth Economic Conference in the next month. Commonwealth finance ministers subsequently agreed to extend the import cuts to all member states. All these steps, of course, merely served to exacerbate US fears about the direction of our policy.

At the end of June, a few days after ministers had accepted his emergency measures, Cripps circulated to the Economic Policy Committee a paper reviewing the external situation and offering three possible lines of policy for the future.[9] These were: severe deflation, devaluation, or the on-going policy of improving competitive power through exhortations for higher productivity. Severe fiscal deflation was out of the question as it ran completely against party policy and, it was believed, would ruin Labour's chances of success at the next general election. Cripps, however, was prepared to see some mild deflation, and made it clear that he would demand compensatory cuts in food subsidies if various Supplementary Estimates were added to current public expenditure levels. The Treasury and Bank of England also suggested a tightening of monetary policy at this stage but, with Dalton declaiming about the reincarnation of Montagu Norman, Cripps was unwilling to raise short-term interest rates to satisfy City opinion.[10]

The unwillingness of ministers to raise Bank Rate was another example of their dislike of the price mechanism and preference for controls which they did not really know how to use. There was a tendency to associate the price system with the profit motive which they saw as inherently evil.

As for devaluation, Cripps made clear his agreement with the Bank of England's arguments against such a step. These he circulated as an appendix to his main memorandum. He stressed, too, that all his advisers were agreed that devaluation alone was not enough. Thus ministers were left only with the current policy which he proposed to bolster by import cuts, strict economy with regard to public expenditure, a reaffirmation of the wages policy of the previous year, an appeal for help from North America, a form of selective tax or subsidy scheme to encourage dollar exporters, and a movement towards freer trade with Europe to compensate for the restriction of the dollar trade.[11] When this memorandum was discussed by ministers on 1st July only Morrison – urged on by his closest adviser, Max Nicholson, and seeing it as the least of the evils put to them – supported devaluation.[12]

Among officials, opinion about devaluation was still at this stage divided. Those who favoured devaluation, now including Leslie Rowan, put the case thus: there was little prospect of an end to the dollar shortage in the near future, we could not go on borrowing to finance our dollar deficit *ad infinitum*, and there was abundant evidence that our exports were uncompetitive in North American markets in terms of price. How else could we simultaneously reduce the dollar gap and make our exports more competitive except by devaluation? As Robert Hall put it, severe deflation 'would be a fantastic reversal of all we have striven for in economics since 1931', while to hope we could overcome the current crisis by productivity increases was no more than wishful thinking and, in effect, merely added up to a policy of drift. At the same time, a retreat into an independent sterling block, as was being proposed in some quarters, would have been against all our post-war political and economic goals. There was, in reality, no logical alternative to devaluation. We could take the step ourselves sooner, or be forced into it later when the reserves ran out.[13]

Those against devaluation, of whom the most persistent was the Bank of England, did not believe it would remedy for any length of time the root causes of Britain's external problems. These they diagnosed as excessive government expenditure, nationalisation, the burden of sterling liabilities, and the current recession in the United States. They believed that Britain's financial credibility and stability could be restored only by drastic action to cut public expenditure, particularly on food subsidies and the National Health Services, and a deferment of further nationalisation plans. The Bank of England believed that a devaluation would most likely cause our closest competitors to devalue with us, so that there would be no real benefit to our balance of payments with third countries. In trade with North America they saw 'no reason to foresee any immediate increase in the dollar income of the Sterling Area' while our imports were already tightly controlled and unlikely to fall much in response to higher prices. Their conclusion, therefore, was that, given their view of the price elasticities of demand for Britain's exports and imports, devaluation would have an adverse effect on our dollar balance.[14]

Edward Bridges, as Permanent Secretary to the Treasury, had a crucial role to play as far as both sides of official opinion were concerned. The protagonists of both policies did their best to convince him that their policy was right. To him the disadvantages of devaluation had long been obvious, while the advantages remained uncertain. Like Stafford Cripps, he also saw devaluation as a dishonest, almost sordid action. This is amply illustrated by the fact he gave the policy of devaluation the code name of 'Caliban', which he told Robert Hall stood for all that was unsavoury and underhand. Moreover, to the end he remained determined to see that ministers should never view devaluation as a universal panacea, but that they should see it in the context of a series of measures necessary to stabilise the economy. He was frightened by the possibility that one devaluation might be followed by another. This was something that both Robert Hall and I were also always conscious of. We had maintained all along that cuts in government expenditure, a tighter monetary policy and, indeed, a stronger incomes policy would be necessary to make room for increased export production, and to head off the possibility of wages following prices in an upward spiral. It was not until well into July that Bridges became convinced that there was no practical alternative to devaluation.

On the 7th July the Secretary of the US Treasury, John Snyder, arrived in London for two days of talks with British ministers and officials which we hoped would find 'some compromise solution to the long term [dollar] problem which would be acceptable to American and Canadian opinion as well as to ourselves'.[15] John Snyder was a conservative from a small-town background. Unlike most US officials with whom I dealt, he was often overtly anti-British and difficult to deal with. I never managed to discover the cause of this attitude, nor did I or others succeed in softening it. By the time of this meeting, Stafford Cripp's health was failing fast. He was suffering from a serious gastric ailment which made it difficult for him to sleep or eat. Moreover, the strain of the last few months, added to his insatiable appetite for work, meant that he was close to the end of his tether. He had made arrangements to enter a sanatorium in Switzerland on 19th July.

Despite the frailty of his physical condition, Cripps conducted the London talks with his usual skill. Snyder emphasised from the start that his government was convinced that devaluation was 'an essential element in any long-term solution' to Britain's dollar and general balance of payments problems, but he got little reaction from Cripps on this subject. Cripps told the US Treasury Secretary that devaluation would be acceptable only within the limits of a general settlement, the nature of which he was unprepared to elaborate. Furthermore, he even tried to convince Snyder that he should allow Britain to insert a sentence into the final communiqué from the talks implying that the United States did not consider the devaluation of sterling to be an appropriate measure in present circumstances. Snyder, not surprisingly, refused, although in the end he was persuaded to sign a statement claiming that devaluation had not been mentioned during the talks. A disgruntled Snyder returned home talking of 'a fundamental difference between US and UK in [their] approach to the problem of economic recovery and stability'.[16] The only truly positive development from the talks was an agreement to hold further official and ministerial discussions in Washington at the end of August and the beginning of September. Indeed, had it not been for the diplomatic skills of Oliver Franks, we might not have even achieved this. It was only through his interventions at the meeting that any sort of meaningful dialogue was established.[17]

In the middle of July, Douglas Jay, Economic Secretary to the Treasury, and Hugh Gaitskell, Minister for Fuel and Power, became convinced of the inevitability of devaluation. As Jay and Gaitskell, neither of whom was at the time a member of the Cabinet, were to form two-thirds of the ministerial triumvirate to whom Attlee passed the

Chancellor's duties during his convalescence in Switzerland, their change of heart was to prove decisive. What is more, although he was still, as Jay has put it, apt to take 'refuge in ambiguity',[18] the last third of the triumvirate, Harold Wilson, President of the Board of Trade, was at this stage also coming around to this view as it became increasingly apparent to him that severe cuts in public expenditure would soon be the only alternative.

Jay claims that he was greatly influenced in his decision by evidence produced at the Commonwealth Economic Conference by Edgar Whitehead, the Finance Minister of Southern Rhodesia, that British exports were uncompetitive in terms of price.[19] Gaitskell's conversion is said to have been the result of a conversation on Hampstead Heath with Paul Rosenstein-Rodan, a close personal friend and Economic Adviser to the World Bank, although Lord Kaldor has also claimed to have played a part.[20] Even though when any important decision is made everyone involved is apt to exaggerate his own influence, I am also convinced that the many discussions Robert Hall and I had with Gaitskell and Jay in previous months played a part in convincing them of the need for devaluation.

On 21st July, by which time our gold and dollar reserves had fallen below the £400 million mark, Gaitskell, Jay and Wilson met and decided to advise the Prime Minister to devalue sterling. The same day Bevan agreed to the need for a lower exchange rate and Dalton also was soon converted. On the 25th July, Gaitskell, Jay and Wilson explained their views to Attlee, who was convinced. Gaitskell took the lead in all this, and in doing so made such an impression on Attlee as to make him the obvious successor to Cripps if and when his health failed completely.[21] Senior officials were informed of these developments the next day in Edward Bridges' room. We knew, however, that the saga of devaluation still had some way to run and that, even if it was now assured that devaluation would take place, the questions of when, by how much and with what supporting measures, remained.

A few days later, Edward Bridges sent a note to Attlee expressing the combined views of himself and his two Second Secretaries – Wilson-Smith and Eady – Robert Hall and myself.[22] We told the Prime Minister that while we supported a 'substantial' devaluation to bring British costs back into line, it was 'essential' that other accompanying steps were taken to reduce the inflationary pressures operative in the economy which 'would soon cancel any benefits to be obtained from devaluation'. We had in mind a 5 per cent reduction in public expenditure for the current year which should be maintained in the next financial year and a 'moderate rise in money rates of interest as a supporting measure'. Attlee's immediate response to this minute and to a further explanatory note written by Robert Hall was disappointing. Initially, he seemed unwilling or unable to grasp what was to us the obvious connection between budgetary policy and the external account. Eventually, we managed to convince him that some deflation was necessary in order to provide capacity for the increased export production that would be needed.

The Cabinet met on 29th July and 'agreed in principle that the pound might be devalued'.[23] They granted the Prime Minister authority to take the action he thought necessary. A few days later, he sent a letter to Cripps in Switzerland drafted in the main by Douglas Jay, and delivered by Harold Wilson who was to spend his vacation close by. It began,

> My Dear Stafford,
> Though most reluctant to inflict official business on you at this time, I feel compelled to seek your views on certain issues arising out of the dollar situation. I have been considering further, together with those of my colleagues most closely concerned, and the officials charged with responsibility for preparing materials for the Washington talks, the question of devaluation. All of us are now agreed, including the responsible officials, that this is a necessary step (though not of course the only step) if we are to stop the present dollar drain before our reserves fall to a level so dangerous as to impair the Government's ability to handle the situation.

The reasons given for this decision were cited as: an expectation of devaluation which was leading to an unwillingness to hold sterling, or to buy British goods; the unlikelihood of short-term financial help from North America; the fact that substantial long-term assistance could not be expected from the Americans before the reserves fell to crisis levels.

The letter went on to mention how officials 'unanimously' believed that inflationary pressures would have to be tackled urgently if there was to be 'any lasting benefit from devaluation', and then dealt with the timing of such a move. Attlee favoured a date before the Washington talks in order to make sure that it did not appear that Britain was 'trading an offer of devaluation for concessions' from the Americans.[24]

When Harold Wilson reported back to Attlee on Cripps's response to this letter, it appeared that it was the timetable of devaluation, rather than the taking of the decision itself, which concerned the Chancellor most. Assuming there was not to be an early general election, Cripps wanted to decide on a date on his return in consultation with Attlee, Bevin and Wilson. His own opinion was, however, that no announcement should be made before the Washington talks, since this would seem to undermine confidence in the new rate and be seen by the Americans as 'a piece of sharp practice'. He favoured announcing the decision to the nation on 18th September, after he had returned from Washington, even though this implied that the rundown in reserves would be allowed to continue for a dangerously long time.[25]

When Cripps returned to England on 19th August senior ministers, together with Edward Bridges, assembled at Chequers to discuss the subject. The Chancellor's health remained poor. He was still not sleeping without the aid of drugs and he was anxious not to take on his full duties for another ten days or so. Moreover, it soon became clear that Cripps was still not wholly convinced that, on balance, we should benefit from devaluation. In the end, however, he was persuaded to overcome his moral objections and acquiesce in the decision, provided Britain could secure firm US backing for a new rate when we informed the IMF.[26] He also insisted that no announcement be made until 18th September.

There is no doubt in my mind that after his repeated declarations, both public and private, that he would not countenance it, the decision to devalue left Cripps with a great sense of frustration and personal humiliation. However, to my knowledge he never seriously contemplated resignation.

The Chequers decision to delay devaluation until Cripps and Bevin had returned from Washington was made known to the Cabinet on 29th August, the day that the British delegation set sail on the *Mauretania* for the United States. Those who travelled on the *Mauretania* were Mr and Mrs Bevin, Stafford Cripps, Roger Makins, myself and the two private secretaries. Roderick Barclay and William Armstrong, Robert Hall, George Bolton of the Bank of England, and Henry Wilson-Smith had gone on ahead by air. The trip across the Atlantic was extremely rough and, on one day, Roger Makins and I were forced to retire to bed. However, the weather had much less effect on either Bevin or Cripps, and the latter, despite his poor health, was to be found endlessly pacing the deck, frequently before dawn. On one occasion he actually persuaded the Captain to refill the swimming pool so that he might swim in it. When he did so, every time the ship rolled or pitched one end of the pool was almost empty!

One day when I was standing idly by the ship's rail looking at the sea, someone came up to me and said, 'You don't know me but we have something in common.' He continued, 'You once had a governess called Leda Sesti who taught you to read and at the same time to speak Italian. Many years later she taught me to speak English.' He was Guido Carli, subsequently Governor of the Bank of Italy. Years after I left the Treasury he and I were to serve together on two international advisory boards.

I am reminded by Roger Makins (Lord Sherfield) that perhaps the strangest aspect of the crossing was that the two ministers did not actually meet for the first three or four days. Cripps, who had joined our party late at Southampton, used to get up at 4 or 5 a.m. and go to bed around 4 or 5 p.m. Bevin would not get up until after that time. We officials would brief Cripps in the morning and Bevin in the later afternoon. It was not until the third or fourth day, when Cripps consented to stay up a little later, that we had the opportunity to speak to them together.

When we arrived in New York, after a press conference we had supper on board. On the way into the dining room Bevin turned to me and said, 'Come and sit next to me and let's have some champagne.' We did. Part way through the first course someone came and whispered in his ear that there was a high-ranking official of the State Department present who should have been sitting next to him. He turned to me and said, 'Well, Edwin, I suppose you'd better let him take your place,' and as an afterthought, 'here, take the bottle.'

After dinner we drove through New York to catch the train to Washington in a convoy of cars with a police escort, passing one red light after another – something I have never done before or since. At the station we had to walk some way to the train and it became obvious that Bevin was far from well. He was gasping for air and having difficulty moving his bulky frame. He revived himself with some heart pills, saying to me, 'The old ticker is not what it was.' It dawned on me then that the Foreign Secretary might soon have to retire.

Conversation during the crossing mainly centred on our brief for the talks and how we would present it. We hoped to secure from the Americans more favourable administration of the ERP, a resumption of stockpiling, loans from the Export-Import Bank, drawing rights from the IMF, reciprocal tariff reductions, help with regard to the burden of our sterling balances, and an increase in the dollar price of gold.[27]

The one subject which we did not touch on until we reached Washington was the question of the rate. This was not decided until we reached the British Embassy. The Economic Section had for some months been making calculations about what rate would be the most suitable, bearing in mind their estimates of Britain's import and export elasticities of demand and the likely effects on wages and prices. Estimates varied from 20 to 30 per cent.[28] Robert Hall had also discussed with Hugh Gaitskell and me the possibility of allowing the pound to float for 'an experimental period' before a new fixed rate was finally decided upon. The Bank of England, however, was against such a move for a number of reasons. It was of the opinion that it represented 'the antithesis of the exchange stability in which the UK has rightly taken the lead in the past'; that it was 'inconsistent with IMF obligations'; that it would encourage 'uncertainty' and 'nervousness which would affect all other countries and every section of world trade'; and that the reserves were by then insufficient for us to manage a float effectively.[29]

The Chancellor took the Bank's advice, and rightly. We then set about deciding what would be the most effective new fixed parity for sterling. The general concensus amongst officials was that it was better to go too low and risk upward pressure on the rate than to go too high and risk going through another devaluation, especially when, as yet, no accompanying measures had been decided on. At a meeting in Oliver Franks' study, Robert Hall, George Bolton, Henry Wilson-Smith and I decided that the final choice lay between rates of $2.80 (30 per cent devaluation) and $3.00 (25 per cent devaluation), and that $2.80 was probably best. We put these conclusions to Cripps and Bevin in the latter's sitting room at the Embassy. At the Chequers meeting of 19th August, Cripps had favoured a rate no lower than $3.00, and Bevin a rate of $3.20. They were both, I believe, a little surprised by our advice.

Cripps had to be dissuaded from asking the Americans and the Canadians what rate they would suggest in view of the dangerous precedent this would create. In the end, Cripps turned to Bevin – who, still far from well, was dressed in his pyjamas and dressing gown – and asked his opinion. Bevin turned to me and asked, 'What effect will a rate of $2.80 have on the price of the standard loaf of bread?' Bevin was always concerned about the cost of the loaf. As a child and as a young man he had been very poor and, as a consequence, always had a deep concern for the living standards of the under-privileged. Anticipating such a question, I had cabled to London for this information. I was able to give him an immediate reply and he nodded, saying that this would be acceptable but he hoped we could have a whiter loaf. $2.80 to the pound was to be the new rate. Modern-day economists, accustomed to using complex computer models to decide on policy changes, will no doubt find it hard to believe that this was the manner by which the new exchange rate was chosen.[30]

The Washington talks, after a somewhat frosty beginning, went well, and Anglo-American economic relations, which had for a time been rather strained, improved thereafter. The Americans promised lower tariffs, simpler customs procedures, more overseas investment, and agreed to allow us to use ERP dollars to buy Canadian wheat.[31] There is no doubt that they were pleasantly and greatly surprised by our choosing to inform them of our decision to devalue, and indeed the extent and timing of the move.[32] Looking back on the Washington discussions, Dean Acheson, the US Secretary of State commented: 'As we foresaw the talks, discussion of devaluation was a possibility but an improbability ... It seemed quite impossible that the British would tell us when and how much.'[33] This surprise, more than anything else, helped to smooth negotiations and enabled us to obtain the concessions detailed above. It illustrated to the Americans that we were willing to take action to help ourselves and to place confidence in them.

On his return from Washington, Cripps duly announced the decision to devalue to the nation and to the world. He attached great importance to his radio broadcast and had rejected a draft that Robert Hall and I had prepared in the empty offices of the wartime Raw Materials Mission at 1800 K Street, before his departure from the United States. Our draft began by admitting that the devaluation was a defeat for our previous policy, but Cripps changed all this. He said Bevin had told him never to apologise for your actions as a minister. He also told me that he feared that if he announced the decision to devalue at the beginning of the broadcast people would switch off their sets and not listen to the economic reasons that had forced it upon us. This re-draft, according to Clem Leslie, was to damage Cripps's reputation, as people thought he was trying to brazen it out, something the public thought was unlike him.

Despite the fact that when Cripps made his broadcast on 18th September almost two months had elapsed since the decision to devalue had been made, there had been no leaks to speak of. Most foreign governments were officially informed of our intentions on the weekend that it was announced, and the IMF was given less than twenty-four hours' notice. Ministers and officials had for six months been so preoccupied with reaching a decision to devalue that little detailed consideration had been given to the impact of a 30 per cent devaluation of sterling on other countries, even those who held their reserves in sterling. Nor had the significance, as far as the world dollar shortage was concerned, of getting other countries to follow our lead been stressed.

Although there had been speculation about an imminent devaluation for some time, the suddenness of the announcement took foreign governments by surprise. Many Commonwealth countries which only a short time ago had agreed to a 25 per cent reduction in dollar imports to help stave off a forced devaluation, were angry and made their feelings known. In the end, all Sterling Area nations, with the exception of Pakistan, moved with sterling. Most OEEC countries followed sterling all or part of the way, with only the Swiss franc and Swedish krona remaining at their old dollar parity.[34]

The most vocal protests came from the French. From their acting Foreign Minister, British representatives at the OEEC received 'a serious remonstrance regarding the lack of confidence shown to the French Government by His Majesty's Government in the manner in which devaluation had been carried out'.[35] Jean Monnet, for his part, was upset and took it as an indication that Britain did not take a close Anglo-French relationship seriously.

While it was true that, at this time, the French government was itself in the midst of an economic and political crisis and a sudden sterling devaluation was unlikely to help matters, it was, we believed, impossible for us to give the French more warning than we in fact did. Because of our fears of provoking speculation against the pound, we felt that we really could not trust anyone except the Americans with an early warning.

The announcement of the devaluation by no means signalled the end of the external crisis of 1949; there was still to be decided the question of what additional measures should be taken to stabilise the economy. Robert Hall and I immediately joined with other senior officials in trying to convince ministers to grasp the nettle of a complementary austerity package. We repeated our view that cuts in public expenditure, a tightening of the cheap money policy pursued by Labour since the end of the war, and a stronger incomes policy were vital to the success of devaluation. Many Cabinet members, however, were loath to accept deflation to the extent required because, like Attlee, they failed to grasp adequately the connection between financial policy and the external account. Others suspected a conspiracy amongst officials designed to force the Labour government to abandon its socialist policies and revert to pre-war orthodoxies. I remember that Dalton was particularly wary of official advice.[36]

As a result of pressure from Herbert Morrison and the Treasury, the Prime Minister had in early August already circulated a request for all civil departments to review public expenditure with the object of securing such economies as could be obtained without prejudice to major government policy. It was hoped that by eliminating waste and by more efficient administration, net expenditure could be reduced by some 5 per cent (£100 million). If not, ministers were instructed to offer cuts in programmes which would enable this objective to be achieved.[37] Reductions in public expenditure under the headings of waste and inefficiency eradication amounting to only £26 million had been offered by the end of September, when Cripps circulated an Economic Section paper on 'The Internal Financial Situation' to the ministerial Economic Policy Committee.[38] This paper, drafted in the main by Robert Hall, sought to estimate the cuts in government expenditure and investment needed to accompany devaluation. Hall judged that because of excessive spending on defence, health and food subsidies in the first half of the financial year, the Budget surplus would be about £160 million less than originally hoped for. Added to this, a decline in the personal savings ratio indicated that cuts of some £200 million in total would be required merely to keep the pressure of demand to that originally deemed appropriate in the spring. Changes in the foreign balance over the same period supported these findings. Some deflation was required, even without devaluation. But devaluation, according to Robert Hall's estimates, necessitated at least a further £100 million of cuts, otherwise there would be no resources available to reap the benefits of the change in the relative prices of imports and exports. Action had to be taken soon or the advantages conferred by devaluation would be lost.

Robert Hall was the first to admit that his figures were little more than rough estimates and could easily prove to be wide of the mark. He wrote to me setting out his fears that the total of £300 million of cuts could prove to be too low and leave dangerous inflationary pressures in the economy. He was worried that the existing supplementary estimates submitted by departments were likely to underestimate the overshoot in government expenditure: no allowances had been made for an overshoot in investment programmes; not all estimates of the increased costs to government departments resulting from devaluation had been received, and in his original calculations wages had been assumed to remain constant. He concluded, 'We would be justified in asking for a higher target on the ground that performance always falls short of target.'[39]

Ministers were also concerned about the potential inaccuracy of Robert Hall's figures, but mainly for the opposite reason. They feared that his recommendations would prove too deflationary and result in unemployment and broken promises. Dalton, for one, saw them as being set deliberately too high and characterised the paper as 'another flank attack by officials'.[40] After a series of meetings of the Economic Policy Committee at which it was assumed that the suggested budgetary change would prove equal to the impact on final demand, ministers succeeded in reducing the target for economies to £280 million, to be divided equally between investment and government expenditure, as devaluation would bring higher profits to trading departments such as the Ministry of Food.[41] Moreover, before Attlee came to announce the cuts in the House of Commons on 24th October, the Cabinet was rocked by a series of resignation threats from Bevan, Alexander and Bevin, as ministers sought to stop the axe falling on their own particular department, and from an exhausted and infuriated Cripps, because although the Cabinet had agreed to a policy of some deflation indi-vidual ministers were unwilling to shoulder the burdens necessary.[42]

In the end, the expenditure cuts left the social services and the food subsidies virtually intact, the Ministry of Defence got away with a very small reduction in expenditure of some £30 million, and some economies would not come into effect for some time and would be hard to trace even then. What is more, the cut in investment was largely on paper, except for housing.[43] Anthony Eden was not far wrong in describing this austerity package as 'just scratched together in the last fortnight ... sketchy and inadequate ... only effective in the distant future' and 'the maximum that can be agreed without Cabinet resigna-tion'.[44] The initial reaction of the City was that the cuts did not go far enough, and that there was the threat of a further exchange crisis soon in the absence of a second package of measures. The Americans shared the view, blaming the government's timidity on the forthcoming general election.[45] Robert Hall and I certainly would have liked firmer action but were forced to recognise the political realities of the situation.

While the Cabinet would not budge on the subject of Bank Rate at this stage, we did manage to convince them of the vital need to strengthen the voluntary incomes policy outlined the previous year in the *Statement on Personal Incomes, Costs and Prices*. An official working party was set up at the end of August to look into short-term options in this direction. The chairman was Bernard Gilbert, a Third Secretary in the Treasury, who in 1940 had given me financial authority to spend £100,000 to buy up all the aluminium pots and pans in the shops to be melted down for aircraft production. I served on the working party with, among others, Alec Cairncross, then Economic Adviser at the Board of Trade. We eventually decided to support a further voluntary freeze of wages for at least six months, but this time we hoped we could cast the net of the policy wider and, in particular, include the one and a half million workers whose wages were linked directly to the cost of living through 'sliding-scales'. We also recommended more stringent price control and an extension of voluntary dividend limitation. The working party specifically rejected a suggestion from Cripps that all wages, prices and profits should be frozen by statute for three months. This was both because of the administrative burden it implied and on the grounds of the political and legal implications it involved. An idea floated by the Ministry of Labour that the taxation of employers should be used as a sanction against wage claims was rejected for similar reasons.[46]

Initial ministerial consideration of the working party's report and discussion with the TUC resulted in the inclusion of an increase in profits tax in the package, and the exemption of especially low-paid workers. After several further meetings with Cripps, Bevin, Bevan and Isaacs, a new and tighter wage policy received the endorsement of senior trade unionists. On 23rd November the TUC General Council announced its recommendation of a one-year stabilisation of wage rates, and the suspension of cost of living agreements, provided that the retail price index did not increase by more than 5 per cent. Despite Bevin's observation that the narrowing of differentials effected by the 1948 pay guidelines had already caused 'great unrest', and his antipathy to the further exemption of low-paid workers from the freeze, this single exemption from the general rule was retained.[47] For a year after devaluation the government kept its side of the bargain made with the unions. Retail prices rose by only 2 per cent over this period in comparison with 3.2 per cent over the year to September 1949. Domestic wage inflation averaged a mere 1.4 per cent per annum in the twelve months after devaluation, about half the pre-devaluation rate, while hourly earnings continued to rise at a rate of about 3 per cent per annum. Thus the effect of devaluation on costs and prices was remarkably small, and fears of a wage-price spiral's eroding the beneficial effects of a lower exchange rate proved unfounded.

The change in exchange rates went far beyond sterling and the Sterling Area making it, in effect, a dollar revaluation. Nine months after devaluation the Korean War broke out, bringing in its wake massive repercussions for world trade, prices and national budgets. For these reasons it is difficult to isolate the impact of the exchange rate movements in 1949 from other events and to make a firm judgement about their long-term success. What one can say is that our gold and dollar reserves, reduced to some £330 million on 18th September 1949, had within nine months increased by 70 per cent, and were to increase by an even greater extent in the following nine months. Moreover, the lion's share of the competitive advantage of devaluation remained after the Korean War. Between 1949 and 1954 the American GDP price deflator rose by 13.3 per cent, while in Britain it increased by 16.4 per cent. Britain also enjoyed a current account surplus in every year between 1950 and 1954, except 1951, and a cumulative surplus of more than £500 million over this period.

In 1950 there was an improvement in Britain's current account deficit with the Dollar Area of £200 million, and a slightly greater improvement in the dollar balance of the rest of the Sterling Area. During the Korean War Britain's deficit with the Dollar Area increased, but after hostilities ended it started to improve again. As far as the rest of the Sterling Area was concerned, after 1950 a small and consistent surplus came to replace what previously had tended to be habitual deficit. There is thus also evidence to suggest a change in the balance between the dollar and non-dollar worlds after devaluation which persisted well into the 1950s, and no doubt helped to ease the continuation of post-war reconstruction.

We can conclude, therefore, that although devaluation was delayed for too long, leading to an excessive loss of reserves, and although the financial measures which accompanied it were by no means as wide-ranging as they should have been, its results were satisfactory in terms of both the short and the longer term, both from the point of view of Britain and the world as a whole. The rate of $2.80 to the pound was subsequently maintained for eighteen years, and this period of almost two decades witnessed unprecedented exchange rate stability, economic growth and employment levels throughout the world.

If Stafford Cripps had not been a sick man during this period would the outcome have been different? I do not think so. He would no doubt have argued more forcefully against devaluation, but he could always be persuaded if he thought the argument was sound. The inevitability of a forced devaluation if a voluntary one was not decided upon would, I believe, have convinced him, perhaps even earlier than actually was done. Once devaluation was decided upon I think he would have insisted upon tougher supplementary measures than were accepted.

CHAPTER SEVEN

A First Attempt at
Anglo-French Co-operation

In 1949 there were a series of Anglo-French discussions which foreshadowed the development of the European Coal and Steel Community in 1950. Soon after Britain and France had submitted their Long-Term Programmes, the French delegation to the OEEC in Paris proposed a series of informal bilateral talks so that the two countries' plans for 1950–2 could be integrated and made more consistent. Reporting on the attitude of the French government machine to this suggestion, a British official remarked,

> there were some in the French administration who thought something could come of it. For instance, Monnet (Head of the French Planning Commissariat) had said that if Plowden and some of his colleagues could come over and work for two months with the French Planners to produce a scheme for production which could leave out of account all the difficulties of financial transfer and country boundaries, he believed something could come out of it.[1]

The French suggestion immediately caused considerable consternation at the Foreign Office, which was compounded when the French sought to send a massive official delegation to what was scheduled to be a low-key meeting of French and British officials in February. The Foreign Office succeeded in postponing the talks and the French were politely asked to limit their party to Hervé Alphand, head of the Economic Section of the French Ministry of Foreign Affairs, and his immediate subordinate officials.

Despite the Foreign Office's wariness of joint planning I met Jean

Monnet in London on 17th February 1949. I had lunch privately with him and one of his principal assistants, Etienne Hirsch. I had first met Jean Monnet in the early autumn of 1947. He was a most remarkable man. The day he died, the BBC asked me to say something about him. I cannot remember my exact words but what I tried to convey was that he had by imagination, single-mindedness, persistence and determination done more to unite Europe on a permanent basis than all the emperors, kings, generals and dictators since the Fall of the Roman Empire. I still believe this to be true.

He was born in Cognac, the son of the man who founded the brandy firm of J. G. Monnet. He never went to university, but as a young man he was sent to London and Canada to learn English and meet potential customers. Although at the outbreak of the First World War he was found unfit for active service he still felt that he had a contribution to make. He early formed the impression that the British and the French were fighting two unco-ordinated wars. They were, for example, bidding against each other for scarce raw materials and there was no co-ordinated use of shipping. Through a mutual friend he obtained an introduction to Viviani, the Prime Minister of France. He explained his views on the need for the pooling of the two war efforts and to set up joint Anglo-French bodies to do this. As a result, he was sent to London as a member of the civil supplies service where he worked throughout the war. He was 27 years old.

In 1919, at the age of 31, he was asked by the British and French governments to be Deputy Secretary-General of the League of Nations. Two years later he learnt that his father was having trouble with his business and resigned from the League of Nations post and returned home. From then until the time of Munich he was engaged in various business enterprises throughout the world.

Within three months of the outbreak of the Second World War he was made chairman of the Franco-British Committee for Economic Co-ordination. With the fall of France he was appointed by Churchill to work in association with the head of the British Purchasing Commission in the United States, not a grand-sounding title but a position from which he exercised great influence, particularly with the United States administration.

After the war, he proposed to General de Gaulle that a council should be created to be served by a Planning Commissioner and staff to plan the modernisation of the French economy. His ideas were accepted and he became the Planning Commissioner. It was in that capacity that I was to work closely with him for six years.

He had a most charming personality and no matter how often and how greatly we might differ we never quarrelled. Our contacts soon developed into a close friendship and long after I left Whitehall we tried to meet whenever he came to London or I went to Paris.

At our meeting in February 1949 he repeated the proposal that representatives of the CEPS should sit down together with their French counterparts and discuss the integration of the two countries' plans with a view to making recommendations on policy directly to their respective governments. Monnet was convinced that I would carry sufficient weight with senior Cabinet ministers for our recommendations to be taken seriously. I had to tell him, however, that while it might be possible for him to do such an exercise independently of the main French Civil Service machine, it was quite impossible for the CEPS to do so. Since we had been established in 1947 we had done our best to make ourselves part of the official machine and, should the two governments decide to carry out such an exercise, we, for our part, could only do it in the normal way, that is to say through that official machinery and under ministerial direction.[2]

After further pressure from the French and a meeting between Cripps and his opposite number in Paris, Maurice Petsche, ministers decided to allow the two planning staffs jointly to examine the Long-Term Programmes during April. I had a further series of private discussions with Monnet in early March, at one of which Cripps was also present. During this second series of meetings Monnet elaborated on his hopes for the talks. Subsequently, I reported his views thus:

> M. Monnet explained that in his view Western Europe was a vacuum, on either side of which were the two great dynamic forces of communism and American capitalism. He felt that this vacuum could be filled either by one of these two outside forces, or by the development of a Western European Way of Life.[3]

At the time, we were becoming increasingly preoccupied with the problem of devaluation and the difficulty of persuading ministers of the need for it. Consequently, I fear we did not pay enough attention to

Monnet's analysis. I did, however, agree to his suggestion that the proposed April talks on Anglo-French co-operation should be held at his country house outside Paris and that I should attend together with two or three members of the CEPS and Economic Section.

Subsequently, I approached the Foreign Office for its guidance on the importance attached to Anglo-French co-operation and what line we should take during the talks. Roger Makins told me that the Foreign Office was wary of Monnet's motives. He also made it clear to me that while France was an extremely important ally of the United Kingdom, and the Foreign Office was anxious to see a consolidation of the good relations we shared with the French government, at the end of the day our 'special' relationship with the United States was 'paramount' and to be maintained at all costs. His conclusion was that 'we should obviously not agree ... to anything which would render us incapable of sustaining an independent resistance if France were overrun'.[4] That is to say, in helping Europe nothing was to be done which might undermine Britain's basic economic structure. In effect, this meant that we should avoid any surrender of Britain's national sovereignty and keep the discussions as much as possible to bilateral agreements and tariff reductions.

Armed with this brief, Robert Hall, Alan Hitchman and I left for Monnet's country house at Bazôches. On the French side Monnet was joined by his two closest confidants, Etienne Hirsch and Pierre Uri. For several days we discussed with them ways of advancing Anglo-French economic co-operation. The talks were conducted in a cordial and informal atmosphere. As Dr Richard Mayne has said in his book *The Recovery of Europe*:

> Plowden arrived on the morning of Thursday, 21st April 1949 accompanied by his deputy and by Robert Hall, the Head of the Economic Section of the Cabinet Office. With Monnet were Etienne Hirsch, already familiar in wartime London as 'le Commandant Bernard' and the mercurial Pierre Uri. The advantage of the meeting as Monnet saw it was its total informality. Gathered in the long, low stone-floored drawing-room with its family bibelots, its paintings by Madame Monnet and its tall french windows overlooking the fields towards Rambouillet, it was possible to discuss ideas frankly rather than negotiate from pre-arranged positions. On this friendly basis, Monnet and Plowden reviewed and compared the economic situation in Britain

and France and the plans and problems the Governments had before them.[5]

Our discussions were, in the main, of a practical and technical nature, rarely touching on wider issues of politics. We identified our individual problems, such as shortages of key commodities, and tried to find ways to solve them together. At the end of the discussions we drew up a list of limited proposals to take back to our governments, including an idea to ameliorate the shortages of food and coal in the United Kingdom and France by a system of mutual exchange. When on our return, however, we put these proposals to Bevin via Cripps, they were immediately rejected as Bevin felt that even these would go too far in the direction of a surrender of British sovereignty.

The talks between the two Planning Staffs went no further and were largely forgotten in Whitehall as the devaluation crisis absorbed our attention. Towards the end of the year, however, Monnet resurrected the issue of Anglo-French co-operation while talking to Robert Hall, and after consulting those concerned, particularly the Foreign Office, I wrote to Monnet to clarify the British position. My letter began thus:

My Dear Monnet,

Robert Hall has mentioned to me his recent conversation with you in the course of which you reverted to the idea of exchanging UK coal for French foodstuffs in a manner which would make plain to the world the reality of Anglo-French co-operation. Without challenging your underlying idea, I think we must take account of the facts as they exist at present which suggest that there is at present little basis for an arrangement of the kind you suggest outside the ordinary commercial exchanges.[6]

The implication was that it would be fruitless at that time for Monnet to try to push Anglo-French co-operation beyond the point that it encroached upon British sovereignty.

It became obvious in the following year that Monnet was anxious for the April discussions to lead to an Anglo-French nucleus around which a European Community could be built. He hoped that an agreement between the United Kingdom and France to co-operate on economic matters could provide a stepping stone for further developments with West Germany and other countries. At the time, however, it was by no means clear to us that this was Monnet's objective. He was never this explicit about his hopes for the talks and we in the British delegation did not realise how far, in fact, he wanted to go. But, in any case, this does not mean that had we known, a different outcome would have resulted; indeed I think such knowledge would have made us even more cautious. The three of us who went to Paris never thought in terms of going as far as Monnet did and, given Britain's position in the world and the general outlook of British ministers, officials and the country as a whole at that time, this is not surprising.

I am also convinced that Monnet never really grasped the difference between his position, which was highly influential but somewhat outside the regular French official machine, and my own which was very fully inside the British one. As such, I had to keep to what had already been decided at ministerial level as official policy. I could not, as Monnet wished, agree to full co-operation with the French without first knowing the details. On my return I would have to explain to ministers exactly what was involved for the United Kingdom and how any new scheme would fit in with our current policies.

The upshot was that a disappointed Monnet was forced to find another way to bring to fruition his ideas for the creation of a European Community. Having been rebuffed by us, he turned to Adenauer and West Germany for support. It is easy to look back now and say that the British position towards European co-operation was shortsighted and that we missed the boat, but such a judgement neglects to take into account political attitudes and the strategic outlook in this country at the time.

CHAPTER EIGHT

1950:
Fundamentals and the
European Payments Union

By late 1949 the Labour government had enacted all the major Bills promised in their 1945 election manifesto and the party had agreed on a new programme for a second five-year term of office. The question of a date for a general election arose. Most of the younger members of the Cabinet, together with Herbert Morrison, thought that a date in May or June 1950 would be most suitable. Cripps, however, would not hear of this as it implied that the election would take place after the Budget. He believed that any Budget introduced before an election would be an 'Election Budget', and as such would be immoral. He refused to move on the issue and even went as far as to threaten resignation. Attlee could not accept this as it would have been a shattering blow to the government and duly called an election for 23rd February.[1]

Thus Labour was forced to fight a general election just a few months after a major devaluation and the introduction of a series of austerity measures. This was hardly the most auspicious moment to go to the country and although Labour gained considerably more votes than in 1945, their overall parliamentary majority was reduced to six. As a result, Labour governed for the next eighteen months under constant pressure from the Opposition and with the threat of defeat in the House being a habitual worry.

Several senior ministers had by this stage been in government for ten of the most difficult and taxing years in British history and were beyond their mental and physical peaks. The endless round of three-line whips meant that they began to show increasing signs of strain. Initially, Cripps continued as Chancellor but his health remained poor and, in

March, Attlee decided to appoint Gaitskell as Minister of State for Economic Affairs to assist him. Until October 1950 when Cripps felt compelled to retire, Gaitskell acted as a kind of 'Vice-Chancellor of the Exchequer', at first assuming responsibility for external economic policy but, as illness took an increasing toll on Cripps, gradually taking on more and more duties.

In the spring of 1950 the trials and tribulations of the previous summer and autumn seemed very distant and in May it was felt that points rationing could be abandoned. Britain's external position had improved in spectacular fashion. Sixty per cent of the reserves lost during the devaluation crisis had been recovered by the end of 1949, and at the beginning of April 1950 Cripps could tell the House that the rest had been regained.[2] In the wake of devaluation, speculation had been reversed and British dollar exports recovered. Moreover, the United States increased her imports from the Sterling Area as she pulled out of recession, while the dollar import curbs of the previous year meant that the Sterling Area was buying significantly less from the Dollar Area.

In his latest Budget, anxious that we did not 'risk losing the advantages we [had] built up with such difficulty over [the] post-war years',[3] Cripps continued his policy of disinflation. He made no effort to reduce the overall burden of taxation, lower tax on the lower range of incomes being more or less offset by higher tax on petrol in an effort to save more dollars. According to recent estimates, over the years 1948–9 to 1950–1, during which Cripps was Chancellor, the Budget surplus for the public sector as a whole averaged some £700 million per annum, or about 7 per cent of GNP.[4] In fact, Cripps was always concerned that he might be taking too deflationary a fiscal stance and throughout his term as Chancellor had to put up with constant pressure from his Cabinet colleagues to reduce his Budget surplus. The year 1950 was no exception and just before the Budget the Lord Privy Seal, Viscount Addison, questioned the wisdom of a policy of such large Budget surpluses. As a result, Cripps circulated to the Cabinet a memorandum prepared by the Treasury which set out how the government's primary aim in economic policy should be to manage demand and offset cyclical fluctuations in the economy through fiscal policy without producing inflation or allowing unemployment.[5] This approach was endorsed by the Cabinet, illustrating both that ministers and officials were at this time moving towards Keynesianism and that planning was increasingly being seen in terms of demand-management.[6]

In the months after the Budget three policy issues took up much of our time in the Treasury. These were the debate with the United States over the 'fundamentals' of economic policy, a European Payments Union, the setting up of and the question of whether or not we should take part in the Schuman Plan for the Western European Coal and Steel industries (which I shall deal with in Chapter 9). I will turn first to the question of 'fundamentals'.

It had always been the intention after the September 1949 Washington discussions that there should be a continuing dialogue between Britain and the United States on economic policy issues. In mid-February Leslie Rowan, who was Economic Minister at the Embassy in Washington, reported to Alan Hitchman that the Americans were increasingly interested in the underlying thrust of British economic policy and were keen to discuss this, together with the essentials of their own economic policy. They were especially keen to know when we considered a return to convertibility would be prudent and were talking vaguely in terms of an Anglo-American economic partnership. Rowan's conclusion was that 'we must be prepared to have talks with the Americans about fundamentals, that they may ask us to do so in the near future, and that the climate of opinion is likely to be favourable'.[7] A meeting of senior officials soon after agreed that we should make preparations for such discussions,[8] and following an exchange of letters between Snyder and Cripps, a series of meetings between US and UK officials was set up for the end of June.[9]

A paper on 'Fundamentals' was prepared for the ministerial Economic Policy Committee. This described how the basic objectives of British external economic policy were full employment, a rising standard of living, the closing of the dollar gap, and a general improvement in the balance of payments. However, neither full convertibility, even on current transactions, nor the abandonment of discrimination against dollar supplies could be a possibility until Britain had built up her gold and dollar reserves and the United States balance of payments surplus had been eliminated. Although the reserves had increased, they remained lower than before Marshall Aid and the suspension of convertibility. At the end of 1951 Britain's obligations would increase by some $200 million a year in the form of repayments for the American loan. The conclusion was that for the sterling-dollar problem and discrimination to be reduced, action from both sides of the Atlantic was required. In view of the fact that sterling had recently been devalued, the major onus was on the United States to make dollars more plentiful. The Americans should be urged to pursue a more expansionary domestic economic policy, especially in the event of a slump, to continue long-term aid, and to stimulate imports by reducing tariffs. For our part, in order to make sterling more scarce it was thought prudent that we continue our policy of disinflation, try to resolve the problem of the sterling balances, and maintain an adequate balance of payments surplus with the rest of the world.[10]

Hugh Gaitskell was closely involved in the drafting of this brief, and before it was finalised Robert Hall, Henry Wilson-Smith and I had some considerable disagreements with him over its contents. For our part, we believed that the draft favoured by Gaitskell contained too little emphasis on how we proposed to move towards convertibility and non-discrimination. It was all very well asking the Americans to take action, but we feared that the draft was too negative as far as our own policy was concerned. We wanted to 'chart a course' towards convertibility and suggested that we offered the Americans a plan for the gradual and controlled introduction of convertibility in Europe.[11]

Gaitskell got his way in the end as much by political muscle as intellectual argument. When talks between the US Treasury and UK officials led by Leslie Rowan got under way in June, the Economic Policy Committee paper formed the basis of our position. From the start, the Americans repeated their complaint of the previous year that 'whatever may have been the virtues of our policies, our specific actions had in some cases moved us away rather than towards the objectives of [convertibility and non-discrimination outlined in] the Loan Agreement of 1945'. They cited as an example the fact that the 25 per cent cut in Sterling Area dollar imports of the previous summer seemed to have become a permanent policy. They believed that in recent years they had taken a number of political risks to help Britain, and urged us to 'give some sign by early action that we too [were] ready to make experiments which it will be clear to Congress and the American people [were] directed towards our agreed aim'. Rowan could only reply that we could not risk going too fast, too soon and chance a second premature movement to convertibility; we had no real examples of 'experiments' to offer the Americans.[12]

A few days after this meeting the Korean War broke out and, for a time, more urgent matters became uppermost in Anglo-American relations. The question of a more rapid return by Britain to a policy of convertibility and non-discrimination did not go away completely, however, and it was soon again to be in the forefront of officials' minds.

The initial post-war recovery in intra-European trade was underpinned by a whole series of bilateral payments agreements. However, as recovery gathered pace these began to prove increasingly inelastic and restrictive. The first steps towards the multilateral settlement of European payments came in November 1947 but, because of the effects of the convertibility crisis, Britain did not feel able to take part. In October 1948 and 1949 Britain was party to two successive Intra-European Payments Agreements. These two agreements introduced a system of drawing rights under which countries receiving ERP aid could be required to make part of their aid available to other participants to finance their forecast bilateral deficit with any other European country concerned. The drawing rights did not mean that a country had to transfer dollars at any stage. It merely had to allow its own currency to be drawn upon up to the amount forecast, this amount being made good in additional aid. As we had feared at the outset, these schemes proved to be unsatisfactory. Settlements were monthly and bilateral rather than cumulative over the whole year and net of surpluses and deficits with other countries. The forecasts used were often extremely inaccurate and the overall effect of the agreements was to distort trade still further and actually to stimulate bilateralism rather than to reduce it.

In the aftermath of the round of devaluations towards the end of 1949 it was widely recognised that a more simple and comprehensive scheme was required to go hand in hand with the measures taken by the OEEC in that year to liberalise European trade. On 2nd November 1949 the OEEC Council decided 'to widen the area of transferability of currencies among the member countries by suitable measures in the next Intra-European Payments Scheme'.[13] Differing schemes were put forward by the ECA, the OEEC Secretariat and the UK Treasury and it was the ECA's proposals which eventually were to form the basis of the European Payments Union (EPU).

The final terms of the scheme were not agreed until August and a treaty was not signed until September. The EPU, as it was finally established, consisted of three basic features. First of all it made all 'authorised payments among the member countries of the OEEC and their associated monetary areas fully multilateral'. In short, only the net surplus or deficit of each country with the rest of the EPU had to be settled. Second, the scheme was cumulative. At any particular stage the net position represented the sum of all surpluses and deficits since the inception of the Union. Third, under the EPU the net balance was settled up to an agreed 'quota', partly in gold and partly in credit extended by member countries to each other on prearranged principles. For debtors, the 'gold portion rose gradually from zero to 100 per cent ... so as to put more and more pressure on them to correct persistent disequilibria in their payments'. For a creditor, the gold portion rose from zero to 50 per cent when its cumulative surplus reached 20 per cent of the country's quota. Thereafter, settlements were made on an *ad hoc* basis.[14]

Although neither Robert Hall nor I was greatly involved in the negotiations – as these were, for the most part, left to the Treasury Overseas Finance Division and Robert Hall's deputy, Marcus Fleming – I can remember that the EPU was not established without a long and difficult series of meetings and that Britain was extremely reluctant to join it. In the aftermath of the convertibility crisis and devaluation, the government was understandably unwilling to experiment with anything to do with the external account. The Bank of England, in particular, feared that any new payments scheme providing for a wide degree of transferability between OEEC nations would pose a threat to the special position of sterling as an international currency, especially if such a scheme was perceived as the first step towards a rival European currency unit.[15] The Treasury was more concerned with the danger that the EPU might result in large dollar and gold outflows, and wanted to maximise the credit margin and minimise gold payments in settlements between OEEC members. Naturally, it was also keen to maintain the many agreements we already had with European countries for sterling settlements. As such, therefore, the British position was that we wanted the EPU facilities only to be used as an additional means of payment after existing credit lines had been exhausted. This contrasted sharply with the ECA view that the EPU should replace all bilateral agreements.[16]

A further bone of contention with the Americans – and indeed with many OEEC nations during the negotiations – was, as might have been expected, the question of discrimination. Unlike the ECA and most of our European neighbours, we wanted to keep a system of bilateral agreements on import quotas rather than replace them by a non-discriminatory set of global quotas. There were two reasons for this stand. In the first place, we saw the imposition of qualitative restrictions against creditors as a means to encourage them to act to eliminate balance of payments disequilibria, rather than against debtors. Debtors, of course, would have to deflate to balance their external account and this would raise unemployment. Creditors, however, would reflate and thereby offer a further guarantee against unemployment. Second, and quite separately, Britain was keen to retain freedom to deal with serious balance of payments deficits by directly restricting imports, as we were to do in in 1951 and 1952.[17]

A third point of conflict between Britain and the United States government related to the overall management of the EPU. The Americans wanted to set up a 'supervisory board' to run the EPU with widespread powers to exert influence over the make-up of individual nations' economic policies. We saw that as a potential means by which the United States would seek to impose freer trade and deflationary policies on those countries in fundamental disequilibria, and preferred instead that the EPU should as far as practicable operate automatically. On this issue we eventually got our way.[18]

In the end, the differences of opinion between the Americans and ourselves were settled only after the introduction of Gaitskell into the negotiations as minister with responsibility for external economic policy. He was much more adaptable and at home with this complex economic subject than Cripps.[19] The stalemate was further loosened by the rapid increase in British reserves from $1,340 million before devaluation to $2,422 million in mid-1950. Most important of all, however, was the offer of a series of compromises from Washington which sought to allay British fears about the system. In effect, the Americans introduced measures to multilateralise the sterling balances held by EPU countries without posing a threat to Britain.

Under the two previous Intra-European Payments Agreements we had actually ended up paying out dollars to OEEC members when we had a balance of payments surplus with the OEEC as a whole. Under the EPU, we could be in net deficit of up to £379 million (our quota) and the loss of reserves would not exceed one-half of the net amount. In addition, the credit we could obtain if necessary was considerably more than under the old system of bilateral agreements.

The ECA placed $350 million in the EPU as initial working capital, together with an additional $150 million to multilateralise the sterling balances. The EPU was to run initially for two years. In the end, it lasted until the return to general European convertibility in 1958. Despite British suspicion, as Robert Triffin, who devised the ECA's initial scheme and took a large part in the negotiations, has said, 'It loosened overnight the stranglehold of bilateralism on intra-European Trade and Payments [and] paved the way toward the resumption of multilateral trade and the resumption of currency convertibility.'[20] As such, it was one of the major achievements of post-war European economic co-operation. What was more, it soon proved vital in helping the world to overcome the payments disequilibria thrown up by the Korean War and the Western rearmament programme.

CHAPTER NINE

The Schuman Plan

As described in Chapter 7, by the end of 1949 Jean Monnet's efforts to build real collective European action around Anglo-French industrial co-operation had come to nothing. Never one to allow a single setback to deflect him from his ultimate goal, his response was to turn away from Britain and look instead to West Germany. His plan was to forge a bond between France and the new Federal Republic which would form 'the germ of European unity', and rule out any chance of future conflict between these two nations which for so long had been at each other's throats.[1]

Historically, the coal and steel industries had formed the basis of both of these nations' economic and military power. Monnet's hope was that the joint control of these industries on an equal and fair basis would usher in a new age of peace, prosperity and co-operation in Europe. It could simultaneously reduce the chances of any rekindling of German militarism and nationalism, and end the mistrust and fear that the French and German people felt for one another. It could offer an example which would encourage other European countries, Britain included, to solve their economic problems together and work towards the establishment of a single European state.[2]

In April 1950, with the help of Etienne Hirsch and a young lawyer called Paul Reuter, Monnet set about translating his vision into a more concrete plan. By early May an outline had received the approval of Robert Schuman, the French Foreign Minister. This Monnet/Schuman plan in turn received the support of Adenauer, the German Chancellor, and on 8th May the proposals for the French and German coal and steel industries were outlined informally to Dean Acheson, the American Secretary of State, who was stopping over in Paris *en route* to London.[3] The following day Schuman announced to the world that 'the entire Franco-German production of coal and steel [would] be placed under a joint High Authority within an organisation open to the participation of other European nations'. He added that:

> By pooling basic production and by creating a new High Authority whose decisions will be binding on France, Germany and the other countries who may subsequently join, this proposal will create the first concrete foundation for a European federation which is so indispensable for the preservation of peace.[4]

Bevin was told of the content of Schuman's speech by the French Ambassador in London a few hours before the official announcement. At the meeting between Bevin and Acheson for which Acheson had come to London, Bevin soon realised that Acheson was considerably better informed on this proposal than he was. As is clear from the EPU negotiations discussed above, the Americans had in recent months made it abundantly clear that they believed that we could and should be doing more to lead and to participate in an integrated economic system in Western Europe.[5] As a result, Bevin saw what he thought was a Franco-American plot, hatched behind his back, to force the pace on European integration. He was furious and made clear his anger to both the American Secretary of State and the French Foreign Minister who arrived in London for tripartite discussions a few days later. Indeed, it took all Acheson's diplomatic skills to stop Bevin from immediately issuing a statement condemning Schuman's announcement.

Initial reaction to the Schuman Plan at an official level was cautiously supportive both within the Foreign Office and elsewhere. For my own part I predicted, wrongly, that the setting up of a common authority as proposed would most likely lead to the formation of a cartel 'of the more or less conventional type'. If this was the case, I was convinced that it would be foolish if we declined to join as it would mean that our coal and steel industries would be subject to unfair competition. I therefore concluded in a minute to the Chancellor that 'it would be right for this country to welcome in principle the proposed formation of such an Authority but to wait to see how it progresses before committing itself to enter or not'.[6] Robert Hall was of a similar mind. He declared that although he foresaw 'immense practical and adminis-trative difficulties in carrying through any scheme of this kind' he saw no option 'but to welcome the move and wish for luck', while in the meantime making a thorough investigation of the French proposals.[7]

There was no doubt that politically it would have been most unwise to condemn the French initiative *ab initio*. Thus when, on 11th May, Attlee announced in the House of Commons that 'His Majesty's Government will approach the problem [of further investigation] of the Schuman Plan in a sympathetic spirit, and desire to make it clear at the outset that they welcome this French initiative to end the age-long feud with Germany and to bring unity and peace to Europe'[8] he had the wholehearted support of virtually the whole of Whitehall, ministers and officials alike.

An official committee chaired by Edward Bridges was set up on the same day to obtain more information on the Schuman Plan and to report to ministers on its findings. I was a member. Monnet had announced his intention to visit London in the next few days. Because of my friendship with him, I was given the job of finding out from him exactly what the implications of the French plan would be for Britain, and seeing if we could enter into any international talks on the subject without commitment.[9] In the evening of 15th May Stafford Cripps had a meeting with Jean Monnet. Roger Makins and I were present. It was Cripps's intention to listen to what Monnet had to say. To our astonish-ment, after listening to Monnet, he said he thought that Britain should accept to negotiate on the basis proposed by the French, subject to clarification of certain points of which the principal ones were (a) that there was no danger of a capitalist cartel, and (b) that the Americans should not participate in working out the scheme. He said he realised that the proposal might lead to political federation but thought that this would not come until later. I felt it necessary to tell Monnet that the views expressed by the Chancellor were his personal views and had not been discussed with his colleagues. Monnet said he understood and would tell no one of the conversation except Schuman. After the meet-ing, Roger Makins and I felt that Ernest Bevin should immediately be told of it. This was done and he informed the Prime Minister.

At a meeting of the Economic Policy Committee the next day, the Chancellor told the committee of his meeting with Monnet the previ-ous day. The committee decided that officials should take part in discussions with an international study group to examine the proposals in detail

> on the understanding that their association with this work would not commit the UK government to adopt either in principle or in detail the scheme evolved. Care would also have to be taken to prevent this plan from becoming involved with proposals for federalism in Europe. Any Authority administering these industries should derive its sanctions from inter-governmental agreements.

This intervention by Cripps had not the slightest chance of succeeding if participation meant accepting the surrender of sovereignty to a coal and steel authority, as was shown by the decision of the Economic Policy Committee the following day. Moreover, Cripps would never have argued for it against the strongly held views on this subject of Ernest Bevin, for whose judgement he had the highest regard. I was surprised at his intervention and can only explain it partly by a desire to see what Monnet would say but, more important, by his strong belief that British industry needed to become more efficient and that perhaps here was a way of achieving it for two of our most important basic industries, in particular by rationalisation between the steel industries of the participating countries.[10]

Accompanied by Roger Makins and Alan Hitchman, on 16th May I met Monnet for breakfast at the Hyde Park Hotel where, since the First World War, he had always stayed on his visits to London. Our discussions made three things abundantly clear. First, the establishment of the proposed High Authority would involve the surrender of national sovereignty over a wide strategic and economic field. While some system would be provided for individual governments to appeal against the Authority's decisions, France would not allow this merely to re-establish individual governments' national sovereignty over the Authority's decisions. Second, Monnet intended France to proceed with the negotiation of a treaty with the Germans, no matter what were the opinions of other European countries. Thus while Monnet was ready to welcome British participation, he was also ready to press ahead without us if we would not accept their conditions. As he put it in his memoirs, he believed that once the announcement of the Schuman Plan had been made 'Europe was on the move. Whatever the British decided would be their own affair.'[11] Third, we became aware, on our side, that

Monnet's ideas on exactly how the mechanics of the whole plan would work were vague in the extreme. He had, as yet, given no real thought to the pricing and investment policies of the High Authority. We found it hard to separate the *dirigiste* from the liberal in his thinking. Above all, it was the political principles of the whole arrangement that were sacrosanct. The technical details were all secondary.[12]

When I came to report my findings to the official committee, my conclusion was that, despite the 'extremely nebulous' character of the proposal at this stage, association was likely to prove economically advantageous to Britain, and we should therefore seek to involve ourselves in any further international discussions in order to find out more and to mould the Authority into a shape favourable to Britain's interests. Like the Foreign Office, however, I did not want us to do so without reservations.[13]

An 'Interim Report by the Official Committee on the Proposed Coal and Steel Authority' was presented to the ministerial Economic Policy Committee on 23rd May. It emphasised that there was no doubt that full British involvement in, and acceptance of, the scheme as it stood would 'involve some abatement of British sovereignty so far as concerned the coal and steel industries of the United Kingdom'. This was not something any official felt they could recommend to ministers, especially when so little of the detail of the final scheme was known. As the report put it, 'It is quite clear to us that we should not commit ourselves in the dark.' We suggested, instead, that Britain should seek association with further negotiations between the French and Germans in a constructive spirit, but we should make explicit our non-acceptance of all the political implications of the announcement of 9th May.[14]

This policy was accepted by ministers and outlined to the French in a message sent on 25th May.[15] Ministerial hopes that the French would accept it had received a fillip when, at his final press conference before leaving Britain, Schuman seemed to leave the door open for British participation on this basis. Monnet, however, had other ideas. He did not want the British to sit in on negotiations in a special position and thereby hold what, to his mind, amounted to a virtual veto over any proposals we did not accept. He feared that if this was the case the proposed discussions were unlikely to achieve a satisfactory outcome. They would merely produce a loose arrangement or 'another OEEC' which from his point of view was useless. To Monnet it was vital that those taking part in further negotiations were bound by the intention to conclude a treaty on the lines of the original announcement.

For these reasons, on leaving Britain, Monnet acted quickly to head off any compromise deal which Schuman might be tempted to strike with Bevin. He went straight to Bonn, where he had talks with Adenauer. These resulted in a joint communiqué announcing agreement between the French and German governments to accept the original principles of the French plan and the setting up of an international conference to discuss its details.[16] A copy of this communiqué for the signature of the Foreign Secretary crossed with our message of 25th May. Bevin could not sign such a document, and the next day he replied 'that if the French Government intend to insist on a commitment to pool resources and set up an authority with certain sovereign powers as a prior condition to joining in talks, His Majesty's Government would reluctantly be unable to accept such a condition'.[17]

Over the next week, further cables were exchanged between the two governments in an effort to clarify matters and to find some common ground, but as neither side was willing to move far from its original position, there was little progress.[18] During this period I received a letter which Monnet had promised to send me giving some clarification of what, to his mind, should be the role of the High Authority.[19] On 29th May he contacted me by telephone at home and invited me to secret talks at Bazôches, where I suppose he hoped to convince me that I should recommend that my government accept the original spirit of the Schuman Plan. In a minute to senior officials detailing our conversation, I noted how I told Monnet that 'it would be for Ministers to decide whether I should visit him in France or not', and that, in any case, 'I could see no useful purpose in my doing so unless there had been any new developments since our last discussion [in London]'.[20] I am convinced that Monnet was still failing to grasp the difference between his role in the French government machine and my own in ours. I did not go to Bazôches.

On 1st June the French government sent us an ultimatum stating that the establishment of the High Authority had become an 'immediate objective'. A final decision on whether or not we accepted its supranational status was required by 7 p.m. London time on the following day.[21] It was clear that Monnet had convinced his government that it should not allow Britain to draw things out any longer. The British

Cabinet at that time was widely dispersed. Bevin had been taken ill again and was back in hospital, Attlee and Cripps were both in France on holiday, and other senior Cabinet ministers were also relaxing out of London over the Whitsun break. Although I had realised for some time that sooner or later we would be forced to choose, the ultimatum came as a shock to those officials and ministers who were in Whitehall when it arrived.

Kenneth Younger, who was in charge of the Foreign Office in Bevin's absence, telephoned me and asked what I thought we should do. I said that we must see Herbert Morrison, who in Attlee's absence was in charge of the government, as soon as possible. We found that he was at the theatre and was going to have supper afterwards at the Ivy Restaurant. We went to the Ivy and found him having supper with his friends. I said, 'Lord President we must have a word with you in private.' He, not unreasonably, said, 'Why can't it wait until tomorrow morning?' When I said it could not, we retired to a sort of passage at the back of the restaurant where spare tables and chairs were stored. We explained the French ultimatum. After a pause for thought he said, 'It's no good. We can't do it: the Durham miners wouldn't like it.' He was right, the Durham miners, and indeed all workers in the coal and steel industries, would not have liked it.

After talking to Bevin, who was far from happy at being dictated to, Morrison called what turned out to be a sparsely attended Cabinet the next day to obtain formal approval for British rejection of the French ultimatum. Before the Cabinet meeting, which I attended, Edward Bridges hastily drafted an introductory note for those who were to be present. This emphasised that 'It has been our settled policy hitherto that in view of our world position and interests we should not commit ourselves irrevocably to Europe either in the political or the economic field unless we could measure the extent and effects of the commitment.' He added that, to his mind, the most important aspect of the Schuman Plan was that it represented 'a new and constructive approach to Franco-German relations', which was in our interest from both the political and the defence points of view, and that our exclusion from the scheme now would not prevent our participation at a later date on rather better terms. He concluded that the difference of opinion between Britain and France could not be 'glossed over by mere verbal ingenuity in the drafting of a communiqué', and that therefore there was no alternative but to reject the French demand.[22]

At the Cabinet, ministers expressed their shock and dismay at the way the French had gone about this whole business. Some said that they suspected that the French had never wanted us included in the scheme from the outset. Not surprisingly, they agreed with Bridges' analysis, adding that 'No British Government could be expected to accept such a communiqué without having had any opportunity to assess the consequences which it might involve for our key industries, our export trade and our level of employment.'[23]

The French ultimatum was ignored, although the Cabinet did make a token effort to keep discussions going by proposing to the French that there should be a meeting of ministers of all the countries concerned to find a new method of negotiation. This, in turn, was rejected. A few days later Attlee summed up the situation when he told the French Ambassador over dinner that 'it was quite impossible for us to sign a blank cheque'.[24]

On 3rd June a joint communiqué was published in Paris on behalf of the six governments which accepted the French proposals. In signing this communiqué, the Dutch reserved the right to leave any future negotiations whenever they wished. It has been suggested that the British, too, could have participated in the Schuman Plan on this basis, but this was never really a viable option. We would still have had to have agreed to the basic principle of surrender of sovereignty, while Monnet, for his part, would have seen this rider as strong enough to undermine the whole exercise. The British leaving any conference on the Schuman Plan would have been a very different matter from the Dutch doing so.

Within three weeks the 'Six' had begun to discuss the details of the pooling of their coal and steel production. Subsequently, an official committee and a ministerial committee both drafted reports on what were considered more palatable alternative schemes of concerted production policies for Western European coal and steel in the event that the Schuman-inspired negotiations failed. Not surprisingly, the two reports put emphasis on advisory rather than mandatory powers for a High Authority.[25] When the negotiations amongst the 'Six' produced a document which laid stress on the very aspects of the Schuman Plan which the British Cabinet felt it could not accept, the alternative plans were shelved. They were certainly never put to other governments for discussion.

The refusal of the British government to take part in the negotiations for a European Coal and Steel Authority resulted in Britain's losing the leadership of Europe which she had enjoyed since the war. In retrospect, it has been called one of the turning points in British post-war history, a serious error of judgement and a missed opportunity. Dean Acheson even went so far as to call it 'the greatest mistake of the post-war period' and one from which both Britain and Europe were not to recover from for a long time.[26]

It was an opportunity but not, in my view, a missed opportunity. There was no possibility of persuading the British people or any British government at that time to enter into the Coal and Steel Community on the terms laid down by the French. The terms were to cede control of two basic industries, coal and steel, to some supra-national body. To believe that it was a missed opportunity is to judge the events of nearly forty years ago in the light of what we know and believe today.

What was the situation, then, four or five years after the end of the war – a war in which Britain and the Commonwealth had alone fought from the beginning to the end? In spite of the independence granted to India and Burma, Britain was still the centre of a great empire. It was the focal point and manager of the Sterling Area. A large part of world trade was conducted in sterling. Nearly twice as much of UK trade was done with the Commonwealth as with Europe. The British standard of living was then higher than that of any European country except the neutrals. After the United States, Britain maintained the largest armed forces in the Western world. They were stretched across the globe from Europe to the Far East.

To put it crudely, in the terms that a forthright colleague of mine used, 'We were being asked to join the Germans, who had started two world wars, the French, who had in 1940 collapsed in the face of German aggression, the Italians, who had changed sides, and the Low Countries, of whom not much was known but who seemed to have put up little resistance to Germany.' To cede control of coal and steel to a supra-national body which would also cover these six countries seemed incompatible with the 'ability to sustain independent resistance should France be overrun'.[27]

Two of Labour's most experienced politicians perfectly summed up the population's feelings about Europe. Herbert Morrison, when faced with the French ultimatum on the European Coal and Steel Community (ECSC) on 1st June 1950, said, 'the Durham miners wouldn't like it'.

I can also remember Ernest Bevin, at a meeting in August 1950 with Charles Spofford, the American representative on the NATO Council of Deputies, saying, while discussing the rearmament programme, that the United States must realise that Britain was not part of Europe – 'she was not simply a Luxembourg'. He added quite candidly that the people of Britain were pinning their faith on a policy of defence built on a Commonwealth/USA basis – an English-speaking basis. They were doubtful about Europe. He asked, and I remember this quite clearly, how could he go down to his constituency (Woolwich), which had been bombed night after night by the Germans, and tell the people there that they should rely on German help in a war against Russia? Londoners simply would not rely on the Germans; if they came to their help so much the better, but reliance must be placed on the Commonwealth and the United States.

The views of ministers and officials, both in the Foreign Office and in other parts of Whitehall, tended to mirror public opinion. The feeling was that a grouping of Britain with the countries of Western Europe was not in itself strong enough to stand alone in the post-war world. Any movement towards exclusivity for Europe in foreign policy was therefore a non-starter. A wider grouping was essential if Britain and, indeed, Europe were to be rendered secure from Soviet aggression. We had been saved from defeat in two world wars by American intervention and if the United States had been involved in Europe before the Second World War the latter almost certainly would not have happened. We could not afford to allow the Americans to return to their old policy of isolationism after binding us with Europe, as much of their domestic opinion desired. If we let this happen, we feared that Russia would soon overrun not only continental Europe but the British Isles as well. In short, we believed in an 'Atlantic Community' as the best form of strategic defence. The 'special' relationship with the United States was, in the words of the Foreign Office brief to me for my talks with Monnet in 1949, 'paramount'.[28] Notwithstanding all this, however, we also had to consider our responsibilities to the Commonwealth and the Sterling Area, and indeed to the Middle East and South-East Asia where we were performing a policing role.

Would a Conservative government have been able to convince the British people to join with Europe? I personally doubt that, had it come to the crunch, it would have wanted to. I shall cite three pieces of evidence to support this belief. First, in October 1953 Harold Macmillan and Robert Hall came to my flat to discuss the housing programme over dinner. When we had finished with housing, Macmillan asked whether we thought he ought to have resigned and whether he should do so now. Astonished, we asked him why. He said that while they were in opposition under Churchill's leadership, the Conservatives and he in particular had made many speeches advocating European unity and integration, but now that they were in power Churchill was only interested in our special relationship with the United States and in the relationship of the West, and the United States in particular, with Russia. Naturally, we urged him not to resign. After all, it was not the first time that a political party had dropped an important issue when it came to power.[29]

Second, in the summer of 1954, when I had left the Treasury and was chairman of the Atomic Energy Authority, I was asked by Churchill to estimate what it would cost to develop and make 'the hydrogen bomb'. Some weeks later, in his room at the House of Commons, I explained our estimate. When I had finished, he nodded and said, 'We must do it. It is the price we must pay to sit at the top table.' By this he meant to sit with the United States and Russia – nothing about Europe.

Finally, in December 1985 I asked Lord Home if he thought any government under any leader could have taken us into the ECSC in 1950. He wrote me a letter which he has allowed me to quote. His conclusion was that 'the British public was still too near to the glory of Empire to accept the role for Britain of just another country in Europe. A British P.M. cannot make that sort of deal over the heads of the people.'[30]

This was well understood by Monnet when, at the time, he said to me, 'With the exception of the UK and the neutrals every country in Western Europe has been defeated in war and every country has been occupied by an enemy army of occupation. So we are disillusioned with our institutions and are ready for change and a new approach. You are not, but when you see that it works you will want to join.' He was right and we did.

Had we been able to seize the opportunity to join the ECSC at the outset and then the EEC, I am sure we should have greatly benefited, as would have the EEC. I believe our influence would have made it more outward looking and more willing to accept real free trade within the Community. At the very least, the excesses of the Common Agricultural Policy would have been, if not avoided, mitigated. But it must be remembered that since Elizabethan times Britain had looked outwards from Europe and had founded the largest empire in history. She had avoided entanglement in Europe, except to prevent any one power from dominating it. The beliefs engendered by four hundred years of history are not changed overnight by intellectual argument. This takes time unless it is brought about by the shock of defeat in war. Even today, if we consider the attitude of the British public since we joined the EEC it could not exactly be described as enthusiastic. At the most, the majority have accepted that it is probably in our best interests to be members. But in 1950 attitudes were quite different.

CHAPTER TEN

The Korean War

In the same week as the Commons debate on the Schuman Plan, Russian-backed North Korean troops launched an unprovoked attack on their American-backed southern neighbours. The Cabinet's immediate response was to offer British support to the Americans in calling for United Nations action against the communist aggressors. Within weeks, and five years after the end of the Second World War, Britain was to find herself caught up in another costly period of war.

In June 1950 the British economy was performing in a manner we had hardly dared dream of a few years earlier. Internally, we had full employment, near-stable prices and rapid growth in production and productivity. Externally, the previous months had witnessed a rapid increase in our gold and dollar reserves and a sizeable balance of payments surplus. Provided that US economic activity remained high, officials had no reason to expect any dramatic change in this picture. The Korean War, however, was to change everything. It brought in its wake a reallocation of resources to support a heavy armaments programme, enormous imported inflation which, in turn, acted on domestic wages and prices, and a massive balance of payments deficit. Its effects played a major part in the eventual downfall of the second Attlee administration.

On first hearing of the North Korean invasion, Robert Hall and I feared that this could prove to be the prelude to a Third World War, especially if there was no positive response against it by the Americans and the new NATO Alliance. We were both firm believers in the view that had the British and the other Allies rearmed and reacted against the Nazi menace earlier we might never have had a Second World War, or at least we would have been better prepared to fight a war than we actually were. We feared that the same mistake might be made again and the Russian appetite for imperialist ventures elsewhere enhanced. We both quickly expressed our support for an increase in defence expenditure and strategic stocks.

Ministers were equally alive to the need to combat Russian expansionism. They recognised that the response of Britain, as the strongest nation in Western Europe, in terms of rearmament would be a key element in eliciting worthwhile co-operation from other European NATO countries. As a result, officials were soon instructed to look into what could be done by way of increasing defence expenditure without threatening serious damage to our vital export industries. These investigations had not gone far when, on 24th July, the American government asked all Alliance countries to provide by 5th August information about the plans they had for increases in the armed forces and military production. This request was coupled with personal assurances from Lew Douglas, the US Ambassador in London, to the Prime Minister that 'it was the purpose of President Truman to make available very large resources to the Western Union Powers to assist in any stepping-up of armaments necessitated by the present world state of affairs'. Douglas went on to add that this would include 'arrangements for making good any interruption in the economic plans for balance of payments which might be caused by the need for switching over from production of goods for exports to armament'.[1] Both officials and ministers took this to mean that at least we should have insurance against the effects of rearmament on the external account. In fact we should have known better than to believe this. Under the American constitution it is Congress which has the final say on the disposal of federal funds, no matter what the current administration might propose. We did not take this fact sufficiently into account and our assumptions about American aid were to prove wildly over-optimistic.

I was at this stage put in charge of a working party set up to formulate an official reply to the Americans and, over the next year or so, was to be responsible for the general economic supervision of the rearmament programme. Even before the working party reported to the Cabinet via the Chancellor, additional expenditure of £200 million on increased recruitment, forces pay and essential military equipment had been authorised, as had an extra £137 million for the civil defence programme. Our report concluded that in addition to this it would be possible over the three years after April 1951 to spend a further £800 million on defence, making a total defence expenditure of £3,400 million for the period 1951–2 to 1953–4. We added that financial support amounting to £550 million, or half the increase from the pre-Korea total of £2,300 million, in the form of 'free dollars', should be sought from the United States to cover the cost of extra imports and the loss of exports. As such, we calculated that the maximum we could afford from our own resources was £950 million per annum, a figure which in terms of a percentage of national income put our defence expenditure on a par with the United States.[2] The burden was, of course, small compared with what we had borne in the war.

This programme was accepted by the Cabinet on 1st August[3] and announced to the public on 3rd August, even though at that stage we had no guarantee that the Americans would, in the end, agree to provide the assistance requested. At the beginning of September the programme was raised by a further £200 million to meet the additional cost of further rises in service pay and an extension of the length of National Service from eighteen months to two years.[4]

The only minister who voiced misgivings about these proposals was Aneurin Bevan. In a statement to his fellow ministers which foreshadowed events over the following year, he made clear his serious doubts about the substitution of rearmament for a social and political defence against Soviet imperialism. While Britain could perhaps sustain the burden of additional defence expenditure, he was doubtful if other European countries could. Their efforts to do so might well bring about social and political problems in resisting the domestic communist threat.[5]

In the light of Bevan's resignation and that of Harold Wilson in 1951, it is widely believed that the left were opposed to resistance in Korea. This was not so. In fact Western minds generally were alarmed by the communists' elimination of rival regimes in Eastern Europe. Socialists were shocked, above all, by the Prague putsch, threats against Yugoslavia, and the Berlin blockade. While nobody knew what part Russia had played in Korea, some feared that she might either directly, or more probably by means of a satellite army, attack Yugoslavia, West Germany or Iran. Among those who had made their fears known were Aneurin Bevan and Richard Crossman.[6]

The American reaction to this rearmament programme was also unfavourable, but for quite different reasons. When I outlined the details to US Embassy officials, I emphasised that its major objective was to preserve peace and avoid war. They reported back to Washington that while they found this, in itself, 'unobjectionable in principle' they believed that we had used this formula as 'a mandate to develop a rearmament programme with a strong "business as usual" flavor ... involving the minimum economic dislocations'. To their mind, it was 'inadequate for present and forseeable future needs', and would encourage other European countries to present small programmes which would 'seriously jeopardise NAT[O] objectives'.[7]

The feeling both in the London Embassy and in Washington was that the amount and form of US aid requested went well beyond anything the Americans had been contemplating. There was considerable shock when it was made clear to them that £550 million of 'free dollars' was a basic assumption of the UK programme, and that without it we would have to reconsider our whole rearmament effort. American public opinion was equally dismissive of the scale of the British programme and request for aid, especially at a time when our reserves had recently doubled. People questioned why the American taxpayer should subsidise a continuation of Britain's high standard of living and socialist welfare policies.[8]

Discussions with the Americans on defence aid went on simultaneously in London, Washington and Paris with various branches of their government machine and within NATO. The whole process was terribly confused and we were frequently at a loss to comprehend exactly which set of talks should be considered the most crucial, which US department was the key authority, how firm a commitment the Americans had made in July, and what role congressional voting would play in all this. It was not until the beginning of September that we began to form a picture of exactly where we stood, and when we did so our original expectations for American aid proved misguided. At this juncture the State Department made it clear that while the US government had earmarked some $4.5 billion of aid for NATO in the financial year 1950–1, the great bulk of this was to be given in the form of military equipment manufactured in the United States. Only some $475 million was singled out for direct aid to support NATO production programmes, and the lion's share of this was designated for the finance of raw-material imports, components, capital equipment and technical aid. A mere $150 million was set aside for off-shore purchases by NATO countries and, as such, could be described as 'free dollars'. Moreover, it was stressed that the figure of $475 million for direct aid was conditional on defence expenditure by the European NATO countries far beyond the levels contemplated at that time.

We were faced with a situation in which, instead of the full funds for our balance of payments we had been counting on, we could, at most, hope to receive one-sixth of the meagre amount of dollars available. As Bill Strath put it to me at the time:

It is evident that the position adopted at present by the Americans does not offer a basis for negotiation of even an interim settlement which would yield more than a small fraction of the total assistance for which the UK has asked ... A satisfactory settlement from our point of view would ... require a revolution in current American thinking, and there is no evidence that this revolution is likely to take place either easily or quickly at the official level. [9]

The choices presented to the British government by the clarification of US defence aid policy were extremely difficult. The government could either criticise the Americans for the misleading statements of July and thereby risk a political rift with them at a most sensitive and inopportune moment for the Western Alliance, or it could admit that there was a gap in the plans to finance the rearmament programme. If it tried to play down the size of this gap and its implications it would be playing into the hands of those Americans who had maintained all along that the British rearmament programme would, at most, exert a minor destabilising effect on the economy. If it described the gap as large, the government would undermine confidence in industry and the City, and increase pressure for wage increases at a time when all the signs were already pointing to a major upsurge in prices and a deterioration in the current account.

At the instigation of Edward Bridges this situation led in the first week of September to the drafting by the CEPS, Economic Section and other interested departments of a report for ministers indicating how far it would be prudent to increase our defence expenditure relying on our own resources, or on the expectation of less US aid than was at first assumed. The conclusion was that it would be possible to sustain the

£3,600 million programme without reducing our standard of living, home investment or expenditure on social services with £350 million of aid rather than the £550 million originally requested. We should therefore scale down our request for assistance to this level.[10]

A Cabinet sub-committee met on 8th September to consider the report but was far from happy about its conclusions on both economic and political grounds. Ministers thought our projections for the balance of payments were too optimistic and that, in particular, we had under-estimated the effect of raw-material prices and domestic inflation on the external account. They also continued to insist that 'the Americans should be held to the promises they had made to assist in maintaining the general balance of payments'. They would not sanction a lower figure for aid, and suggested that in future negotiations we should emphasise to the Americans that the usefulness of this country in a military and political sense 'would be seriously jeopardised if it ceased to be economically viable as a result of shouldering the full defence programme'.[11] To a degree I shared these ministerial misgivings.

Some other officials also disagreed with the report. In the Treasury, Herbert Brittain and 'Otto' Clarke doubted if there was, in statistical terms, any real justification for a figure of £350 million rather than any other, and thought that any request for 'free aid' was unlikely to succeed. They preferred instead to submit a number of specific requests which included asking the Americans to underwrite our reserves at a particular figure, assist us with stockpiling and, most importantly, waive the interest and capital repayments on the 1945 loan.[12] In Washington, because he thought any request for direct aid would undermine our economic independence, Oliver Franks favoured a similar course of action and had found Dean Acheson to be supportive.[13]

Gaitskell pointed out to Attlee that there were several major drawbacks with this kind of approach. In the first place, the Americans were likely to ask the Canadians to match any waiver on loan repayments, and the Canadians were unlikely to agree. Second, any waiver or underwriting of the reserves would also still be subject to congressional approval and would be on an unsatisfactory annual basis. Finally, any abrogation of British contractual obligations was likely to have an adverse effect on our credit rating and the international standing of sterling.[14]

Thus for a while we continued to press for £550 million of 'free dollars' and to seek the revolution in US opinion that Bill Strath spoke of. Bevin, in Washington for a NATO Council meeting in mid-September, made representations, but to no avail. By the end of September it had become clear to all that the American government had no intention of granting us £550 million, £350 million or any lump-sum, bilateral aid package. All it would agree to do was to provide varied *ad hoc* aid for the £200 million of rearmament expenditure to which we had already committed ourselves. It agreed to instigate a multilateral process suggested by the Assistant Secretary of State, Paul Nitze, whereby the economic burden of rearmament would be shared out fairly and tolerably amongst all NATO countries, including the Americans themselves.

On 6th October, Gaitskell, having obtained the Prime Minister's approval, left for Washington. His brief was to try to obtain more definite information on the method of assessing contributions within NATO, and to discuss ways of reducing the problems of the boom in raw-material prices, which was reaching dangerous proportions because of American purchasing policy. He was accompanied by Robert Hall, Henry Wilson-Smith, William Armstrong and myself. Gaitskell's visit helped to build up connections with the American administration for the future, but on neither of the main issues under consideration was much headway made.[15] On the subject of 'Burden-Sharing' within NATO, Gaitskell was to record later in his diary that 'We did not carry any distance talks [*sic*] on the kind of formula which may have to be adopted to settle the question of equitable distribution. The chief attitude of the Americans on this was entirely to fight shy of formulae altogether.'[16] This was to be the attitude to this procedure for some time after Gaitskell's visit to Washington.

When we came to discuss raw materials we made an impassioned plea for American action both to increase supplies and to control domestic demand. We received some support for our viewpoint from the State Department and Averell Harriman, but the American administration as a whole was not, at that stage, ready to agree to speedy and concerted action to stop the damaging escalation of prices and the decline in available supplies.[17] With the major economic indicators still showing the British economy to be in excellent health, the Americans saw no urgent need to offer to change their policies. Even though they accepted that conditions would deteriorate in 1951, in October 1950 they saw an economy with minimal inflation, full employment, a unique welfare system, large reserves, a strong currency and a policy of discrimination against the dollar in many areas. Indeed, so strong did they think the British economy was at this time that the ECA made clear that it would be very difficult for ERP aid to Britain to be continued after that year. Before our arrival in Washington, rumours had been circulating there that Gaitskell's visit was to obtain American approval for a sterling revaluation.[18]

It should also be remembered that we were dealing with a country which was so economically strong, and had so much capacity to draw upon, that it could cope with a war or major rearmament programme with relatively little disruption to its own economy and society. Despite the huge burden carried by the American economy in the Second World War, American living standards had actually risen between 1941 and 1945 when ours and those of the rest of the combatants had fallen substantially. This experience made it hard for Americans to understand the pressures which wars and rearmament could exert on other nations smaller and less flexible that the United States.

After the Washington talks, we went on to Ottawa for three days of informal talks with the Canadians, before returning to New York to pick up our flight home. During our brief stay in New York, Hugh Gaitskell was informed, late at night, that Stafford Cripps had resigned on grounds of ill health and that Attlee wanted him to take over. I soon found myself being summoned from my bed from what I considered to be a well-earned early night to accompany him for a celebratory drink at the Blue Angel Night Club. Although most reluctant, I agreed to go. We walked from our hotel to the night club. On entering we were greeted by two attractive young ladies who took the money for our entry fee and then asked, I suppose because of our English accents, if we were actors. I replied, 'I am not an actor, but he is.' We sat down to enjoy the cabaret but our visit was brief. Gaitskell had entrusted me with our cash, of which, in keeping with Britain's shortage of dollars, we did not possess much. On finding out that our glasses of whisky and soda cost $10 each we were unable to afford another and felt obliged to leave. Hugh Gaitskell accused me of excessive austerity in the Crippsian mould. It was only later that we discovered that the $10 actually entitled us to several drinks.

Cripps's departure was not unexpected. He had been ready to resign some months earlier because of his health. Soon after the general election I can remember walking with him from the Treasury to Downing Street to attend a meeting. After walking along in silence for a few yards, he turned to me and said, 'Edwin, I'm trapped. I intended to go after the election, but with a majority of six I can't possibly do so now.' Over the next few months, Hugh Gaitskell and I had to emphasise repeatedly to him how much the nation needed him in order to keep up his spirits and to stop him from resigning.[19] Finally, however, he felt it necessary to return to his favoured Swiss clinic and was there advised that if he did not take at least a year's break from politics he might soon be dead. In the meantime, Edward Bridges and I were deputed by the Prime Minister to sound out various Cabinet ministers on their choice for the Treasury post if and when Cripps had to stand down. Herbert Morrison, because of his political weight in the Labour Party, obtained some support, and indeed Edward Bridges thought he would make a good Chancellor. However, after his experiences as Economic co-ordinator in 1945–7, this was a job he was very reluctant to take on. When I asked him if he would accept the job if it was offered he said, 'When I listen to Stafford in Cabinet explaining all those figures I just know I couldn't do it.'[20]

When we had completed our discussions, Edward Bridges said to me, 'The kind of talks you and I have been having with ministers in the last few days are an example of why no civil servant should ever keep a diary. The temptation to publish eventually would be too great and the result, the destruction of trust between civil servants and ministers.' Laziness has always inhibited me from keeping a diary.

With Morrison effectively out of the running, Gaitskell was really the only choice. Although only 44 years old and without having held any of the most important ministerial posts, he had the support of both of the previous incumbents – Dalton and Cripps.[21] He was a good, practical economist and had taken a vital lead in policy-making during the devaluation crisis and generally while serving as Minister of State for Economic Affairs. Gaitskell had greatly enhanced his reputation in the summer of 1949. Harold Wilson, through his hesitations at that time, had engendered a lot of distrust amongst his senior colleagues and had thereby undermined his chances of succeeding Cripps. Bevan, for his part and to his eternal disappointment, was viewed by Attlee as being too unstable and unlikely to carry confidence abroad. His appointment might also have posed a threat to party unity.[22]

Gaitskell was of a different generation from Cripps, and in his private life was in a number of ways the antithesis of his predecessor. He was energetic, outgoing and extremely good company. Away from politics he loved nothing better than parties, dancing and a night on the town. He became a friend of mine in a way that, close though we were, Cripps never did. When he became Chancellor, Gaitskell was as well qualified for the job of running the economy as any holder of that office before or since. It has always struck me how unlucky he was that events conspired to make his period at the Treasury so difficult. He was destined never to become a truly experienced politician in the sense of winning elections or holding all the three great Cabinet portfolios. None the less, his many excellent qualities made him a man of great potential. He was a highly intelligent and courageous man who was never afraid to cut through petty prejudices. He was also a great patriot and there was never any doubt in my mind about his keen social conscience.

If he did have any faults they were an occasional arrogance, indeed at times a pig-headedness, and a tendency to become bogged down in the detail of his work. He would sometimes behave more like the official he had been during the war than a minister. His interest in economics led him to become, as it were, more concerned with the trees of economic theory than the wood of political judgement. This aptitude, on occasions, made life difficult for his staff. He would re-draft speeches, engage in highbrow academic debate when decisions were needed urgently, and be perennially late for appointments. It also meant that, like his predecessor, he overworked.

The early months of the Korean War were disastrous for the South Koreans and their Western allies. They soon found themselves hemmed in on a small and precariously held beachhead on the southerly tip of the Korean peninsula. However, after a daring landing behind enemy lines on the west coast at Inchon, the allied forces were able by the end of September to push the North Koreans back to the 38th Parallel which originally divided the peninsula. Rather than stopping there, the UN troops, led by General MacArthur, continued to press northwards until two months later they had all but removed the communists from their own country. It was at this stage that the Chinese attacked across the Yalu River in large numbers and once again forced the UN troops into headlong retreat. With MacArthur threatening to launch bombing raids on targets in China, and a statement from President Truman which appeared to imply that the Americans were even ready to use the atomic bomb, the British Cabinet feared that the Korean War was about to escalate out of hand.[23]

Attlee's response was to set off to Washington in search of reassurance from Truman that Britain's worst fears would not be realised. Although his visit had mainly political aims, he also sought to encourage the Americans to set up bodies along lines similar to the bipartite Combined Boards which had yielded effective international control of raw materials in the Second World War. As a result, on 3rd December 1950 I once again found myself flying across the Atlantic. In addition to the Prime Minister there was Denis Rickett, Attlee's Private Secretary, and William Slim, Chief of the Imperial General Staff. Roger Makins and Robert Hall also went to Washington, although they travelled separately.

When discussions got under way in Washington, Attlee was quickly assured that Truman's remark concerning the use of the atomic bomb 'was ... an unpremeditated answer to a question at a press conference. He had evidently never seriously considered use of the bomb in Korea.'[24] The Americans also satisfied the Prime Minister that their policy was as far as possible to limit the hostilities to the Korean peninsula.

When the talks turned to economic matters, we once again put forward our case that a lack of co-ordination and thought in American policies for the purchase, stockpiling and control of raw materials was, on top of general Western rearmament, having grave effects on our economy, and indeed on the European economy as a whole. We made clear our belief that we were suffering special difficulties because of the prices and short supply of zinc, sulphur, nickel, cotton, wool and rubber. We emphasised that we considered the grim outlook for inflation, the balance of payments and industrial production in Britain in the forthcoming year was to a great extent the result of American selfishness and lack of foresight.[25]

Although the Americans were convinced that our problems were as much the result of excess demand as their own actions,[26] they appeared considerably more forthcoming than had been the case in October. For the first time, all the various US agencies concerned with raw materials were brought together to talk to us.[27] A joint working party was set up and within a few days had agreed to establish a steering committee consisting of American, French and British representatives and a number of autonomous commodity committees upon which representatives of all the countries directly concerned would sit in order to help alleviate the world raw-material shortage.[28] On the British side we were generally satisfied that these arrangements were a major step forward. As it turned out, however, the system finally established was very different and never remotely as successful as the wartime Joint Boards. Our price and supply problems continued to worsen for some time. After a long series of negotiations, the central steering committee was swollen by the additional inclusion of Canadian, Australian, Indian, Brazilian, OEEC and Organisation of American States (OAS) representatives, and it became a slow-moving and ponderous body. At the same time, the Americans to a large degree continued their policy of self-interest and indifference to the needs of other nations. As long as this was the case there was little hope of an easing of the situation.

During the economic discussions the Americans also requested us to initiate a larger defence programme. They stressed that Britain was their major ally, and indeed the only ally on which they could really depend.[29] Attlee was immediately struck by their arguments, as I think were all the officials present, and, although we again pointed out the difficulties we were already facing because of rearmament, he agreed that we should consider a further expansion of military expenditure.[30]

The atmosphere during the talks in Washington was a most serious one. There was a sense that this meeting between Truman and Attlee was overdue and was needed to clear the air on a number of issues. Both sides got on well, and while it would be wrong to describe Attlee and Truman as intimate friends, they rapidly developed a profound respect and regard for each other. After the differences of opinion between the two countries over the European Payments Union and European integration in 1950, Attlee's visit seemed to revive the 'Special Relationship' between the two countries.

I had met and briefed the Prime Minister on a great number of occasions, but the trip to Washington in December 1950 was the first time that I had been in close contact with him over a protracted period. My observations of him at this time served to confirm what I already thought to be true. Despite his taciturn nature and the fact that he was never a character in the sense that Churchill or Bevin was, he was a remarkable man, an astute political manipulator, somebody who was rarely ruffled by events and who always retained a great dignity.

There were two particular episodes on the trip to Washington which will always stand out in my mind. First, while the British party was alone and discussing rearmament prior to attending some meeting, Attlee turned to Slim and asked how long it would take him to create from the African colonies an army comparable in size and quality with the Indian Army, an army which we could use to support our foreign policy just as the Indian Army had done. Slim, who had spent his life in the Indian Army, said he could do something in eight or ten years, but to do anything really worthwhile would take at least twenty or probably more. This I think amply sums up where senior politicians at that time believed our priorities and responsibilities lay. They naturally looked to the colonies and the Commonwealth rather than to Europe. What is more important, I think it shows how little we had come to understand our changed position in the world and our true weakness if someone as realistic as Attlee, who had been instrumental in granting independence to India, could contemplate using the African colonies for such a purpose.

The second incident occurred during our flight home. Attlee and I were about to retire to the special bunks provided for the Prime Minister's party when a young junior minister, who had joined us in New York after performing some departmental business, began to talk at length about the difficulties and problems he was having in his work. As Attlee pulled his pyjamas on over his skinny frame he interjected in his clipped, military tones, 'Well, I've got one piece of advice for you that I have always followed. Never take your troubles to bed with you. Goodnight.' Within a few moments the Prime Minister was fast asleep. Perhaps this is one of the secrets of a successful political career.

On our return home Attlee reported to his Cabinet colleagues that he accepted that 'some acceleration of the defence programme was now unavoidable'. Dean Acheson followed us back across the Atlantic and was expected to begin pressing Western European countries to double their pre-Korean armaments programmes, while the Americans had already committed themselves to spend some $42 billion in the fiscal year 1950–1 and to complete their share of NATO's ambitious Medium-Term Defence Plan in two years rather than three. If Britain did not want to be treated merely as another European country, and if we wanted to be sure that the Americans did not lose interest in the defence of Europe, Attlee concluded that 'we should align ourselves with the Americans in urging the others to do more'.[31]

Bevin was immediately authorised to tell the NATO Council, at what was to be his last international conference, that 'the United Kingdom Government in view of the disturbed and dangerous situation, had decided to increase and accelerate their defence preparations still further ... and were now considering the form and direction this additional effort should take'. Although the American Chiefs of Staff were talking in terms of a £6,000 million programme over the next three years, no figure was mentioned at that stage. This was to wait for a detailed analysis of what was required, what was physically possible and what it all would cost.

The Chancellor had by now announced to the public that the US and UK governments had agreed to suspend Marshall Aid to Britain from 1st January 1951.[32] Nevertheless, no new general financial assistance from the United States was expected although, of course, the 'Burden Sharing' exercise was still to be completed.[33] Douglas Allen of the CEPS, Jack Downie of the Economic Section and Christopher Saunders of the Central Statistical Office were given the job of working out the economics of the new rearmament programme under my supervision. We had a far from restful Christmas and New Year.

CHAPTER ELEVEN

The Defence Programme, January 1951

Within a month we had completed our investigations into the scope for a further increase in defence expenditure. On 25th January, in the absence of both Shinwell (Minister of Defence) and Bevin, Gaitskell presented the new programme to the Cabinet. Total defence expenditure for the years 1951–4 was raised to £4,700 million, a doubling of the pre-Korea level which raised its share of GNP to 14 per cent. Among NATO countries only the United States exceeded this proportion. Expenditure would rise particularly steeply in the first year, and continue at a high level for the following two years. At the peak, 2,500,000 people, or some 11 per cent of the active population, were expected to be engaged in defence work or to be in the armed forces. Defence expenditure would be concentrated on the metal-using and textile industries in particular. These sectors provided around half of our exports and investment at that time. Given that the economy was already fully employed, that the terms of trade were expected to continue to deteriorate, that serious shortages of raw materials were predicted and that we could depend on no general assistance from the Americans, the resource allocation problems were clearly formidable.

The policy evolved to meet these problems was 'to take as much as possible of the necessary sacrifices on current consumption rather than to burden the future by any serious reduction in investment or the incurring of overseas debt'.[1] The large current account surplus for 1950, then put at £229 million, would be allowed to run down but it was hoped to maintain a net balance excluding the cost of stockpiling in 1951. The remainder of the resources would be released by fiscal and monetary measures and direct controls on consumption which at that stage were unspecified. 'Very roughly', we estimated that 'the supply to the home market of manufactured consumer goods (excluding food, drink and tobacco) will have to fall by about 2 per cent per annum or by 5 per cent by 1953.'[2] We had no doubts that this would be extremely unpopular. People had become used to rising standards of living since the war and would resent any reverse in this trend.

The programme was approved by the Cabinet, although not without some doubt and dissent, and on 29th January the Prime Minister announced it to the House of Commons. He put special emphasis on a number of points. In the first place, he stressed that 'the Government do not believe that war is inevitable. Their purpose is to prevent war.' He added, however, that 'peace cannot be ensured unless the defences of the free nations are made sufficiently strong to deter aggression'. It is worth remembering that at that time, the Russians had 175 divisions in Europe, with 27 in East Germany alone, while NATO had 12.[3] Second, Attlee warned that the completion of the programme within the allotted timescale depended on a number of factors – such as the supply of materials and machine tools – largely out of our direct control. Finally, he underlined his intention not to see Britain mortgage her future by running up huge external debts, and slashing domestic investment to pay for the programme.[4]

Robert Hall and I had given US Embassy officials an indication of the size of the new rearmament programme early in January and at that stage I had also indicated my personal belief, wrongly as it happened, that the expanded programme could not be achieved without the compulsory direction of labour.[5] The final details were passed on to Dean Acheson by Oliver Franks on the same day as Attlee announced them to Parliament. In doing so, Franks stressed the need for US assistance in obtaining enough machine tools and raw materials.[6] The American Ambassador reported to Washington that the new programme was 'an effort which in size does not fall too short of what might reasonably be expected from the British at this time', and the lack of conditions regarding 'free' dollar aid as a definite step forward. His recommendation, however, was that US praise should be restrained. The hope was to get US public opinion to support it, while maintaining some pressure on us for more in the long run.[7]

Back in Whitehall some officials and ministers were far from confident about the Prime Minister's assurances over the balance of payments. This view was compounded when, in April 1951, Oliver Franks reported to Gaitskell that because Britain was continuing to add to her reserves the American government was unlikely to authorise any assistance for us in the next financial year. Aid was to be made available only to countries with external deficits and declining reserves. The fact that the swelling of our reserves at that time reflected a Sterling Area surplus rather than a UK surplus was of no relevance to Congress, nor indeed was the fact that British balance of payments forecasts were becoming increasingly pessimistic.

Gaitskell was furious about this. He felt that American policy 'prejudge[d] the results of the so-called "Nitze exercise" ', which was still in its early stages. It also failed to take into account the size of our liabilities in comparison with our reserves and therefore was too simplistic a formula.[8] He sent a copy of the latest Treasury balance of payments projections to the United States and hastily arranged a meeting with the US Ambassador to encourage the Americans to review their position on the matter.[9] He made little progress. The Americans were not at that stage ready to change their criteria for aid distribution.

As it happened, the total balance of payments deficit for 1951 was to rise eventually to £369 million, embodying a massive swing of some £700 million over the previous year. This surprisingly large deterioration gained its initial momentum from a continued rise in raw-material prices caused by rearmament, the general buoyancy of the world economy and American selfishness. At the same time, the unfettered world demand brought worsening shortages of non-ferrous metals and export production began to be held up. The government had no choice but to reintroduce a number of controls over the use of these metals and to limit the manufacture of durable consumer goods.[10]

In addition to the widespread ignorance in the United States of the supply and price problems faced in Britain and elsewhere, Lord Knollys, our chief representative at the unwieldy and ineffective International Materials Conference in Washington,[11] identified three reasons why the Americans continued in 1951 to behave in a self-interested manner in their raw-materials policy. In the first place, the failure of countries like Britain to impose a total embargo on strategic exports to Russia, China and the Eastern bloc had an unfavourable effect on American decision-making. Second, American public opinion was no longer convinced that a world war was imminent and was therefore less ready than ever to accept cuts in civilian consumption. Third, responsiblity for American raw-materials policy was still dispersed chaotically among a wide range of competing agencies.[12]

American officials were constantly lobbied by our Embassy staff about our need for raw-materials assistance. In May, first Robert Hall and Roger Makins, and then Richard Stokes, the Lord Privy Seal, were sent on missions to try to educate the Americans about the predicament faced by Britain and to change their attitudes. By the end of that month there were at last indications that the atmosphere on the subject of raw materials had really changed for the better and that the Americans were ready to take action to ensure sufficient supplies at reasonable prices.[13] Ironically, however, by this time raw-material prices were, in any case, beginning to level off and in some cases to fall.

The wage freeze negotiated by Cripps and Bevin after devaluation had lasted for only six months before internal discontent forced the TUC, in its own words, to 'adopt the practical course of recognising that there must be a greater flexibility of wage movements in the future'.[14] Thus as the cost of living moved up in response to the rise in raw-material prices, wages began to follow suit. By the early months of 1951 domestic inflation was moving steadily upwards. Gaitskell was always alive to the dangers of inflation; and, at the instigation of Robert Hall, in late 1950 work had been going on in the Economic Section and the CEPS to try to construct a formula for long-term wage restraint in the context of full employment. A wide range of options were discussed, many of which were to resurface in the 1960s and 1970s when incomes policy was seen as a vital facet of economic management.

With the Chancellor taking the lead, it was decided early in 1951 to present to the trade unions the idea of an independent 'Wages Advisory Council'. At the same time, the government was to issue a document following up the 1944 White Paper on *Employment Policy* and detailing the macroeconomic lessons learned since the war, with an emphasis on boom control rather than on slump avoidance. The 'Wages Advisory Council' was to consist of a number of 'honest brokers', employers and trade union leaders. It would provide published comment on all collective negotiations on rates of remuneration, taking into account a periodically announced definition of what the government considered to be an average wage increase commensurate with the national interest.[15] 'The idea,' as Edward Bridges put it, 'preserved the principle of collective bargaining, but involved some modification of the process by which that bargaining is carried out.'[16]

The proposal for a 'Wages Advisory Council' was presented to trade union representatives in February 1951 by Gaitskell and Bevan, who was by this time at the Ministry of Labour. Bevan assured Gaitskell that, as he was on good terms with all the union leaders, he would be able to talk them round to the government's standpoint.[17] As it turned out, however, Bevan's optimism was misplaced. The Chancellor reported afterwards that the TUC, while not showing a wholly irresponsible attitude, could not sanction any such advisory committee, nor did they think that there was any chance that formal wage restraint could be accepted without rigid price control.[18]

Gaitskell chose to abandon the 'Wages Advisory Council' rather than set it up without union backing. The government also dropped the plan to publish a second Employment Policy White Paper. For a while, wages were left more or less to market forces and by the summer of 1951 the annual rate of increase in both wages and prices was fast approaching double figures. At this stage the Chancellor warned other ministers that the public were becoming increasingly inflation-conscious and that inflation was likely to escalate further in the absence of new measures.[19] The implications for exports were obvious and hardly comforting. His response was to strengthen price controls and, against the wishes and advice of many of us in the Treasury, he announced the government's intention to introduce legislation to limit company dividends to the average of the two previous years. By this latter measure he hoped to create the right atmosphere for a further approach to the trade unions for a policy of income stabilisation later in the year.[20] Before much more could be done to bring this to fruition, however, Labour fell from office.

Not surprisingly, the continuing raw-material crisis caused officials and ministers much anxiety in the lead-up to the Budget of April 1951. Indeed we identified it as the greatest threat to our calculations for the next fiscal year. At that stage we were confident that, given sterling's recent devaluation and Britain's competitiveness in 1950, the general balance of payments would not prove to be a cause for too much concern. Likewise it was accepted, although not without some ministerial misgivings, that the threat of excess domestic demand could be dismissed to a large extent. Robert Hall and the Economic Section pointed out that £700 million of additional armaments expenditure would be offset largely by the deflationary impetus of the higher import prices.[21] With the abolition of initial allowances on investment, this meant that only about £150 million of additional tax revenue had to be sought. This was realised by raising income tax by 6d in the pound and by increases in profits tax, petrol tax and purchase tax on major consumption items competing with defence.[22]

However, the Budget of 1951 is remembered for other reasons. It precipitated the resignation of Aneurin Bevan, Harold Wilson and John Freeman from the Labour government.

On becoming Chancellor, Gaitskell was anxious to keep social expenditure in check at a time when the country could least afford to let it get out of control. Since the inception of the NHS in July 1948 the growth of its expenditure had been a constant source of anxiety to the Treasury and, in the aftermath of the previous year's Budget, a special sub-committee, presided over by Attlee himself, had been set up to monitor NHS expenditure on a weekly basis.[23] In April 1951 Gaitskell proposed to introduce charges for half the cost of dentures and spectacles further to circumscribe the growth in NHS expenditure. This measure was expected to raise £13 million in 1951–2 and £25 million in a full year.[24]

Aneurin Bevan had been in many ways the father of the NHS and, although by this stage he was Minister of Labour, he still regarded it as his own special field and responsibility. He had clashed with Gaitskell in 1950 over its finances when the latter was Minister of State for Economic Affairs and he reacted violently to the Chancellor's plan to institute charges for dentures and spectacles in 1951. Not only was the principle of a free Health Service being infringed, but this was being done to help finance a growing rearmament programme, the wisdom of which he had been unsure of for the previous nine months. Moreover, he became convinced that the shortage of raw materials and machine tools would make it impossible to spend the full defence Budget in 1951. As he put it in his resignation letter, 'the scale of military expenditure in the coming year would be unobtainable physically'.[25] Surely, he argued, a mere £13 million of additional social expenditure could therefore be accommodated.

In arguing in this manner, Bevan was resorting to the method used by all spending ministers when they wish to squeeze more of the taxpayers' money from the Chancellor. The problem is, of course, that when all the £13 millions are added up the total amount to be added to public expenditure can be very large.

In customary fashion, Gaitskell informed his Cabinet colleagues of his Budget proposals the day before he presented them to the House. Attlee was in hospital suffering from an ulcer and Morrison was in the chair. Bevan opposed the new charges and threatened resignation. Wilson and George Tomlinson, the Minister for Education, made clear their support for him.[26] After a lengthy debate the Cabinet was adjourned until the evening and, in the meantime, Morrison went to see Attlee to seek his advice. The Prime Minister supported Gaitskell and gave Morrison a message urging the rest of the Cabinet to do likewise.[27] When ministers met a second time that day Bevan and Wilson remained unmoved. The matter was put to a vote which gave a large majority to the Chancellor, and Bevan said he would offer his resignation to the Prime Minister the next day.[28]

The following morning first the two dissident Cabinet Ministers and then Gaitskell saw Attlee in hospital. At this stage the Prime Minister tried to persuade Gaitskell to withdraw the charges, but he refused and Attlee reluctantly agreed that he would have to lose the Minister of Labour and the President of the Board of Trade. Gaitskell subsequently told me that even as late as 12.30 p.m. that day he was unsure as to whether or not he would present his Budget, but present it he did. Moreover, at the last minute, on the advice of Herbert Morrison, he deleted a phrase from his speech and thereby delayed the implementation of the charges and opened the way for a continuing dialogue with the rebel ministers.[29] This strategy had some success in that Bevan and Wilson did not resign immediately. Efforts to reach a compromise formula acceptable to both sides continued for some weeks and centred on the question of whether the charges should be announced as 'temporary' or 'permanent'. Ultimately, however, with Attlee unable to play much more than a spectator's role in events, and Bevan being encouraged by his left-wing supporters to stand firm, these efforts came to nothing. On 21st April, Bevan resigned. Wilson followed on the 23rd and John Freeman, a junior minister at the Ministry of Supply, soon after.

The dispute between Gaitskell and Bevan was complicated. On the one hand, it was bound up with political matters as varied as the socialist principles of the government, the rights and wrongs of rearmament as a means to combat communist imperialism, the extent of rearmament, the control of social expenditure, and the question of excessive deference to American foreign policy. On the other hand, it encompassed a personal feud between two Cabinet ministers who were socially, intellectually and temperamentally very different.

Gaitskell was the middle-class intellectual, educated at Winchester and Oxford, and a former economics don. He was a realistic and practical socialist on the right of the Labour Party with no real roots in the working class. Bevan, by contrast, was the fiery and unpredictable working-class hero from the Welsh valleys. A self-educated 'gut' socialist with a flair for politics, he was one of the great orators of the twentieth century. He could hold any audience spellbound, be it made up of Members of Parliament, trade unionists, or the general public. Bevan was not only a passionate politician but also something of an intellectual with a wide range of interests. Indeed, he once told me how he was trying to arrange a holiday in a remote part of Italy so that he might be able to see a particular painting in the church of a tiny village.

Bevan, because of his capricious nature, was passed over for the jobs of Chancellor and Foreign Secretary in quick succession.[30] He grew bitter and jealous, especially when he saw the rapid rise of his young colleague Gaitskell, and reacted accordingly. At the same time, Gaitskell became increasingly exasperated by Bevan's personal attacks on him. Their dislike became mutual.

Looking back on this episode now, I remain convinced that the finances of the NHS had got out of control and that a stand had to be taken in order to try to prevent a continued rise in government expenditure at an inopportune moment. Edward Bridges, Robert Hall and other senior officials were in agreement on this at the time and we all lent our support to Gaitskell. The housing, education and national insurance budgets had all recently been restrained and we saw no reason why the NHS should be an exception.

Bevan had more of a case on the size of the defence programme, as the *Economic Survey for 1952* makes plain. The defence programme of January 1951 did not reach its targets for the first year. Scare raw materials, machine tools and components, labour shortages and the general strain on the metal-using and textile industries saw to this.[31] When the Conservatives came to power in October 1951 they immediately began to review the programme and were content to let it run into a fourth year.

This was not a great surprise to senior officials. We always believed it might be necessary once the immediate military emergency had passed, and were not too perturbed when it did. The fact is, the political aspects of the rearmament programme in January 1951 were of great importance. British rearmament was as much as anything else a political statement designed to encourage similar reactions in other NATO countries and to convince the American Congress and people that we in Europe were willing to make sacrifices in order to defend ourselves. If we could achieve these goals, we believed we could keep the American forces in Europe in sufficient numbers to guarantee our security and nip in the bud any thought of further communist expansionism. Like the rejection of the Schuman Plan, the extent of the rearmament programme can be seen as an indication of where we believed our priorities to lie in foreign policy.

It has been asserted recently by, amongst others, my old friend and colleague, Lord Croham (Douglas Allen), that the size of the rearmament programme after January 1951, by arresting the momentum of the post-war export and investment boom, curtailed an economic miracle in Britain that might have matched that of the Germans or the Japanese over the last forty years.[32] While rearmament undoubtedly did set back our recovery, it is, in my view, extremely doubtful that a German- or Japanese-style miracle was then possible. Even if there had been no Korean War, the obstacles to an economic miracle were and still are formidable. Perhaps the most important are a national resistance to change, poor management in much of industry, reactionary trade unions, the poor education and training of much of the workforce and too great a concentration on old and declining industries. These characteristics have prevailed since the middle of the previous century. We must hope that many of the changes begun in the last eight to ten years will continue, in particular the acceptance of the need for change and for the creation of an educational system suited to the modern world.

Even with a smaller rearmament programme our economy would have suffered from imported inflation caused by the rearmament programme of the United States. But, in any case, the point is largely irrelevant, for without the British rearmament programme and the influence this had in persuading Congress to adopt the very large

American rearmament programme, Western Europe might have been overrun and there might have been no British economy left at all.[33]

The vast majority of the Cabinet, together with senior officials like Edward Bridges, Robert Hall and myself, believed that there was a real threat of another world war. We felt it was essential to try to forestall this threat by helping to redress the balance of power in the world. If this meant endangering economic recovery, then it was a chance we had to take. The crucial question one must ask is, 'What would have happened without the British commitment to rearm on the scale announced in January 1951?' To my mind, at the very least we would have undermined Anglo-American relations for a long time, with serious consequences for our economy. At the most, we might have helped to trigger a communist invasion of Western Europe with all its horrific repercussions. If rearmament is successful in preventing a war it must always seem to have been too large; if it fails, as in the later 1930s, it always appears to have been too small.

Whatever the rights and wrongs of the rearmament programme of January 1951, one thing is certain. The resignations of Bevan and Wilson which it helped to bring about split the Labour Party for many years and contributed greatly to the downfall of the Attlee government six months later. They further weakened and undermined the confidence of an aging administration which was already weary and beleaguered after six momentous and exhausting years in office, and which was coming under ever more intense pressure in the House of Commons. The government had, moreover, two months before it suffered the loss of a second major figure.

Ernest Bevin, like Cripps, was dogged by ill health throughout the post-war years. Indeed, it was remarkable that he managed to continue to work and to be so successful in his job for so long. He suffered from a chronic heart condition and underwent a number of serious operations. Finally, however, no longer able to stand the strain and a shadow of his former self, in March 1951 he was forced by Attlee to stand down as Foreign Secretary. He died a month later.

As Alan Bullock's superb three-volume biography of the man makes clear, Ernest Bevin was, without doubt, a great Foreign Secretary and one of the most powerful and influential figures in the history of the Labour and trade union movements. His was a remarkable story. In 1921, aged 40, he became General Secretary of the Transport and

General Workers' Union and was soon recognised as the leading trade unionist of his day. Churchill brought him into Parliament and the War Cabinet in 1940 as Minister of Labour. During the war he played a vital role in Britain's mobilisation and in sustaining morale and productivity. Then, in June 1945 when Labour came to power, Attlee appointed him as Foreign Secretary and over the next six years he helped to shape many of the political and economic characteristics of the modern world.

Bevin would always listen to his officials and his years as a trade union leader had given him a marked feel for economics. This was unlike his two immediate successors, Morrison and Eden, who did not enjoy the subject and often appeared to be frightened by it. Bevin was, moreover, one of the most fervent supporters of the basic policy to secure full employment and stable prices. In discussions with trade unionists about wage restraint, his knowledge and experience could make the difference between success and failure. It is noticeable that, after his death, Labour was unable to secure another round of wage restraint.

If at times a vain man, he never lost his roots in the working class of the nation. He was 'the People's Ernie'; a colourful and larger than life figure about whom everybody who worked close to him had his own favourite anecdote. My own most abiding memory of Bevin, however, relates to a meeting I had with him just before his death. One afternoon I ran into him in Storey's Gate, not far from the Foreign Office. I was struck by the deterioration in his physical condition since I had last seen him. Attlee had kept him in the Cabinet and made him Lord Privy Seal on his resignation from the Foreign Office. He had been given a room in what had been Churchill's wartime headquarters which was much less grand than the one he was used to. Guiding me into that room, he remarked resentfully, 'Look what they've done to me Edwin, look what they've done to me, look at the office they have given me.' He believed to the end that he could have done his old job and felt bitter and heartbroken that Attlee, for many years his greatest political ally and confidant, could force him to stand down and replace him with his greatest political enemy, Herbert Morrison. It was truly a sad end for a great man. But Attlee was right; Bevin was no longer physically able to shoulder the burden of being Foreign Secretary.

From the first quarter of 1951, as was widely predicted, the balance of payments showed a sharp turn around. However, over the summer months the deterioration, especially in the dollar balance, was far more dramatic than was expected.[34] Three new, unforeseen factors conspired to bring about what Gaitskell himself referred to as a 'serious' position.[35] First, in May 1951 the Iranian Parliament passed a law to nationalise that country's oil wells and refineries and to end the British concession there. Iran was Britain's main source of oil under non-dollar control and, as a result of this action, we both lost income from oil sales and had to buy supplies elsewhere from expensive dollar sources. Second, falls in the international prices of wool, rubber and tin cut heavily into the Sterling Area's dollar earnings at a time when many of these countries were spending heavily on imports. Third, Britain began to run a large deficit with the EPU, amounting to £387 million, in the last six months of 1951.[36]

Economic policy in general was under constant review at all levels over the summer months, but little of substance was done to arrest the rapidly developing crisis. I advised other senior officials that I believed the situation to be in such a state of flux and uncertainty that what was needed was not an immediate, drastic revision of policy but a change of attitude to certain important issues, such as exports.[37] The government contented itself with measures to limit some dollar imports, to cut some food rations and to tighten controls over steel and other vital commodities.[38] In addition, Gaitskell left for Washington in early September. His purpose was ostensibly to attend meetings of the IMF and World Bank but he was also authorised by the Cabinet fully to inform the US administration of the worsening situation in Britain, and to discuss a number of remedial measures with them.[39] It was to be his last trip as Chancellor and, indeed, although few would have believed it then, his last trip as a minister. He took with him William Armstrong, Clem Leslie and Eric Roll. Leslie Rowan, by this time head of the Treasury's Overseas Finance Division, and I travelled on ahead.

Our first task in Washington was to present the relevant members of the administration and officials with a memorandum outlining the extreme seriousness of our external position. In it we stressed the effects of American purchasing and stockpiling policy over the last year or so, and informed them that we expected a dollar deficit for the third quarter of more than $500 million and that the position would change little in 1952.[40] Although the American Embassy in London had given the State Department some prior indication of the extent of our plight, as usual the Americans appeared to think we were being unduly pessimistic.[41]

We asked them for action to assist us in two areas: raw materials – particularly steel – and general dollar aid. On the former subject we obtained some further assurances from the relevant departments that the United States would in future be more supportive and alive to our problems, but they were extremely reluctant to give their explicit backing to Gaitskell's plans for a joint Anglo-American initiative to stabilise world commodity prices. They did not wish to be seen to be colluding with us to the exclusion of their other allies.[42] When it came to the subject of general aid, Gaitskell began by indicating that fulfilment of the rearmament programme might well hinge upon 'United States action in some form'.[43] Subsequently, we raised with them a number of ideas we had on aid although these were not presented as specific requests. They included US assistance for British stockpiling, additional end-item defence aid, and guarantees of dollar oil supplies to replace those lost because of the Iranian crisis. With a presidential election looming, however, there was no hope of our receiving assistance in the financial year 1951–2. Gaitskell also had talks with the Treasury Secretary, Snyder, on the question of a waiver of the interest payments on the 1945 Anglo-American loan. This was something which under the original agreement we could request if our economic position was truly dire. However, as Snyder pointed out, such a step would have had a disastrous effect on American public opinion and was never viewed by our side as anything other than a last resort.[44]

By the end of our visit to Washington no firm aid package had been agreed. This did not mean that we had failed. Our major aim was always to make the American politicians and officials fully understand our position. This we achieved, particularly with the State Department and the ECA. Moreover, just before we left Washington for Ottawa and the NATO Council meeting which Gaitskell was to attend there, we had a most productive tripartite meeting in the State Department with French officials and Dean Acheson, Averell Harriman and Robert Lovett, US Secretary of Defence. The French at the time had similar economic difficulties to our own; like us, they were worried that the United States would use the Ottawa Conference to press Western Europe into yet larger defence programmes. They proposed that a committee of four outside experts should be appointed to report to the NATO Council on the whole issue of rearmament and the dispersal of its economic burdens amongst member countries. Neither Acheson nor Gaitskell was keen on such a serious and complex matter being left to outside experts, but they were attracted by the basic idea of establishing a process for quickly and realistically harmonising the military requirements of the developing political situation with the economic capabilities of individual NATO countries. The original Nitze Burden-Sharing exercise had got bogged down and had taken an inordinate length of time to produce little progress. A new initiative was needed and it was agreed to discuss the matter further in Ottawa.[45]

CHAPTER TWELVE

'Operation Wise Man'

On our arrival in Ottawa, talks on the subject resumed at once at both ministerial and official level, and were quickly extended to include representatives of all NATO countries. It was soon established that members of the committee should be 'insiders' rather than 'outsiders', as in the original proposal. Gaitskell was convinced that they should all be of ministerial rank. We then moved on to the size of the committee. Not every NATO country, by any means, was keen to have a four-man committee. The smaller nations naturally wanted to obtain direct representation for themselves. On the British side we were anxious to keep the new committee small so as to ensure it could fulfil its functions quickly and efficiently. To get around the difficulties with the smaller NATO nations we suggested that a three-man 'Executive Bureau' consisting of an American, a Frenchman and a Briton should do the bulk of the work, but that it should issue its report through a twelve-man 'Temporary Council Committee' (TCC) on which all NATO countries were represented. This formula was accepted, although not without some protests, particularly from the Italians.[1]

Subsequently, Averell Harriman, President Truman's Special Assistant, was made chairman of the TCC. Jean Monnet and Hugh Gaitskell were appointed as vice-chairmen. These three men also made up the Executive Bureau, or the 'Wise Men' as they were called. I was appointed as Gaitskell's 'alternate' to act on his behalf when he was not available. In fact, because of the Chancellor's duties on the hustings and in Whitehall in October 1951, Gaitskell was not able to

125

attend a single working session of the 'Wise Men' before the Labour government fell from office. Thereafter, I formally took over from Gaitskell as Britain's 'Wise Man' and became a vice-chairman of the TCC.

In 1951 Averell Harriman was already a man of great experience in the worlds of industry and politics. A former businessman and merchant banker, he had served during the war as US Ambassador both in London and Moscow. Between 1948 and 1950 he was US Special Representative in Europe whose job it was to oversee the ERP. It was while he was performing this latter role that I first met him and learned to appreciate his great experience and wisdom. His knowledge of the political worlds of both the United States and Europe was to prove of inestimable value in surmounting the many and diverse problems thrown up by NATO rearmament. I retain a lasting admiration for his courage and skill in negotiation, and the way he managed the whole 'Wise Man Exercise', as our task was known. He, as much as anyone else, ensured that our work was a success.

As 'Wise Men' we each had a deputy to assist us and to attend to much of the detailed work. Harriman brought with him Dr Lincoln Gordon, a brilliant former Rhodes scholar with whom he had worked closely at the State Department and the ECA, and who has since 1951 spent a life divided between the academic world and government service, a combination the Americans are better at arranging than we are. In the years 1952–5 he served as US Economic Minister in London and made an invaluable contribution to Anglo-American economic relations. Later he became President of The Johns Hopkins University and Professor of International Economic Relations at Harvard. Monnet's number two was Etienne Hirsch whom, like his superior, I knew well from our discussions on European integration in 1949 and 1950. Eric Roll was appointed as my deputy. I knew him well as he had served in the CEPS in 1948 and then went on to become British Minister at the OEEC. He did a splendid job and took much of the burden from my shoulders. It was therefore no surprise to me that he went on to have such a distinguished career both in Whitehall and the City.

I was also assisted by Richard Coleridge, a naval captain who advised me on military matters, Anthony Rumbold of our Paris Embassy staff who provided political briefing, and E. C. Gough of the Ministry of Defence, an expert on defence production. Moreover, in Whitehall a committee under Edmund Compton of the Treasury, and on which 'Otto'

126

Clarke and Robert Hall served, was established to monitor our progress.[2]

The 'Wise Man Exercise' began on 9th October 1951 in Paris, where the work already done on burden-sharing had taken place. We were put up in some luxury at the Bristol Hotel, situated conveniently near to the Embassy. We worked in an attractive house in Rue de la Faisandrie, off the Avenue Foch; the meetings of the 'Wise Men' taking place in the octagonal music room. We could hardly have asked for more pleasant surroundings.

The NATO resolution on the 'Wise Man Exercise' described its object as follows:

> There is required as an immediate next step an analysis of the issues involved in reconciling on the one hand the requirements of external security, in particular of fulfilling a militarily acceptable, NATO plan for the defence of Western Europe with, on the other hand, the realistic politico-economic capabilities of member countries.

The procedure we adopted in our analysis was as follows. In the first place, the defence costs of NATO countries' current programmes for rearmament were screened individually and collectively, as were the costs of forces, infrastructure, and materials for a revised version of the US-backed Medium-Term Defence Plan for NATO. This was undertaken by a specially appointed Screening and Costing Committee chaired by General J. T. McNarney of the US Airforce. It included representatives from Belgium, France and the United Kingdom. Their findings were passed on to the Executive Bureau for analysis and then discussed jointly with representatives of each NATO country, both official and ministerial. Whenever the programme of one of the three 'Wise Men's' countries was discussed, a representative from another NATO country joined the Executive Bureau.

In the second stage, each country submitted a memorandum on the political and economic implications of both their present and the proposed enlarged programmes. These memoranda were examined by a Temporary Economic Analysis Staff. This was made up of officials borrowed from the NATO and OEEC secretariats. Its findings were then also discussed by the 'Wise Men' with official and ministerial representatives of each individual NATO nation.

The third stage was the drafting of a report by the 'Wise Men' which sought to reconcile the military, economic and political factors operating on each country, with a view to providing NATO with a militarily balanced and effective programme which was also politically and economically feasible.

Finally, our draft report was discussed by the whole TCC and amended in the light of its comments.[3]

This was not at all an easy process and the 'Wise Man Exercise', although often fascinating, proved also to be frequently frustrating and terribly exhausting. Indeed, the experience made such an impact on me that when a few months later Anthony Eden asked me to agree to his putting forward my name as Secretary-General of NATO, I had no hesitation in refusing.[4] The thought of doing something similar to the 'Wise Man Exercise' full-time filled me with horror. It involved, as Eric Roll has put it in his memoirs, the complex 'combination of economic analysis, hard bargaining and diplomacy, which had to take account of political realities, both international and domestic, and which it is virtually impossible to describe in terms of a political science textbook'.[5] He might well have added that it also required the stamina of a marathon runner and the patience of a saint. Time was short. We were originally meant to complete our report by 1st December, in fact we were two and a half weeks late. Even so, we would often work twelve or fourteen hours a day, seven days a week. I can well remember finishing our Draft Report at about 7 a.m., and a number of other nights when we saw the dawn. Moreover, to obtain updated briefings we would also have to pay a number of exhaustingly hurried trips back to London.

There were, in addition, some less obvious difficulties. For example, military costing and screening of this type and scale had never before been attempted. We were very much treading in the dark and with hindsight the methods we used were, to say the least, primitive and rather unscientific. Moreover, while the OEEC had gone some way towards standardising statistics on European balances of payments and national income, differences in the quality of different nations' figures were substantial. Those of us without a military background also had great difficulties in coming to terms with both military jargon and the logistical complexities of military organisation.

By far the greatest difficulty which the 'Wise Man Exercise' faced, however, materialised in the form of the attitude of Monnet and his government to the whole process. From the outset the French began to make conditions about their participation which neither Averell

Harriman nor I could accept. In particular, they were anxious to make the defence effort as effective as possible in the immediate future and to confine the TCC report's content and recommendations to the year 1952 and, to a lesser extent, to 1953. It was our policy and that of the Americans to look further ahead and aim for a fully adequate defence as early as possible.

To make matters worse, their own submissions were often useless, containing unrealistic and incredible figures. Furthermore, Monnet himself was unhelpful and uninterested throughout, frequently giving the impression that he thought himself above the whole exercise. On several occasions I cabled London to express my utter despair about his attitude.[6] Once Averell Harriman and I sought the help of Eisenhower, as Supreme Allied Commander in Europe, in talking the French round. All he could offer, however, was the rather optimistic advice that 'if you look into your hearts you will find the solution there'. We did not find the solution in our hearts and for some time there was considerable doubt as to whether we would ever be able to find any solution and to produce an agreed report. In the end, however, we succeeded, perhaps because the French saw that the whole 'Wise Man Exercise' might collapse because of them.

Monnet maintained a poor opinion of 'Operation Wise Man' for many years. Early in 1976 my wife and I were in Paris. We arranged to drive out to Bazôches to have lunch with Jean and Sylvia Monnet. Soon after we arrived he told me that he had almost finished his memoirs and that he had said some nice things about me. I asked him what he had said about the 'Wise Man Exercise'. He replied that he had said nothing because it was of no importance. When I said that I thought it had been a major factor in the development of the NATO Alliance, he gradually accepted this and agreed to insert a small section about it into his book. As it turned out, it hardly did justice to those months of toil and turmoil.[7]

I am convinced that the reasons behind Monnet's indifference to the proceedings at the time and his tendency to erase them from his memory in later years went very deep. They extended beyond French fears that they might be pushed into a commitment to too much military expenditure over too long a period. I believe that Monnet was not interested in 'Operation Wise Man' because it was bound up with what he saw as an old-fashioned military alliance involving no surrender of sovereignty.

Moreover, this old-fashioned alliance was not exclusively European. Monnet looked forward impatiently to the day when a European army drawn from a United States of Europe would be doing NATO's job without excessive American interference. He wanted to get on with the job of realising this dream as soon as possible. NATO was to him merely a short-term expedient. He did not want to see it gather a momentum which would deflect the attention of the peoples of Europe from federation. When NATO did gather momentum, and I believe the 'Wise Man Exercise' played a major role in this, he was resentful.

In spite of our difficulties with Monnet we remained, as always, good friends. One evening, in order to try and resolve some difficulty, I asked him to come and have a late supper with me. We dined at the Bristol Hotel in a private sitting room provided for me by His Majesty's government. It was late and Monnet said he did not want much. I think he had some oysters and *épinards en branches*. Afterwards he said he would like some brandy. The waiter recommended what he said was some excellent house brandy. When it came Monnet rolled it round his mouth and said that it was not good. The waiter indignantly replied that it was the best brandy there was. When I informed him that this was Monsieur Monnet himself, a look of horror came over his face and he seized the bottle and rushed from the room. He returned triumphantly soon after with a bottle of Monnet brandy. Never have I seen a wine waiter so cowed.

The 'Wise Man Exercise' did have some compensations. I made new friends and found myself in strange relationships with my seniors. When a country's defence programme was to be examined by the Executive Bureau, that country was usually represented by its Minister of Finance and its Defence Minister. I found myself, a Treasury official, masquerading as a 'Wise Man', cross-examining the Chancellor of the Exchequer on the British defence effort and why it should not be greater.

The Final Report of the Temporary Council Committee was completed on 17th December 1951. It was a long and complicated document which Eisenhower subsequently described as a 'truly monumental piece of work'.[8] It set out a provisional plan for the build-up of forces for the defence of the North Atlantic Area, detailing the national defence expenditures required for this purpose up to mid-1954. There were clear targets and a plan of action for 1952, targets and a less pre-

cise programme for 1953, and targets and an indication of a programme for 1954 and beyond. On Britain the Report stated that, in
view of the strain already being exerted on us by rearmament, the TCC
did not believe that any increase in Britain's defence effort should be
considered. It further recognised that Britain's existing programme
required the solutions of steel supply and of the dollar and general
balance of payments problems. It viewed the latter as unlikely even after
deflation and therefore, in effect, left us some scope actually to reduce
our defence programme.[9] Over the following months this was duly
done. The programme was allowed to spill over into a fourth year.

By contrast, Canada and the Continental countries, except Portugal,
were urged to undertake substantial increases in their defence programmes, on average equivalent to about one-sixth of their existing
programmes in December 1951. The Report made recommendations
concerning the internal economic policies required to make these
expanded programmes possible. It further recognised the exact extent
of dollar deficiency this would throw up, but in fact offered little by way
of a solution to it. We were forced to recognise that political considerations prevented the Americans from expanding their armaments programme and offering more dollar assistance. Averell Harriman had
made it clear from the outset that in an election year, and when there
was the prospect of a Budget deficit of $5–7 billion in fiscal 1953, he
could not sign a report which committed the United States to a greater
defence effort in any form. Nor, indeed, could he offer any firm prom-
ise of aid at all after 1954, although he himself was certain it would be
available. The United States thus received special treatment. She alone
was allowed a political limit to her military effort, even though it was
obvious to all that on economic grounds she was capable of considerably more.[10]

The TCC Report also made a number of suggestions aimed at
making the organisation of NATO tighter and more effective. It proposed the introduction of universal standards of readiness and measures to strengthen NATO logistics and supply channels, the institution
of an annual review of defence plans along the lines of the 'Wise Man
Exercise' and the appointment of a Secretary-General. The latter's job
would be to lead an international planning and co-ordinating staff and
to execute the decisions reached by governments through the NATO
Council and Deputies.[11] In the end, this post was taken up by 'Pug'

Ismay. As a former Cabinet minister and a general he was, in my view and in American eyes, much more suited to the job than I or any other civil servant would have been.

When I first told London informally of the contents of the TCC Report, I received a large number of indignant complaints from officials that it was a hollow document pointing out what was required but offering no real means by which to achieve it. I had repeatedly to impress upon my colleagues the difficulties of achieving unanimous agreement on such a complicated issue in such a short time, and the delicacy of the political situation in the United States. Gradually thereafter, officials began to realise that although the TCC Report did not go as far as we in Britain had originally hoped, it was nevertheless of considerable negative value to us and should be accepted. It did not require us to increase our defence effort and, besides, gave us some justification for a downward review. Moreover, by showing up the dollar problem to its full extent the TCC Report paved the way for progress on this subject in the future after the rhetoric and restraints of an American presidential election campaign had subsided.

The TCC Report was accepted by the British Cabinet.[12] This, however, was not the case everywhere else. The plan of action it proposed for NATO became subject to important qualifications, largely because France felt herself unable to provide the forces required of her, and Canada and Belgium were unwilling to make the financial contributions demanded of them. Before the next NATO Council meeting in Lisbon in February 1952, a resolution was drafted by the Secretariat which proposed that the TCC Report be accepted subject to the reservations of these countries. The British government lent its support to this resolution and it was passed.

In the view of Lincoln Gordon and myself, for all the TCC Report's failings and gaps and the further provisos to the military plan imposed in Lisbon, 'Operation Wise Man' was vitally important to the development and success of NATO and thus to the peace of the last forty years. No previous attempt had been made to develop a plan of action for the defence of the North Atlantic Community which took into account all the relevant factors. NATO itself was a very primitive organisation and the NATO treaty of 1949 was, in many ways, little more than a paper guarantee of security and US non-neutrality. The 'Wise Man Exercise' laid solid foundations for the future and was instrumental in starting the process of bringing about the strong and cohesive alliance which has lasted longer than any other military alliance embracing so many countries in a peacetime environment.

When I returned to London at the end of the 'Wise Man Exercise' in December 1951 it was to work for a new government and for a new Chancellor, 'Rab' Butler.

By the middle of 1951 I had been back in Whitehall for over four years when I had initially only taken on the job of Chief Planner for a year. I knew that I wanted to work in the private sector, and if I was going to do so I felt it was time to make plans to leave Whitehall. This feeling was reinforced by my belief that there would be an election fairly soon and that the Tories would probably win. It was far from clear how they wanted to conduct their economic policy, but I thought it unlikely that they would want to retain someone who was there on a temporary basis, who had already made clear that he wanted to return to the private sector, and who had worked with two Labour Chancellors. Accordingly, I told Edward Bridges and Hugh Gaitskell of my desire to leave at the end of 1951. Hugh Gaitskell, in the nicest possible way, pressed me strongly to stay, but I did not feel able to change my mind.

My decision was announced to the press on 3rd August. I was to be succeeded as Chief Planner by Norman Brook, then Secretary of the Cabinet, who would also become deputy to Edward Bridges. Tom Padmore, a Third Secretary in the Treasury, was to be the new Secretary of the Cabinet.

Two and a half months later there was a general election. The Conservatives won and 'Rab' Butler became Chancellor. He, too, pressed me to stay. He was an old friend and neighbour of mine in Essex. Eventually I agreed to work for him for twelve months. As it turned out, I was to stay for two years. My decision greatly upset Hugh Gaitskell. He reproached me for having refused to stay with him and for having apparently given in so quickly to the persuasions of a Tory Chancellor. He soon forgave me, however, and we remained friends to the end of his life. I was also greatly encouraged by a charming letter from Stafford Cripps who said he welcomed my staying on with 'Rab' Butler.

The first six months or so of the new government's term of office were dominated by the need to do something about the desperate balance of payments position and, as we shall see, were to prove some of the most tense and disconcerting of my Whitehall career.

CHAPTER THIRTEEN

A Change of Government:
Economic Policy under the Conservatives, October 1951 to October 1953

The appointment of 'Rab' Butler as Chancellor in October 1951 came as a surprise to some people. He was no economist, by no means a close associate of Winston Churchill, and a 'Man of Munich'. But with Oliver Stanley's death in October 1950, John Anderson's departure to the Lords, Lord Woolton's reluctance to leave the Upper House even though Churchill offered to introduce legislation to allow him to do so,[1] and Oliver Lyttleton's close association with the City, there was no alternative to Butler if Anthony Eden was to be Foreign Secretary. Nobody else could match his standing in the Conservative Party. Over the previous six years, through his work at Central Office, he had laid to rest the image of the Conservatives as the hard-faced party of unemployment and appeasement.

At first Churchill had little faith in Butler. He quickly established a series of measures designed to keep the Chancellor's room for maneouvre to a minimum. First, feeling that 'Rab' would need support from somebody with training in economics, he appointed Sir Arthur Salter as Minister of State for Economic Affairs, a man he described as 'the greatest economist since Jesus Christ'.[2] Second, he brought into the Cabinet his old friend, Lord Cherwell. Cherwell became Paymaster-General and was asked to re-establish on a more modest scale the wartime 'Statistical Section' so as to provide the Prime Minister's office with a source of alternative economic advice. Finally, and perhaps most significantly of all, he set up a Treasury Ministerial Advisory Committee consisting of senior ministers to watch over Butler.

As it turned out, the checks and balances Churchill initially sought to impose on 'Rab' Butler soon evaporated. Although a most distinguished and experienced economist, Salter was by the early 1950s well past his intellectual peak and was out of touch with more recent developments in economic thinking. He was also a poor speaker. He was moved from the Treasury after a year in which he contributed relatively little to policy-making, except during the 'Robot' episode described in the next chapter. He was replaced as number two at the Treasury by the much more effective Reginald Maudling who a decade later was himself to become Chancellor. Churchill's preoccupation with foreign affairs during his second premiership also meant that he spared little time to watch over his Chancellor and, consequently, Cherwell's Statistical Section had relatively little opportunity to influence policy. Its major contribution was during the 'Robot' episode. In practice, the Treasury Ministerial Advisory Committee also had little status or effect and was largely ignored by Butler. It was not long before it was absorbed into the Ministerial Economic Policy Committee.

Freed from these constraints, Butler went on to become a most able and successful Chancellor who made the most of the favourable world economic environment in the years 1952–5. After the dislocations of rearmament, he supervised the remaining stages of Britain's transition from war to peace and, unlike the majority of his successors, for a considerable time presided over the promised land of full employment and more or less stable prices.

Butler's economic policy differed from Cripps's and Gaitskell's more in rhetoric than in practice. The Tories were committed to the Welfare State and accepted most of Labour's nationalisation programme. In addition, like his Labour predecessors, Butler for the most part put full employment first in his list of priorities. Only during the external crisis of 1951–2 was this not the case. Likewise, although he was responsible for the dismantling of what remained of the system of direct controls, the transition to a freer economy remained gradual and he was not afraid to tighten controls temporarily to meet a crisis. While monetary policy was quickly resurrected, something officials had vainly urged Cripps and Gaitskell to do, budgetary policy remained the prime macroeconomic policy instrument, as it had been since the autumn of 1947. In short, Butler, like Cripps and Gaitskell, was a Keynesian.

On a personal level, Butler brought a number of excellent qualities with him to the Treasury. He was a hard worker who listened to his officials' advice and was always conscious of the need to build up a team spirit. He was also an accomplished performer in the House of Commons. Cool and calm under pressure, he possessed a wonderful grasp of the English language and metaphor, in particular. In debates on the economy he would lead the British people through storms, up mountains, into hospital and through periods of convalescence. He knew how to structure a speech to obtain the maximum effect. Indeed, one of my most abiding memories of him was his habit of attacking speeches that had been drafted for him with scissors and paste until he had come up with what he considered to be a more powerful and effect-ive arrangement of the contents. His modifications were usually a dis-tinct improvement on the original.

Perhaps Butler's two greatest assets, however, were his sharp intel-lect and his acute political judgement, which at times appeared to offi-cials as a kind of second sight. A former Cambridge don, Butler pos-sessed intellectual capabilities which more than compensated for his lack of formal training in economics. This, allied with his appreciation of exactly what the Tory Party, the House of Commons and the elector-ate would and would not accept, made him a truly formidable poli-tician.

'Rab' also had his faults, although with him they were of the most human kind. He could, at times, be infuriatingly indecisive and reluc-tant to confront an issue. This I am convinced was often the corollary of his political sensitivity. Appreciating all the repercussions of a policy and the likely reactions it would provoke, he found it more difficult than those less perceptive than himself to make up his mind. Sometimes after long discussion, at the end of the day one would say, 'Well, Chancellor, it is decided we will do the following.' 'Yes, I agree.' Then the next morning he would send for one and say, 'Well, Edwin, I have been thinking.' One would say to oneself, 'Oh God, not again' and once more one would have to go through all the arguments. But even at his most exasperating he was always pleasant and charming to deal with. Occasionally, however, he would use procrastination as a positive instrument to diffuse a potentially explosive situation.

He was also too easily affected by criticism from his colleagues; he was too nice a man ever to fulfil his political potential. This is why, in my view, he never became more than 'the best Prime Minister we never had'. In 1953, for example, there was a period when both Churchill and

Eden were seriously ill and took little or no part in governing the country. There were doubts as to whether either of them would ever return to office. At this time, in addition to his duties as Chancellor, Butler took the chair at Cabinet meetings and, as such, was in charge of the government, but he was not given any formal authority by the Cabinet.[3] Recalling this period some time afterwards, Lord Cherwell said to me, 'If, after some time, "Rab" had said to the Cabinet, "I cannot go on without holding the office of Prime Minister," there would have been no way he could have been turned down.'[4] But he never said this, and indeed I can remember his remarking to me at the time about Eden 'Anthony must have his chance.' It has always struck me how the vast majority of politicians in his position would have grasped such an opportunity with both hands. 'Rab', however, was different.

Butler's team of officials was very similar to that which had existed under Gaitskell, and before him under Cripps. Edward Bridges, the Permanent Secretary, considered retirement in 1951, but like myself decided to stay on and was not finally to leave Whitehall until 1956. His relationship with Butler, however, was not as close as with his predecessors and, although his influence in the Treasury remained considerable, particularly where the Budget was concerned, he was rather less dominant after 1951 than before. Robert Hall also decided to remain with the Economic Section even though at one time he had been considered to be a Labour supporter. His influence waxed while that of Bridges waned.

At Second Secretary level, Bernard Gilbert looked after Supply expenditure as he had done since 1944. A former mathematician, Gilbert was a pessimist in the finest Treasury tradition. He remained sceptical of Keynesian economics throughout his period in Whitehall and regarded controls and excessive public expenditure with the utmost distrust. The Overseas Finance Division of the Treasury became the responsibility of Leslie Rowan in 1951 on the retirement of Henry Wilson-Smith. Leslie Rowan, an athlete who had captained England at hockey, had been Churchill's Private Secretary during the war. He was very much the rising young star of the Treasury and 'Rab' Butler put great faith in him on matters of external economic policy, particularly during the crisis of 1951–2. The two remaining Second Secretaries were Wilfred Eady and Thomas Padmore. Eady looked after Home Finance until his retirement in April 1952. By this stage, however, his influence was greatly reduced, his reputation never having fully recovered from the convertibility crisis of 1947 when he was in charge of overseas finance. On his retirement his duties were taken over by Gilbert. Padmore, who like Rowan was relatively young, looked after the establishment, that is personnel management, side of the Treasury.

At other levels Butler naturally received much advice from his Private Secretary, William Armstrong, who had also served Cripps and Gaitskell; from Denis Rickett, Economic Minister in Washington; from the Third Secretaries, 'Otto' Clarke, Edmund Compton and Burke Trend; and from C. R. Ross of the Economic Section. As a Conservative, Butler was also more willing than Cripps or Gaitskell to listen to the opinions of the Bank of England, particularly where monetary and external policy were concerned. At the Bank, C. F. Cobbold remained the Governor and George Bolton the most influential adviser.

My relationship with Butler was a most happy one. The fact that I was not an established civil servant but was in Whitehall on a temporary basis, coupled with our long-standing friendship, perhaps allowed me a closer relationship with him than was open to a career civil servant. We were able to exchange ideas and discuss all aspects of policy, economic or political. In his book he generously described our relationship as follows:

> But I depended on Edwin Plowden, as head of the economic planning staff, to interpret and give practical edge to the advice generated by the less voluble and extrovert Hall, to act as '*vulgarisateur*' or publicist for his ideas. Plowden was to become my faithful watchdog-in-chief, and his departure for industry in 1953 undoubtedly weakened my position and that of the British economy.[5]

We have already seen how the British balance of payments on current account went into deficit in 1951 because of the combined effects of a rapid rise in the price of imports, especially raw materials, an increase in the volume of imports that flowed from government stockpiling and a rise in private sector demand, and a shortage of available capacity for export production. From the middle of 1951 this situation was rendered far more serious when our net invisible income was sharply reduced by the seizure of British assets in Persia and the need to make up for the loss of oil imports from that country by buying more from other sources mainly in the Dollar Area. Furthermore, to the effect this worsening British deficit had on reserves was added the deficit run by the rest of the Sterling Area in the second half of 1951. In mid-1951 the prices of materials had begun to fall again. This reduced the earnings of the other sterling nations at a time when their imports were rising, as a result of orders placed in response to the rise in incomes which the earlier commodity boom had caused. The combined deficits of Britain and the rest of the Sterling Area amounted to £750 million in the second half of 1951, reducing the reserves from £1,381 million at the end of June 1951 to £834 milllion six months later, after taking into account loans and capital movements.

'Rab' Butler's reaction on first seeing the national accounts in October 1951 was that 'we are in a balance of payments crisis worse than in 1949, and in many ways worse than 1947'.[6] Senior officials, myself included, had been of this opinion for some weeks, and work was already under way in Whitehall on the assembly of a package of measures to restore confidence in sterling and arrest the drain on the reserves well before the Tories came to power.[7] We had hoped that whichever party won the general election it would put these measures into operation after taking into account loans and capital movements.

After a week or so of hectic discussion with officials and Cabinet colleagues, Butler announced a series of cuts in import quotas, a slow-down in the strategic stockpiling programme and a cut in the foreign-currency allowance for tourist travel. Together, these measures were designed to reduce by £350 million our overseas expenditure. In addition he announced a review of all government expenditure and a three-month moratorium on building work, except for housing and that deemed to be especially vital to the national interest. Most significant of all, however, was his statement that Bank Rate was to be raised from the 2 per cent at which it had stood since before the war to 2.5 per cent.

The background to this modification in monetary policy deserves attention. Of all the measures taken at that time, it was the only one that Labour would have avoided had they been returned to office at the general election. Since I had come back to Whitehall, officials at the Bank of England had been especially keen to resurrect a more active interest rate policy in order to regulate demand and restrain inflation. Their views on this matter were shared by Edward Bridges, Robert Hall, myself and a number of senior officials in the Treasury. We believed that a government should use all the policy levers available to it to manage the economy, and that the manipulation of interest rates could be especially beneficial to confidence in a balance of payments crisis. We campaigned for a change in monetary policy during the crises of 1947, 1949 and for most of 1951, but these pleas to successive Labour Chancellors had fallen on deaf ears. As 'Rab' Butler put it in his memoirs, to the Labour Party cheap money was 'the Ark of the Covenant'. It could not be disturbed.[8]

While in Opposition, senior Tories had consistently berated Labour for not making more use of monetary policy as an alternative to relying on high tax rates and large Budget surpluses to restrain inflation. In the 1951 Budget debate this line of attack was advanced particularly force-fully.[9] We believed, therefore, that in contrast to Labour, the Con-servative Party on assuming power would be more than sympathetic to our pleas for a tighter monetary policy. As it turned out, convincing them of the wisdom of a rise in Bank Rate, initially at least, was not at all easy. I can well remember coming back from Paris in early October to attend a meeting with senior ministers at the House of Commons on the subject. Edward Bridges was there and started the meeting by detailing the deterioration in our external position and the good that would come of a rise in Bank Rate. I then added my own views to his, backing him up. A minister then promptly turned to me and said indig-nantly, 'How would you like to get up on the hustings and say that one of the first things that you had done was to put up the Bank Rate and thereby raise Council House rents?' To this I replied, 'Minister, with respect, you are not on the hustings now. You have just won an election.'

While this anecdote gives an idea of the immediate political dif-ficulties thrown up by the introduction of a more active monetary policy, the antipathy towards dearer money went considerably deeper than this. It was also a hangover from the slump. Keynes and the experience of the years 1932–7 had taught that a cheap money policy was a way to avoid a slump, while the dear money of the 1920s was seen as a partial explanation for the high unemployment of those years and the cata-strophic decline in output after 1929. In 1951 everybody, and City and business opinion in particular, retained fears that at any moment the economy might go into a nose-dive and that we would again be faced with a situation similar to that in the 1930s. It was natural, therefore, that politicians in power were reluctant to put up the Bank Rate.

Nobody wanted to be blamed for resurrecting the misery and waste of the pre-war years, especially a Conservative Party which had only just rid itself of an image as the party of unemployment.

Despite the measures taken early in November, the drain on the reserves continued unabated for the rest of 1951. The Overseas Finance Division's balance of payments and reserves forecasts for 1952 became increasingly depressing. It was soon acknowledged that the economy remained seriously overloaded and that further drastic steps would have to be taken to bring it back into balance and to stabilise the reserves.[10] Debate on what was the best way forward raged over Christmas and well into the new year at all levels. It was even conducted across the Atlantic when Churchill and Eden were in Washington in January 1952.[11] A series of disinflationary measures was introduced over a three-month period.

The timescale of the rearmament programme was extended, hire-purchase restrictions were introduced on certain consumer goods, and a further £150 million cut from overseas expenditure. At the Commonwealth Finance Ministers' Conference in January the other Sterling Area nations agreed to parallel reductions in imports designed to bring the Sterling Area back into balance with the non-sterling world by the second half of the year. In an early Budget, Butler introduced cuts of £200 million in the food subsidies, an increase in petrol duty, a new excess profits levy, yet another £100 million in import cuts and a second rise in Bank Rate, this time to 4 per cent. Income tax was also cut as a spur to production.[12]

Together with officials generally, Robert Hall and I played our part in getting these measures accepted and were broadly satisfied with them. We remained disappointed, however, that not enough was being done to tackle the problem of wage inflation. In our view monetary and fiscal deflation was not enough. A more direct approach was needed too. In the fourth quarter of 1951 retail prices were rising at an annual rate of 12.1 per cent and wages at an annual rate of 11 per cent. This led Robert Hall and me to resurrect the idea of the publication of a second White Paper on *Employment Policy*. In this document we wished to outline clearly the choice the public faced between unemployment, steady cost inflation and a policy of permanent wage moderation. This we hoped might change attitudes in collective bargaining. Butler was at first sympathetic and the Cabinet was even informed at one stage that such a document would be released in early 1952. In the end, however, because of their desire not to undermine industrial relations, the government decided not to go ahead with its publication.[13]

Our satisfaction with the contents of the 1952 Budget and the other measures introduced was increased by the fact that in the weeks preceding the Budget, Lord Cherwell, Sir Arthur Salter, Donald Mac-Dougall and a small number of other officials and ministers, together with Robert Hall and myself had managed to prevent the Chancellor introducing a completely different, and in our view catastrophic, plan to stabilise the economy. I refer to 'Operation Robot'. It merits a chapter on its own.

CHAPTER FOURTEEN

'Operation Robot'

The Commonwealth Finance Ministers meeting in London in January had discussed the notion of convertibility in some depth, and even set up a working party on the subject. It detailed a number of conditions which would have to be met before it could be undertaken. The Commonwealth countries agreed in general terms to work towards the fulfilment of these conditions. It was universally understood that it would not be practicable to make sterling convertible in the immediate future. In spite of this, however, within a few weeks of the end of the Conference the Chancellor was ready to take just such a step there and then.

The basic idea behind 'Robot' originated with 'Otto' Clarke of the Treasury and George Bolton of the Bank of England. The Commonwealth Conference had hardly finished when Clarke circulated a paper calling for immediate convertibility, together with a floating exchange rate and the blocking of the sterling balances. It was his belief that, although in the short term this plan might lead to a large loss of reserves and a sharp fall in sterling's value, it represented the only practicable long-term solution to Britain's economic problems.[1]

By 16th February, Clarke's basic plan had been elaborated in conjunction with George Bolton, and had already been assigned the code name 'Operation Robot' – a title which was meant to indicate its role as an automatic regulator of the economy's performance. Moreover, by this stage Clarke could also rely on the support of Leslie Rowan, head of the Overseas Finance Division of the Treasury, and the Governor of the Bank of England, both of whom were anxious to see 'Robot' introduced in the forthcoming Budget. The three basic elements of the plan were:

(1)   A floating exchange rate for sterling.
(2)   Full convertibility into gold, dollars or other currencies for 'overseas sterling', meaning unblocked sterling balances and new sterling earned abroad by foreigners or acquired by Sterling Area governments.
(3)   The compulsory funding of 80 per cent of the sterling balances held by the Sterling Area and the funding or blocking of 90 per cent of the balances held by those in neither the Sterling nor the Dollar Areas.

The reasoning behind the plan was that, if the pound were set free, the great pressure on the reserves of recent months would be eased before long. We would then no longer have to worry about being forced to devalue again or to float when our reserves ran out. The resultant fall in the exchange rate would also change the relative prices of imports and exports, and thereby set in motion forces which would correct the imbalance in the external account. The phrase used at the time was 'Let the rate take the strain'. By letting the exchange rate move freely in response to market forces, we could simultaneously make sterling convertible and thereby do what the Americans and Canadians had been pressing us to move towards for some time. It was not thought realistic, however, to attempt to shoulder the burden of making all outstanding sterling liabilities convertible. This would put far too great a strain on the exchange rate than was prudent. Hence most of the sterling liabilities would have to be funded or blocked, and restrictions on the gold and dollar transactions of ordinary residents of the Sterling Area retained.

The first I heard of the plan was on the morning of 19th February when I was shown a note from the Governor of the Bank of England on the subject. I was also told at this stage that it was the brainchild of 'Otto' Clarke and George Bolton. My immediate reaction was one of great puzzlement. In the spring of the previous year when our reserves were rising and import prices were also shooting up, we had had a series of discussions with the Bank on sterling revaluation which had also encompassed the idea of letting the pound float upwards. At this time

George Bolton, acting on the Bank's behalf, had been an outspoken critic of freeing sterling and had in fact persuaded me to be extremely cautious of moving to a variable rate. He was convinced that exchange rate stability was a *sine qua non* for an international currency like sterling and that a floating rate would undermine the Sterling Area, the EPU and all monetary agreements worldwide. He added, moreover, that even though they were larger than for some time, our gold reserves were totally inadequate to allow us to manage a floating rate satisfactorily.[2]

Even more surprising to me was 'Otto' Clarke's involvement in the plan. Since the summer of 1947 he had been the chief opponent within the Treasury of any premature move towards convertibility and had also been active in spreading the gospel of inconvertibility at the OEEC. Furthermore, during the discussions on freeing the pound twelve months before I had received a note from him which stated, 'I am opposed to a floating rate. It is bad for traders; it is bad for planners; it is a complete destruction of the IMF.'[3]

In the afternoon of the same day, Robert Hall and I attended a small meeting of officials chaired by Leslie Rowan at which the Bank's memorandum was discussed. After a brief examination of the plan the meeting broke up. Both Robert Hall and I left with the impression that the general consensus was that this whole scheme required a lot more study before a final decision was made on its merits, and that time would be made available for that study. When we met the Chancellor that evening he also seemed to share this view. Later that night I left London with Anthony Eden for the Lisbon NATO Council meeting, satisfied that 'Operation Robot' was not an immediate priority.[4]

At about the same time as the Foreign Secretary and I were taking off for Portugal, Butler was dining at the House of Commons with Churchill, Crookshank (Leader of the House) and the Governor of the Bank of England. During this meeting it was agreed that if such a radical change in economic policy as 'Robot' were to be introduced, it would be wrong for the forthcoming Budget to give no hint of it. If 'Robot' was to become official policy it would have to be announced in the Budget on 4th March.

When he heard of this decision the next day, Robert Hall was flabbergasted. As telegrams would have to be drafted and sent to all Commonwealth countries a week in advance of any formal announcement, it cut the time left for discussion to virtually nothing. A positive decision on a totally new approach to external economic policy might therefore be forced through with only limited consultation and analysis. Robert complained bitterly to Edward Bridges and the Chancellor about this and on 21st February it was agreed that the Budget should be postponed for a week.[5]

On 21st February, Leslie Rowan chaired a meeting of all the permanent secretaries of major departments and the heads of important subsections. They were shown a detailed memorandum on 'Robot' and were told that the external position was now so serious that ministers might well decide to adopt the plan on 4th March. They were further asked to work out during the day what they would have to do from the point of view of their own departments to accommodate such a decision and to report back later. The only officials who expressed any doubts about the plan at this meeting were Frank Lee (Permanent Secretary of the Board of Trade), Robert Hall and Bill Strath, who was deputising for me in my absence.[6]

The following morning Butler outlined the details of the plan to a small group of ministers including the Prime Minister, Lord Cherwell, Crookshank, Lord Woolton (Lord President of the Council), Maxwell Fyfe (Home Secretary) and James Stuart (Secretary of State for Scotland). During the course of the meeting ministers were given a long and complex memorandum on 'Robot' drafted for the Chancellor by 'Otto' Clarke. The Chancellor's paper was a strange document. While arguing that 'Robot' was the only cure for Britain's economic problems, it stated in great detail the awful consequences which introducing 'Robot' would have on the British economy and that of the world as a whole. In short, it played greatly on the idea that any efficacious medicine must taste nasty, indeed the nastier the better. It was freely admitted that 'Robot' would lead to unemployment and inflation, great difficulties for our export industries in the short term, the end of the EPU and possibly even the Bretton Woods international monetary system and the Sterling Area. Yet it was still put forward as the only alternative.[7]

Ministers were given very little time to read the Chancellor's paper and were asked to return it before departing. Despite the wide ramifications of the new proposals only Cherwell opposed them. It seemed most likely at this stage that they would indeed be implemented in the

Budget. Fortunately, it was decided that the introduction of 'Robot' had such wide-ranging implications for Britain's foreign relations that it was quite impossible to go ahead without knowing the Foreign Secretary's views on the proposals.[8]

Two officials, Herbert Brittain, a Third Secretary at the Treasury, and Eric Berthoud, Assistant Under-Secretary at the Foreign Office, were dispatched to Lisbon over the weekend to explain the proposals to Eden. They also carried with them a number of letters and memoranda from various ministers and officials. Two of the letters were for me. One was from Edward Bridges and the other from Robert Hall. The letters explained the dramatic developments in London since my departure and gave the opinions of these two close colleagues of mine on the direction in which events were moving. Edward Bridges' letter seemed to imply that a decision to introduce 'Robot' had more or less been taken; the Foreign Secretary's acquiescence to this being virtually a formality. For his own part, he was glad. He saw 'Robot' as a 'chance of remaining in control of the situation and not just venturing in mid-ocean'.[9] Robert Hall, by contrast, indicated how disturbed and upset he was by developments. He was convinced that ministers did not really understand what the proposals might mean. If we put 'Robot' into operation in the Budget, he envisaged 'a considerable shrinking of world trade' with 'severe' political effects worldwide, 'a considerable increase in unemployment' and more domestic inflation as sterling depreciated. At best, 'Robot' could be successful only at an enormous cost.[10]

After reading Robert Hall's letter I saw that there were, to say the least, strong arguments against the plan and I set off from the hotel where I was staying to see Anthony Eden at the Embassy. He had already seen the papers sent from London and had talked to Herbert Brittain and Eric Berthoud. He was generally supportive of 'Robot', although also in favour of a general election to achieve a mandate for the policy. Eden was never strong on economic issues and I realised that he had been greatly influenced by the rhetoric of a letter Churchill had addressed to him which talked of an economic 'super-crisis'.[11] I told him of the contents of Robert Hall's letter and argued that he simply must not allow a decision on 'Robot' to be made in his absence. After some persuasion he agreed, and I sat down to help draft a letter to be taken back for the Prime Minister. In it Eden said that 'Robot' should be very much a last resort because of its implications for employment and Britain's foreign relations, and that more time should be spent in examining other alternatives.[12]

I returned from Lisbon on the Sunday night. The following morning I found that those against the plan were beginning to mobilise their forces. On the Saturday, Robert Hall had, with the assistance of five members of the Economic Section, drafted a strongly critical memorandum on 'Robot' for circulation to its chief protagonists.[13]

Robert Hall had also been granted permission to consult Lionel Robbins on the subject. Robbins, himself a former Director of the Economic Section, was Professor of Economics at the London School of Economics and one of the most widely respected academics of the time. Robert found him strongly against 'Robot'. In a letter written to me not long before his death, he explained how there were two reasons for his opposition, one theoretical and one practical:

> The theoretical reason is that I have never really believed in floating ... Companies which do business in more than one area have to be continually guessing what prices to quote in the different markets and the movement of capital ... tends to be distorted and its effects are frequently the reverse of optimal.
>
> The practical reason for opposing Robot was that it involved bad faith. I should have had no objection to blocking the abnormal balances accumulated during the war ... but the position at the time of Robot was different. The balances which it proposed to block were new, accumulated in the belief that no blocking was contemplated. This shocked me very much – indeed I recollect that I lay awake long into the night worrying about the loss of international credit which might incur if it were done.[14]

Finally, I learned that Lord Cherwell, with the assistance of Robert Hall and his senior economic adviser, Donald MacDougall, had been working on a paper for the Chancellor critical of 'Robot'. In writing his note Cherwell had made extensive use of the paper shown to ministers by the Chancellor on the previous Friday. He alone had demanded to keep his copy for further study. Cherwell began by pointing out that in all the gloomy predictions for the balance of payments made by those in favour of 'Robot' no allowance had been made for the fact that the measures already taken to correct the external account had not yet had time to work. His main point, however, was that 'Robot' would, in any case, actually increase our trade deficit rather than reduce it as was required. The pound would float down and with it our export earnings, as export sales were at that time largely constrained by supply factors, such as a lack of steel, rather than demand. Where demand was the limiting factor, convertibility would give those abroad a large incentive to restrict imports from us so that they could build up sterling balances and convert them into precious dollars. In addition imports into this country were already tightly controlled; a fall in the exchange rate would therefore merely make them more expensive rather than restrict them further.

Having made this point, much of the remainder of his paper made great play of the difficulties with 'Robot' already pointed out in the Chancellor's own memorandum of the previous week. He added that there was a great danger of sterling's going into an uncontrollable decline, and that really severe deflationary measures might have to be brought in to stop it. He concluded by giving his own alternative pre-scription for the situation. This encompassed further import cuts, a stiff Budget and resort to the IMF for money to tide us over until our circumstances improved.[15]

Over the next few days events moved quickly. There were numerous meetings on the subject at official and ministerial level and an enorm-ous amount of paper was exchanged. Robert Hall and I spent much of our time trying to persuade the Chancellor of the dangers of the pro-posal, and working out an alternative plan of action to be introduced in the Budget. We were greatly encouraged in our task by the fact that, after further consideration, the Foreign Secretary was definitely opposed to the plan. We knew that the Prime Minister greatly valued his judgement on important issues. We were further stiffened by the news that Arthur Salter, the Minister of State for Economic Affairs, was also on our side, and by the efforts Lord Cherwell was making to bring the rest of the Cabinet around to his and our way of thinking.

Matters finally came to a head in successive Cabinet meetings on Thursday 28th February and Friday the 29th.[16] This was a difficult and frustrating time for Robert Hall and myself. We could have no direct impact on the way discussions progressed. We could merely hope that the hasty lobbying of the previous three days would be enough to per-suade ministers to abandon the plan.

During the Cabinet meetings, ministers had in front of them updated copies of both the Chancellor's memorandum of 22nd February and Cherwell's critique.They were also presented with a further memorandum by the Chancellor detailing the alternative courses of action that would have to be taken if 'Robot' were not adopted. This latter document was based predominantly on the analysis of the situation which Robert Hall and I had conducted since my return from Portugal.

The Chancellor opened the Cabinet discussion on 'Robot'. He began by saying that even if the measures already taken to arrest the drain on the reserves began to work favourably, the remaining reserves would, by the second half of the year, be 'so inadequate that the Sterling Area would collapse at the first adverse turn of events'. Drastic action in the form of the 'Robot' plan was necessary, therefore, to protect the currency and should be introduced in the Budget. His exposition of 'Robot' on this occasion contained a number of new elements. For example, Butler said that although sterling would be freed, the Bank of England would be instructed to use the remaining reserves to keep its value within a range of $2.40 to $3.20. This would not be announced publicly, although it would be made clear to Commonwealth governments and central banks.

Butler then went on to describe again how 'Robot' would work. Under the new regime, he predicted that 'the drain on the gold and dollar reserves would cease automatically' as 'the strain of the balance of payments deficit would fall, not on the reserves, but on the exchange rate'. The fall in the rate would then bring into play changes in the relative price of imports and exports which would close the payments gap. Moreover, the funding of the sterling balances would remove the biggest potential threat to our reserves and increase confidence in sterling in the future.

Butler concluded his exposition of 'Robot' by outlining what he saw as the risks and less attractive implications of the plan. He was remarkably candid. He told the Cabinet that Robot

> would mean abrogating our monetary and payments agreements with non-sterling countries. It would be a shock to the Commonwealth members of the Sterling Area, and might bring one or two of them to the point of deciding to leave the Sterling Area altogether. It would disrupt the European Payments Union, and would therefore be viewed with

mixed feelings by the United States Government. Finally, so far as concerned the internal economy of the United Kingdom it would mean abandoning the principle of stability in internal prices and wages; there would in the initial stages be some rise in the cost of living and some measure of unemployment; and there would be a continuous process of change and re-adjustment, much of which would be painful.

His only consolation to those worried about these repercussions was that if the plan were not introduced then 'we would be forced at a later stage ... to take action which had all the unfavourable features of the plan ... without any of its favourable possibilities'.[17]

Cherwell responded to Butler's exposition by repeating the arguments he had worked out with Donald MacDougall and Robert Hall the previous weekend. In short, the economic position was not yet serious enough to warrant such an enormous and far-reaching change in policy and 'Robot' would, in any case, actually make the trade deficit worse by turning the terms of trade against us. It was better to deflate and make further cuts in the import programme than to leap into the dark in the manner proposed by the Chancellor.

When general discussion on the plan got under way the argument swung back and forth. Those in favour of the plan took Cherwell to task for a number of reasons, but primarily they criticised his inconsistency. He argued against floating sterling because it would not bring the external account into balance, yet when he put his case for a fixed exchange rate he assumed external balance in the second half of the year. He was saying that with a variable rate of exchange we would use up our reserves in seeking to prevent the rate's falling below $2.40 but, if our trading performance improved in late 1952 as he suggested, the rate would rise well above $2.40.

Supporters of the plan also expressed their feeling that letting the price mechanism have more freedom to operate, as 'Robot' would, was not at all a bad thing in itself and certainly an advance on the unwieldy planning of recent years. Moreover, they added that sterling was most definitely overvalued and that the sterling balances constituted a sort of sword of Damocles hanging over us which it would be wise to blunt as soon as possible.

Those against the plan argued with similar skill. They emphasised how much of an unknown quantity the operation of the new plan would be. They expressed their distaste at the rough treatment it implied for the Commonwealth, especially when at the meeting of Commonwealth Finance Ministers in January it had been agreed to take a rather different line on the external problem. It was further stressed that the economists under Robert Hall's direction were unanimously against the plan because it would restrict world trade, make sterling too 'hard' a currency, and signal a premature movement away from the prime economic objectives of full employment and price stability. Perhaps the most potent argument of all against 'Robot', however, was advanced by Lord Salisbury, the Lord Privy Seal. In a most powerful exposition he said that 'it would give rise to very great political difficulties' and was against the policies pursued for the previous twenty years. Public opinion was not ready for such a step.[18]

By the middle of the second Cabinet meeting of the 28th, it was obvious that many members of the Cabinet had serious doubts about the wisdom of proceeding immediately with such a violent change of policy. In his summing up of the discussion, the Prime Minister could but conclude that 'at the present time, there was not within the Cabinet a sufficient body of support for this plan to enable the Chancellor to launch it with confidence that he had behind him the conviction, as well as the loyalty of his colleagues'. Thereafter, the Chancellor outlined, with some small amendments, the alternative course of action which Robert Hall and I had developed for presentation in the Budget. This included a sharp cut in food subsidies, a further rise in Bank Rate, more import cuts, both in Britain and the Commonwealth, and an end to initial investment allowances and cuts in the housing and defence programmes. The Chancellor was quick to point out that, in his view, these measures might prove equally unpalatable to the public and the Commonwealth.

The Cabinet's discussions at the final meeting on 'Robot' centred on these alternative measures. They were, in truth, little more than a traditional deflationary package backed up by import restrictions. The majority were introduced in the Budget on 11th March. Butler, Lyttleton, Swinton and Crookshank supported the 'Robot' plan at this stage. Against were Cherwell, Leathers, Salter, the Prime Minister, Eden, Maxwell Fyfe, Salisbury and Macmillan. As to the opinions of the rest, I can only speculate.[19]

After the Budget there was a marked change in both the movement of the reserves and in sterling's strength as world confidence in the British economy returned. The reserves had been falling since mid-1951 and in the first eight weeks of 1952 had fallen by $521 million. In the remainder of the first quarter the pace of the decline fell off markedly and in the last week of March the reserves actually increased by some $50 million. Over the next six months, contrary to the prophesies of doom made by the Bank of England and the Treasury Overseas Finance Division, the reserves steadied. In the autumn they began to rise. Since the new year sterling had stayed at $2.78, the level at which, under IMF rules, the Bank of England was obliged to support it. After the Budget, however, it rapidly gained strength and was soon hovering above $2.80.[20]

Despite these developments the 'Robot' saga did not cease at the end of February 1952. The final Cabinet on the subject had concluded 'that some action on these lines might be taken at a later stage, either if the circumstances became more favourable for the introduction of such a policy, or if the government found themselves compelled ... to take urgent action to protect the currency'.[21] Moreover, a week later Churchill was reported to be still looking forward to the day when sterling could be set free.[22] The supporters of the plan took all this to mean that the Cabinet's rejection of 'Robot' was temporary and continued to bombard the Chancellor with memoranda stating its case, and incorporating amendments designed to answer its opponents' criticisms. The paper drafted by the Treasury Overseas Finance Division ran to more than sixty pages.[23] Thus at a ministerial level Cherwell had to continue to work to stiffen the Prime Minister on the issue, and at an official level Robert Hall, the Economic Section, Donald MacDougall and I spent much time drafting counterblasts to the protagonists' papers.

Robert Hall thought that the best way to silence 'Otto' Clarke, Leslie Rowan and George Bolton was to assemble a more attractive and realistic alternative plan for the future of sterling which was in keeping with the likely nature of Britain's economic circumstances over the next few years. At the end of March he circulated 'The Future of Sterling'. This paper put Britain's problems in terms of the dollar shortage, which because of the blinkered nature of American overseas investment and commercial policy he thought unlikely to end in the foreseeable future. Until the United States changed these policies, his solution was to introduce measures which would further isolate Britain and the Sterling Area from the dollar shortage rather than remove our defences against it, as did 'Robot'. By more discrimination and the development and reform of institutions such as the Sterling Area and the EPU, he sought to develop a 'two-world' international economy. There would be a 'Dollar world' and a 'Sterling world'.[24]

For my own part, I was unconvinced that this alternative plan was the answer to our problems. It seemed to me to make too much of the dollar shortage and to imply the introduction of nearly as radical a change in policy as did 'Robot', only in the opposite direction. It would have been anathema to the Americans and, by accepting we could not go on as before, it might actually play right into the hands of our opponents. The Chancellor was certainly not impressed and, like the Bank and Treasury Overseas Finance Division, thought that it would create an isolated uncompetitive trading group built around sterling. As such, it was likely to perpetuate rather than eliminate the dollar shortage.[25] When, years later, I reminded Robert Hall of his plan, he could hardly believe he had drafted it, and said that he felt ashamed of himself!

The 'Robot' controversy rumbled on through the late spring and early summer before coming to a second climax at the end of June. On the 25th of that month, the Governor of the Bank of England told the Chancellor that there would be another external crisis before the end of August unless 'Robot' was introduced at once. After consultation with senior officials, including Robert Hall, Leslie Rowan, 'Otto' Clarke, Roger Makins of the Foreign Office and myself, Butler decided the matter should be put to ministers again. He was by this stage, however, rather less keen on the plan than had been the case four months before. For some months he had not always agreed with Cobbold, and Leslie Rowan no longer inspired the same confidence in him.[26]

On Friday 27th June, Butler circulated another paper on 'Robot' to a small group of ministers. This was to be discussed the following Monday. The major difference between this version of 'Robot' and that put to the Cabinet in February was that this one contained no provision for the formal funding of the sterling balances. Instead, the Commonwealth was to be asked 'to co-operate with us in producing an agreed assessment of the extent to which the balances represent a "sight liability" upon the United Kingdom economy'. This was not thought to be hard to achieve.[27] Over the weekend Lord Cherwell and Donald

MacDougall again drafted a critique of the Chancellor's paper. This was similar to their February effort and was also circulated before the ministerial meeting. When ministers met, Butler found himself and Oliver Lyttleton isolated in their support for 'Robot'. The subject never reached full Cabinet.[28]

In July 1952 ministers turned their attention to the question of whether or not, instead of introducing 'Robot', Britain should seek to develop a 'two-world' international economy along the lines suggested by Robert Hall in March. This idea received some support from Harold Macmillan, Minister for Housing and Local Government, and Peter Thorneycroft, President of the Board of Trade. After relatively little debate, however, it was decided that a single economic world should remain the basic objective of our external economic policy and with it multilateral trading, convertibility and non-discrimination.[29]

Butler was still anxious to move to the goal set out in 'Robot' as soon as possible and, to the chagrin of Robert Hall and myself, 'Robot' was revived again in the late autumn, although this time in a diluted form known as the 'Collective Approach to Convertibility'. Under this plan we would again float and make sterling convertible, but only if the North Americans and major European countries agreed. The conditions were that France, Belgium and Holland took similar action, that a series of international rules were made to stop countries' cutting imports in order to obtain dollars, and that the American government agreed to provide some $5 billion as an exchange support fund and to cut tariffs. The sterling balances were to be left as they were.[30]

Neither Robert Hall nor I thought this plan was realistic and Cherwell thought it 'might well lead to the worst financial crisis in our history'.[31] Nevertheless, the Chancellor and Prime Minister forced it through Cabinet and it was presented to the Commonwealth Economic Conference in November 1952. Here it was greeted with some scepticism but it was decided that, provided all the preconditions were met, it should persevered with.[32] A variant whereby the IMF would provide a standby credit of $5 billion, rather than the Americans themselves being asked to provide a direct loan, was presented by Butler and Eden in Washington in March 1953.[33] Not surprisingly, however, it was turned down. The new US administration under Eisenhower told Butler and Eden that Congress would not be willing to offer dollar support to Britain of this magnitude through the IMF or in any other form, nor would it be willing to cut tariffs. Above and beyond this, they did not think Britain was ready for convertibility yet.[34] As it turned out full convertibility was not finally introduced until 1958, well after my departure from Whitehall.

The debate on the plan to make sterling convertible at a floating rate of exchange went on for more than a year and for much of that time it dominated life in the Treasury. This was particularly true of the last fortnight in February when, for a while, it seemed to those of us who opposed it that there was little hope of stopping its introduction. The arguments used during the debate were much more sophisticated than those resorted to during either the convertibility crisis of 1947 or the devaluation crisis of 1949, and the line-up of both proponents and opponents at an official level was, in many ways, surprising, given individuals' standpoints in previous reviews of external policy. At the same time, underlying the debate was an enormous amount of back-biting, distrust and hostility which took a long time to dissipate. Indeed, 'Robot' was the focal point of one of the most acrimonious policy disputes Whitehall had seen for many years.

There are a number of reasons why 'Robot' became such an emotive issue and soured so many relationships amongst economic policy-makers, but two spring immediately to mind. First, there was the way 'Robot's' proponents sought to force it through without going through the official machinery set up to analyse new policy proposals. Second, there was a general feeling amongst 'Robot's' opponents that it had become an obsession with those who supported it, to the extent that work on other vital areas of economic policy suffered.

The key figures in stopping 'Robot' were Lord Cherwell and Anthony Eden. It was in February 1952 that 'Robot' came closest to seeing the light of day, and it was at this time that these two ministers made vital contributions. Eden stepped in at a critical moment to arrest the momentum which the plan had developed and gave its opponents more time to organise. Cherwell then made the fullest possible use of this time. He talked round many of his colleagues who were previously ready to go blindly along with the Chancellor's plan and who had given little thought to its consequences. Most important of all, however, he planted seeds of doubt in the mind of his old friend, the Prime Minister.

The fact that I was in Lisbon with Anthony Eden when Herbert

Brittain and Eric Berthoud arrived seeking his agreement to the plan allowed me to intervene at a crucial time. I was able to tell him of Robert Hall's fears and of the controversy that the proposal had caused in London. I impressed upon him that I was sure that because of the far-reaching nature of the proposal and its effect on the Commonwealth and friendly foreign countries, he should not give his consent without having heard the arguments in person. This gave vital time to the opponents, particularly Lord Cherwell, to deploy their arguments against the plan. On my return to London I also helped to strengthen Robert Hall at a time when he was close to despair over the issue. Together we were then able to join forces with Donald MacDougall to help Cherwell in convincing ministers of the dangers of 'Robot'. It was hard for them to ignore the fact that two of the Chancellor's most senior advisers were against the plan.

To this day I remain convinced that the position the opponents took at the time on the subject was absolutely correct. In feeling this I am joined by Lord Roberthall, Sir Donald MacDougall and Lord Sherfield who hold the same view. I believe that the introduction of 'Robot' in 1952 would have been an economic and political disaster for this country and the world. At home, it would have led to higher inflation and unemployment and a worsening of our balance of payments difficulties. Abroad, it would have shattered the EPU, the Sterling Area and the IMF, reduced our credit worthiness and stunted the growth of world trade. In its wake we might well also have seen a return to the beggar-my-neighbour policies of the 1930s. In subsequent years 'Rab' Butler admitted to both Robert Hall and me that he was wrong about 'Robot'. In writing what I have done about 'Robot', I have been greatly helped by Donald MacDougall who allowed me to read in advance of publication the chapter on 'Robot' in his book. Reading it reminded me of the tense atmosphere in Whitehall at the time.

It is worth emphasising the record of the Bretton Woods/IMF fixed exchange rate system which 'Robot' would have destroyed. From 1945 until the early 1970s it was admirable in terms of worldwide growth, inflation and employment. It served as a key permissive factor in a twenty-five-year boom, the like of which the world had never witnessed before. Over the period, the British economy by historical standards, if not those of its competitors, also performed extremely well within this system. Growth averaged between 2.5 and 3 per cent per annum, inflation 4 per cent per annum and unemployment was, for the most part, below half a million. Could a different system, thrown up in the wake of the introduction of 'Robot', have produced similar results? I doubt it, especially bearing in mind the record of the floating exchange rate system in the last decade or so. It has not been good at either a world or a domestic level and, apart from anything else, we have lost the one infallible way in which an official was able to persuade ministers to be less profligate.

By the second half of 1952 the British balance of payments was staging a remarkable recovery. Besides the impact of government policy, this was attributable to two main factors. First, import prices fell by about half as much as they had risen in the previous cyclical phase and, second, an inventory recession led to the first fall in output since the war. Both these factors reversed the accumulation of stocks over the previous year and, as a result, the balance of payments benefited on three scores. Less imports were used, less imports were stocked, and the terms of trade improved. Even though the volume of exports sold fell by some 10 per cent over the year, Britain ended 1952 with a current account surplus of £163 million. This included a UK surplus with the non-sterling world (excluding defence aid) of £123 million and a Rest of the Sterling Area surplus with the non-sterling world of £182 million, making a total of £305 million.

By the late autumn of 1952 it was obvious to us in the Treasury that the economy was running well below full capacity. Unemployment was 100,000 higher than a year before and industrial production was also below the relevant figures for 1951. Gross Domestic Product was likely to show a 2 per cent fall over the year and, unless policy was changed, output in 1953 would fall well short of what we were capable of producing and the inducement to invest in the private sector would be impaired.[35] For the first time in the post-war era there seemed to be considerable scope for expansionary measures in the Budget, especially as trends in import prices pointed to little potential danger for the balance of payments, and the rate of growth of domestic wages and price inflation were falling.

In February 1953 the picture painted above appeared to be even clearer and, in a paper for the Budget Committee on the outlook for 1953–4, Robert Hall put the case for tax reductions. They would both add to demand and improve incentives to production.[36] It was accepted without demur in the Treasury and in the Bank of England that the general thrust of the Budget should be expansionary.[37] The question of exactly how far the tax reductions should go, however, was less clear-cut.

The dilemma facing policy-makers was that if one made a judgement on the expansion required purely on the basis of the capacity of the real economy to meet the extra demand, there would be a case for tax cuts of more than £200 million. This degree of reflation, however, would actually yield a Budget deficit. The psychological effect of running into deficit was thought to be damaging. Externally, holders of internationally mobile funds might withdraw those funds from sterling if they thought a Budget deficit was likely to be so inflationary as to bring about a devaluation. Internally, a deficit might cause entrepreneurs to postpone investment plans because of a belief that the Budget was 'unsound' and likely to lead to economic misfortune. In short, the very act of budgeting for a deficit might do as much harm as the additional spending power injected into the economy would do good.

In the end the Chancellor opted for a margin of reflation of only £150 million. He was worried that the balance of payments had only recently been in a parlous state and recognised that it would be hard politically to take back money he had recently given away if circumstances were to change for the worse again. Most important of all, however, as he told the Prime Minister, he was convinced that 'It would be unsound in itself and bad for confidence not to budget for a reasonable surplus ... say £50 million to £100 million.'[38] As such, he was following the line suggested in the original *Employment Policy* White Paper of 1944. This had stated that: 'None of the proposals contained in this paper involves deliberate planning for a deficit in the National Budget in years of subnormal activity.'[39]

Butler was by no means alone in regarding a deficit as something to be avoided if possible. Edward Bridges, Bernard Gilbert, Leslie Rowan and I all agreed with him in 1953. The officials at the Bank of England thought similarly. It was only the Economic Section which tended to see the performance of the real economy as the prime consideration in Budget policy formulation. Even so they were not supporters of reckless deficit spending.

The £150 million given away in the 1953 Budget was eventually made up of a 6d reduction in income tax, a one-sixth reduction in purchase tax, the abolition of the excess profits levy with effect from the end of the calendar year and the restoration of initial allowances.[40]

On the advice of the Economic Section and the Treasury Home Finance Department, monetary policy remained tight in early 1953. This was because monetary policy was thought to be 'an effective way of moderating an upward movement in stocks', stocks being largely financed on bank credit.[41] In fact Bank Rate was not lowered until mid-September 1953 when it was beyond doubt that interest rates in both the United States and Europe were coming down and that the balance of payments was strong enough to take the strain.

In the aftermath of the 'Robot' controversy and with the upturn in our external circumstances, economic policy-making became easier, and less and less was one looking over one's shoulder for the next crisis. 1953 was a year in which the British economy performed satisfactorily. Output expanded by 4 per cent and real incomes rose as consumer spending and Macmillan's housing drive provided the locomotive force. Unemployment fell steadily to around 350,000 and prices rose more slowly than in any other year since the war. At the same time, the increase in demand over the year did not lead to difficulties with the balance of payments. The increase in the volume of imports was substantially greater than forecast but, largely as a result of import prices falling more than expected, the current account remained in the black. The surplus for the year was £145 million, compared with £163 million in 1952. Within this total, the UK balance with the non-sterling world improved by £148 million and the balance of the Rest of the Sterling Area with the non-sterling world improved by £214 million. The dollar shortage was gradually coming to an end.

The improved performance of the British economy in 1953 allowed the relaxation of a number of controls. By the end of the year the greater part of total imports were free from control and government trading in materials had ceased, except where strategic stockpiling was concerned. The movement to a freer economy at an external level was mirrored internally. General steel licensing ended in May and restrictions on the use of other metals were phased out over the year. Consumer rationing of sweets, sugar and eggs ended; cereals and feeding-stuffs were decontrolled; controls on the prices of raw materials were almost entirely abandoned; and the licensing limits of the building industry were raised in stages.

In October 1953 the British economy was, I believed, if not in prime physical condition, back on its feet. We had full employment, price stability, acceptable growth and, most important of all, a balanced external account and a receding dollar problem. This combination of events would have been hard to envisage at the end of the war. Of course, there was still a vast number of outstanding problems for the British economy, but many of these were firmly rooted in Britain's social, political and institutional past. For me the time had come to return to private industry. I had stayed for six years when I had initially intended to stay for only one. In fact I was asked by the Prime Minister to be the first chairman of the UK Atomic Energy Authority. The prospect was too exciting to refuse, but it postponed my return to private industry for another six years.

After my departure from the Treasury, Bernard Gilbert, the man who in 1940 had played a large if unconscious part in my initial career in Whitehall, took over the CEPS and also became chairman of the Economic Planning Board. The CEPS, however, was not to last for much longer. As the war became more and more of a fading memory, and normal peacetime conditions returned, its functions were absorbed into the Treasury National Resources Group under 'Otto' Clarke.

CHAPTER FIFTEEN

Conclusions

If today we look back to the period 1947–53 with the knowledge of what has happened since then, what conclusions can we draw about the policies of that period?

I believe that the most important was the lack of appreciation of how weak economically this country had become. I do not believe that, at that time, any minister, shadow minister, official, journalist, comment-ator, or the general public truly grasped the real extent of our economic difficulties and our economic weakness.

Doubtless we were misled because we had emerged from the war on the winning side and had endured burdens which were much greater than those which we had expected to bear. We had come to believe that our industry had proved itself in wartime to be more efficient than Ger-man industry. We could see that much of the industry of continental Europe had been severely damaged by bombing, by land fighting, and by the systematic removal of plant and machinery by occupying forces. This country was the largest industrial producer in Western Europe in the years immediately following the war and, although we knew that our productivity was only about a third of that of the United States, we could still believe that we were economically a world power. Because our wartime economic management had been successful we thought we knew better than most how a country and an economy should be run. We believed that we could carry both a substantial defence pro-gramme and develop the Welfare State, the ultimate cost of which was totally miscalculated.

Today one can see that we were weak not only because we had just emerged from a war in which we alone had fought from the first day to the last, but also because we had been more highly mobilised than the Germans, the Americans, or the Japanese. Besides the obvious physical damage wrought by bombing, the war caused tremendous physical wear and tear on the capital infrastructure of the economy. Furthermore, it rendered us all but bankrupt. Britain's financial survival was made possible only by American support during the war in the form of 'Lend-Lease' and through the sale of many of our overseas assets and the running-up of enormous debts. This particular weakness was clear and certainly by 1947 was understood.

The second cause of our weakness, and one that was hardly appreciated at the time, was our long-term industrial decline over the previous eighty or ninety years. All sorts of reasons have been adduced for this relative decline. Many believe that an important cause was the assault made on industrialisation by most, if not all, the intellectual movements of the nineteenth century. Educationalists from Arnold to Morant, authors such as Scott, Trollope and Thackeray, intellectuals such as Ruskin and Morris, and artists such as some of the Pre-Raphaelites all played a part.

Underpinning all this was an educational system which for too long had embodied the triumph of the classics, religion and high moral idealism at the expense of technical and commercial training. In addition many of the most intelligent left to administer an ever-expanding empire.

This decline did not go unnoticed. Many Royal Commissions and committees of inquiry called attention to it. An expert witness before the Royal Commission on Schools Inquiry of 1867 said:

> I am sorry to say that although we may still be unsurpassed in many of our productions we no longer hold that pre-eminence which was accorded us in the Exhibition of 1851 ... it is want of industrial education in this country which prevents our manufacturers from making that progress which other nations are making. From all that I could see and learn I found both masters and foremen of other countries are more scientifically educated than our own. This however is not all. The workmen themselves of other countries have a far superior education than ours. Many of whom have none whatever.[1]

This view was to be repeated to many other commissions and committees of inquiry over the ensuing years, but little was done. Perhaps the most important reason was sheer inertia. The decline was hidden to a large extent by our privileged markets in the Empire and the momentum created by our having been the first supplier in so many fields. Consequently, many saw no need for change.

Great and indeed successful efforts were made to overcome the many effects of the war on the economy. But we were slow to come to terms with our long-term economic decline and the inevitable disappearance of the Empire.

It was a cardinal principle of British foreign policy after the war that the United States must be kept actively involved in Europe to secure both her economic recovery and her defence. In two world wars we and our allies had been rescued from defeat by US intervention. There was the ever-present fear that the United States would retreat back into isolationism and 'Fortress America'.

At the time of Korea, the Truman administration told us that they would be able to persuade Congress to agree to a major rearmament programme only if one of their allies, and that meant Britain, had a substantially increased defence programme. I thought then, and still think, that it was right to do whatever was necessary to persuade the United States to rearm on a massive scale. At the time it seemed there was a real risk of a Third World War unless the Russians were made to believe that the Americans would and could resist aggression anywhere in the world, and particularly in Europe, where it was essential they should maintain and increase their armed forces.[2] This was a view widely held in all political parties, including some prominent people on the left of the Labour Party.[3]

Whether the United States would have rearmed on the scale needed if we had adopted a smaller programme it is impossible to say but, as Attlee said at the time, we were rearming to 'prevent a war'. If such a policy is successful, and it was, inevitably it can seem that the programme was too large, but if it fails, as in the 1930s, it was obviously too small. That failure was in the minds of all concerned.

There is no doubt that the rearmament programme which we adopted did worsen our economic difficulties. The balance of payments went back into deficit and inflation greatly increased.

When the American Ambassador, Lew Douglas, first approached Attlee asking for an increase in the British rearmament programme, he said if Britain ran into balance of payments difficulties because of re-armament, the United States would provide substantial dollar aid. In fact very little was forthcoming. With hindsight, we were misguided to believe that large dollar aid would be provided. Even had we realised this, given the tense atmosphere I doubt that a very different pro-gramme would have been adopted.

Even today, when we have suffered another thirty-five years of rel-ative economic decline, we carry a disproportionately large defence burden, as Table 1 illustrates. I have no doubt that it is necessary for the European members of NATO to contribute substantially to their own defence, particularly at a time when the political gap between the United States and Europe appears to be growing greater, and there are powerful movements advocating the reduction of the American con-tribution to the defence of Europe. It is legitimate to ask whether the other, richer members of NATO should not increase their share of the burden.

Table 1   Defence Expenditure as a Percentage of GDP (at Market Prices) in NATO Countries, 1987

1	United States	6.6%
2	Greece	6.3%
3	United Kingdom	4.7%
4	Turkey	4.7%
5	France	4.0%
6	Norway	3.2%
7	Portugal	3.2%
8	Netherlands	3.1%
9	Germany	3.0%
10	Belgium	3.0%
11	Italy	2.2%
12	Denmark	2.1%
13	Canada	2.1%
14	Spain	2.0%
15	Luxembourg	1.2%

Source: *Statement on the Defence Estimates* 1988, cm 344–1

Our failure to recognise our relative economic weakness and our belief in the continuity of Empire and that we could and should continue, as Churchill put it, 'to sit at the top table', had another effect. It caused us to fail to recognise our identity with Western Europe. Our negative reaction to the overtures of Jean Monnet in 1949 and 1950 meant that the leadership of Europe, which had been ours since the defeat of Germany in 1945, was effectively passed to the French and the Germans. But, as I have said in Chapter 9, I am quite sure no British government of either party would or could have at that time taken Britain into the Coal and Steel Community on the terms proposed by the French.

Nevertheless, the economic policies of the period did enjoy some significant successes. Growth averaged a historically satisfactory rate of about 2.6 per cent, unemployment did not rise above 2 per cent of the workforce until 1952, and in 1951 it was as low as 1.3 per cent (264,000). In sharp contrast to the experience in the period following the First World War, inflation was kept to negligible proportions until rearmament for the Korean War provoked a surge in commodity prices to force it towards double figures. Even then this inflationary burst was relatively short-lived.

Various factors underpinned this success in economic policy-making. First, was the fact that for much of the time the government had the co-operation and support not only of management, but also of the trade unions and the general public. This is illustrated by the two rounds of wage-restraint secured in 1948 and 1949. This co-operation was a testament to the foresight of businessmen like Frederick Bain, Rab Sinclair, Harry Pilkington, Graham Cunningham, who were the Presidents of the Federation of British Industries during this period, and Norman Kipping, Director General of the FBI, to name only a few. Trade union leaders such as Vincent Tewson (TUC General Secretary), Tom Williamson (General and Municipal Workers Union), Will Lowther (National Union of Mineworkers) and Arthur Deakin (Transport and General Workers Union) made a major contribution. Through the medium of the Economic Planning Board and because of my general role in Whitehall, my contacts with industrialists and trade union leaders were frequent. I am convinced that the trade union leaders were very different from many of those who were to follow in the strike-ridden 1960s and 1970s and whose narrow-minded and restrictive practices were to prove such a handicap to economic growth and such an encouragement to inflation and unemployment.

The co-operation we received from both sides of industry owed much to the priority given by the governments of the time to consultation and the sympathetic communication of ideas. The powers of persuasion of Cripps and Bevin were particularly successful in securing the support of the population as a whole. These two politicians, perhaps more than most others, recognised that there were enormous problems involved in transforming the economy from a war footing to a peacetime basis, and that the general public had to be persuaded that the solution would be hard and would take a long time to implement.

Second, there was the fact that from November 1947, economic policy was run from a single department. After Dalton's resignation in November 1947, overall responsibility for economic policy was concentrated in the Treasury: first under Cripps and, subsequently, under Gaitskell and then Butler. A division of responsibility for macroeconomic policy between two departments, as existed in the first two post-war years, causes many problems. It pits minister against minister, and official against official. It often leads to a duplication of effort and confusion as to who is doing what and when. When Cripps resigned in October 1950 he said, 'We must not go back to having the Chancellor of the Exchequer separated from over-riding control in the economic field.'[4]

By all accounts the same difficulties which I witnessed during my first six months in Whitehall manifested themselves again in the mid-1960s when a Department of Economic Affairs was set up alongside the Treasury. After two experiments of this nature, one hopes that in future the same mistake will not be made again.

Third, ministers were soon convinced that to try to plan the economy in minute and elaborate detail over the long term and outside a war situation was an error. In a free democratic society, when supplies are sufficient, the price mechanism must eventually be allowed to allocate the lion's share of resources. Efforts to circumvent this process, and to retain controls for their own sake, result only in frustration on the part of the consumer and failure on the part of the government.

At the same time, however, it was important to recognise that in the situation of recovery from a war, attempts to move too soon towards the free play of market forces could, in themselves, throw up problems and were to be avoided. The attempt to adopt 'Operation Robot' in 1952 is a classic example of trying to go too far, too soon, in the direction of a free economy.

With this in mind, after 1947 planning came increasingly to be expressed in terms of the management of demand in a Keynesian macroeconomic manner in order to counterbalance the natural cyclical behaviour of the economy. This, in turn, further secured the position of the Treasury as the epicentre of economic policy-making. Direct controls were dropped as supplies became sufficient to render them unnecessary. By October 1953 few remained. The unthought-out and nebulous concept of 'democratic planning', with its implication of detailed intervention which Labour had propounded in 1945, fell by the wayside, not just when the Tories came to power in late 1951, but gradually from late 1947. The management of demand was conducted primarily through the medium of budgetary policy although, after the arrival of 'Rab' Butler in the Treasury, the use of Bank Rate and credit controls also came to play an increasing role.

Co-operation on an international level was the fourth element facilitating the change from war to peace. The world economy was dominated by the United States which took considerable responsibility for keeping the world economy in balance without dictating the domestic economic policy each country should pursue. After the convertibility crisis of 1947 the United States reluctantly accepted the continuation of Imperial Preference, the Sterling Area and discrimination against the dollar. Because we were helped by the United States to keep in external balance and because of the Marshall Plan we were able to co-operate in building a freer world economy in association with other European countries, relieved of much of the constraint on domestic policy that our weak external position would otherwise have caused.

The late 1940s and early 1950s witnessed not only the Marshall Aid Programme, but also the setting up of the OEEC (later to be expanded into the OECD), the EPU and NATO. This led to frequent and regular contact between the policy-makers of the major industrial nations and the institutionalisation of the IMF, the World Bank and the fixed exchange rate system. On these institutions were founded two decades of sustained economic growth in the Western world and a long period of world peace. They came about because of the strong and determined leadership, not to say generosity, of the United States. More recently, the international economic framework which it bred has collapsed. America's domination of the world economy was by the early 1970s unsustainable.

Today, by comparison with the 1950s and 1960s, the international economic environment is much more unstable and the problems of economic policy-making have been greatly exacerbated. The United States has now been joined by West Germany and Japan to form a triumvirate of economic super powers, but despite the Group of Seven summit meetings, real co-operation between these three nations is often lacking. In addition, recent years have seen a much greater integration of markets, the institutionalisation of a floating exchange rate system, and the build-up of massive reserves of liquidity which can be switched at a moment's notice from one country to another. If, on top of all this, we recognise that the UK economy has undergone a further forty years of relative decline since 1945, it is obvious that we can no longer pursue an independent economic policy today in the way that was possible in the immediate post-war world.

When I returned to Whitehall in 1947 there were a number of senior civil servants who had come in on a temporary basis during the war and who had elected to become established. The large influx of temporary civil servants during the war and the wartime problems had forced great changes in the attitudes and working practices of the Civil Service and the people who worked in it. Today there is much discussion about the Civil Service and whether it would work better if many more businessmen were brought in to take part in running it. I am sure there would be a advantage in recruiting a number of businessmen in senior positions in Whitehall, particularly in executive posts. There must not be too many as this would undoubtedly undermine the morale of the Civil Service, as indeed it would of any career service.

Pay in the business world tends to be substantially higher than in the Civil Service and businessmen would presumably not come for much less than they were presently receiving. If more than relatively few were to be recruited at these higher salaries this, too, would undermine morale.

Before agreeing to serve in Whitehall, however, the businessmen must realise that working in Whitehall is quite different from working in a private-sector company, no matter how large. In a private-sector company the chief executive or the board decides on policy and, in the final analysis, it is the profit and loss account that demonstrates success or failure. In Whitehall civil servants are responsible to ministers, who are responsible to Parliament. Politicians have to persuade the electorate. Politics inevitably play a major part in the economic policies that a government pursues. Civil servants must therefore become accustomed to, and be ready to work with, constant political interference. In my experience businessmen find this hard. The more successful they have been in business, the harder they seem to find it, perhaps because their strengths are largely in self-confidence and belief in the soundness of their personal judgements.

For my own part, I was fortunate. I had spent the war in a large department and by the end of the war had become its Chief Executive. When I returned to Whitehall in the spring of 1947 I knew how the machine worked. Moreover, I was well paid, I never undertook to stay for more than a year, and I had a job to which I could return whenever I chose. This allowed me much greater independence than would have been the case had I been an established civil servant. Indeed, from time to time established civil servants would ask me to lobby ministers on their behalf because of the greater influence and flexibility the unique nature of my position offered.

Not long before he died, 'Rab' Butler and I were discussing our work together in the Treasury. He said, 'the difference between you and all the others, Edwin, was that you used to burst into my room and say, "Rab, you must do this" or "Rab, you cannot do that". The others used to knock on the door and say, "Chancellor, if I may respectfully suggest ...".' This was, of course, not true but there was an element of truth in what he said. The point is that any organisation benefits from some people who are willing and can afford to stick their necks out.

The Civil Service numbers some 500,000 people and is responsible for spending many billions of pounds. Good management is essential. In a report into Control of Public Expenditure presented to Parliament in July 1961, great emphasis was placed on the importance of management in the Civil Service. The report was made by a committee consisting of some persons outside the government service and a number of senior officials. I was its chairman.[5] The report emphasised that 'it is becoming increasingly necessary for the Permanent Secretary to devote a considerable amount of personal time and attention to problems of management'. We found that permanent secretaries and senior officials tended to devote most of their time to the formulation of policy and advising ministers. This was partly because management problems can nearly always be postponed while matters of policy tend to need immediate attention. But more important were the facts that policy formulation is usually thought to be more interesting than management and that ministers preoccupied with political problems demand immediate advice.

In my experience while more emphasis is today put on the importance of management by senior civil servants, there remains the same tendency to relegate it to second place after policy formulation. The reasons for this remain the same: policy formulation is more interesting and under ministerial pressure, while management usually can be postponed. If ministers really want to see better management of the Civil Service, they will have to accept that senior officials must devote more time to management and less to their political problems. Permanent secretaries will have to accept that they must spend more time on the equally, or perhaps the more important, task of managing their departments. There must be greater acceptance of the need for more and better training for management and, what is more important, a decision to see that it is done.

All organisations can be improved. Our Civil Service, which in spite of its faults (and like all large organisations it has many), I believe to be the best civil service in the world, is no exception.

In the thirty-odd years that have elapsed since I left the Treasury I have often wondered whether I could have used my rather special position to better effect. For example, should I now reproach myself for not having persuaded the governments which I advised to abandon dreams of Empire and to throw in their lot with Europe; to have resisted after a certain point American pressure for larger and larger rearmament programmes at the time of Korea; and so on?

Perhaps I ought to have tried harder, but I would have been swimming against the tide of the time. I am virtually certain I would not have succeeded. In any case, I would not myself have been convinced that this was the right advice to offer; like everyone else my views of the future were heavily influenced by my previous experience. At any time, it is all too easy to look back at our earlier selves and to criticise them for their lack of vision of the future and their preoccupation with the past.

It is particularly easy to do this in Britain today; the speed and extent of the changes in our status since the war have been so great that many people have been unable or unwilling to grasp them. Even if advisers can, occasionally, understand such changes and see clearly the case for taking a new direction, the responsibility for acting on their advice lies with the politicians. Politicians are often the most conservative group of all; their views of the world and of what is possible are likely to reflect the prejudices and beliefs of their constituents, of their parties and of the public at large. They are also conscious of the need not to get too far ahead of public opinion. 'The Durham miners wouldn't like it', said Morrison about the Schuman Plan proposals. It is partly because public opinion tends to be more conscious of the past than far-sighted about the future that politicians can sometimes be so unrealistic, even reactionary, in their aspirations. Even a politician as moderate and as practical as Attlee wondered about the possibility of replacing the Indian Army with an African army. 'The Americans must realise that Britain is not part of Europe,' said Ernest Bevin to a senior American official. 'We must do it. It is the price we must pay to sit at the top table,' said Churchill when deciding to develop and manufacture the hydrogen bomb.

This point is well brought out by Lord Home in his letter to me in 1985: 'The British public was still too near to the glory of Empire to accept the role for Britain of just another country in Europe.'

Were we wrong to believe the United States administration when they told us that the acceptance by Congress of the very large rearmament programme proposed by the administration was crucially dependent on a proportionate increase in the British programme? My American friends tell me that this was so, but who can tell?[6]

This is also indicated by the refusal of Averell Harriman to propose in the 'Wise Men Exercise' any increase in the US rearmament programme, on the grounds that in an election year it would be unacceptable to Congress. Although in fact the United States could, more easily than any other country, undertake an increase.

We, for our part, reluctantly accepted this view because we believed that the defence of the free world and the avoidance of a Third World War depended upon a large rearmament programme by the United States.

One may regret these views and their influence, but they are part and parcel of the democratic process. Advisers to governments have to accept that process and to work within it. So although I certainly wish that some of the advice given by me and my colleagues and some of the decisions taken had been different, I try not to let myself today feel guilty about it. One purpose of this book is to put that advice and those decisions into context and to explain why we thought and acted as we did. A second purpose, though, might be to draw a constructive moral from that experience. If we look at the advice and the decisions of the 1970s and 1980s, can we identify assumptions and prejudices which will seem equally obsolete in thirty years' time? Can we learn from our history rather than being imprisoned by it? I am not altogether sure that we can, but the effort is worth making.

I end by saying that the six years I spent in the Treasury were undoubtedly the most interesting and, in many ways, the most enjoyable of my working life. I owe much to that swim over fifty years ago in the Chelsea Baths where it all began.

Source Notes

Chapter 1

1   Quoted in Richard N. Gardner, *Sterling-Dollar Diplomacy* (Oxford: Oxford University Press, 1956), p. 306.
2   Alec Cairncross, *Years of Recovery: British Economic Policy 1945–51*, (London: Methuen, 1985), p. 383.
3   PRO PREM 8/646: various notes and memoranda on the *Economic Survey for 1947*; Hugh Dalton, *High Tide and After: Memoirs 1945–60* (London: Frederick Muller, 1962); Cairncross, *Years of Recovery*, ch. 6.
4   B. Pimlott, *Hugh Dalton* (London: Jonathan Cape, 1985), ch. 27.
5   R. W. B. Clarke, *Anglo-American Collaboration in War and Peace 1942–49*, ed. Alec Cairncross (Oxford: Oxford University Press, 1982), pp. 157–9, 159–67.

Chapter 2

1   PRO CAB 124/1079: Nicholson to Bridges, 4 Mar. 1947, and E. M. Nicholson, 'Planning, Allocation and the Production Drive', 5 Mar. 1947. See also *Economic Survey for 1947*, Cmnd. 1046, para. 16.
2   PRO CAB 124/078: E. E. Bridges, 'Proposals for Strengthening the Staff for Economic Planning', 6 Mar. 1947.
3   PRO CAB 124/1091: 'Central Planning Organisation'.

4   *ibid.*

5   B. Donoughue and G. W. Jones, *Herbert Morrison: Portrait of a Politician* (London: Weidenfeld & Nicholson, 1973), ch. 30.

6   *House of Commons Debates* (Hansard), 5th series, vol. 439, col. 2150, 8 July 1947.

7   Kenneth O. Morgan, *Labour in Power 1945–51* (Oxford: Oxford University Press, 1984), ch. 8.

8   Alec Cairncross, *Years of Recovery: British Economic Policy, 1945–51* (London: Methuen, 1985), ch. 6.

9   PRO CAB 129/21: CP(47)283, Chancellor of the Exchequer and Minister for Economic Affairs (with annex by officials), 'Dollar Programme in 1948', 16 Oct. 1947.

10 PRO CAB 128/13: CM(47) 82nd Conclusions, 23 Oct. 1947.

11 PRO PREM 8/491: CM(47) 68th Conclusions, 1 Aug. 1947.

12 PRO T229/66: '1947 Investment Programmes Committee: White Paper on Investment Programme 1948'.

13 PRO T229/21: CEPS Staff Meeting, 9 Sept. 1947.

14 PRO T229/66: R. L. Hall, 'The Reduction in Investment in Relation to Inflation', undated, but early December 1947.

15 PRO T171/392: 'November 1947 Budget'.

16 PRO T229/2: 'Note for Ministers on Agricultural Programme from Point of View of London Committee', undated.

17 *ibid.*: LP(47) 23rd Conclusions, 25 July 1947.

18 *ibid.*: 'Report of Officials on Expansion of Agricultural Production in the United Kingdom', 4 Aug. 1947.

19 PRO T230/145: 'The Development of Agriculture' (Note submitted to the Food and Agriculture Committee of OEEC, undated).

20 *ibid.*

21 A. Seldon, *Churchill's Indian Summer: The Conservative Government 1951–55* (London: Hodder and Stoughton, 1981), ch. 6, pt III.

Chapter 3

1   Reference is made to my dissatisfaction in Diary of Hugh Dalton, entry for 5 Aug. 1947, British Library of Political and Economic Science.

2   R. A. Butler, *The Art of the Possible* (London: Hamish Hamilton, 1971), p. 157.

Chapter 4

1   An official committee on which Austin Robinson served was set up in July 1947 to look into 'alternative action in the event of a breakdown of the Marshall Aid initiative'. Its conclusions are contained in PRO T229/136.
2   US Department of State, *The Foreign Relations of the United States 1947. Vol. 3.* (Washington DC: State Dept, 1973), pp. 230–2: Clay to Acheson and Marshall. Henceforth referred to as *FRUS*.
3   CEEC, Vol 1: *General Report* (London: HMSO, 1947).
4   PRO PREM 8/890: EPC(48)2, Note by Secretary of State for Foreign Affairs, 'European Recovery Programme', 5 Jan. 1948.
5   PRO CAB 21/2244: R. L. Hall to Sir N. Brook, 15 July 1948.
6   CEEC, *op. cit.*

Chapter 5

1   *Economic Survey for 1949*, Cmnd. 7647, para. 3.
2   Sir Stafford Cripps, Speech at Workington in January 1949, quoted in *The Economist*, 22 Jan. 1949, p. 130.
3   Russell Jones, *Wages and Employment Policy 1936–85* (London: Allen & Unwin, 1987).
4   Cmnd. 7321.
5   *House of Commons Debates* (Hansard), 5th series, col. 1514, 6 Aug. 1947.
6   Jones, *op. cit.*
7   Cmnd. 7321.
8   TUC, *A Policy For Real Wages* (London: TUC, 1948).
9   *Statement on Personal Incomes, Cost and Prices*, para. 7.
10   PRO T171/394: B. Trend, 'Budget', 20 Jan. 1948; The Treasury, 'Special Measures to Counter Inflationary Pressure', 5 Feb. 1948.
11   PRO T171/395: E. N. Plowden to Chancellor, 31 Mar. 1948.
12   PRO CAB 134/216: EPC(48) 32nd Conclusions, 14 Sept. 1948.

13 PRO CAB 129/24: CP(48)35, Chancellor of the Exchequer, 'The 1948 Dollar Position', 5 Feb. 1948.

14 PRO PREM 8/980: EPC(48) 2nd Conclusions, 9 Jan. 1948.

15 PRO CAB 128/12: CM(48) 42nd Conclusions, 24 June 1948.

16 PRO CAB 129/28: CP(48)161, Chancellor of the Exchequer, 'Economic Consequences of Receiving No European Recovery Aid', 23 June 1948.

17 PRO CAB 128/12: CM(48) 43rd Conclusions, and CAB 134/ 316: EPC(48) 26th Conclusions, 24 June 1948.

18 Information from Professor Sir Austin Robinson. See also Donald MacDougall, *Don and Mandarin. Memoirs of an Economist* (London: John Murray, 1987), p. 72.

19 PRO CAB 134/218: EPC(48)53, European Co-operation Committee, 'European Economic Co-operation: Review of Matters Requiring Urgent Decision by Ministers', 17 June 1948.

20 PRO CAB 134/216: EPC(43) 25th Conclusions, 22 June 1948.

21 *ibid.*

22 PRO CAB 134/191: ED(48) 4th Conclusions, 12 July 1948.

23 PRO T229/29: EPB(47)6, CEPS, 'Economic Survey 1948–51', 1 Aug. 1947.

24 See PRO T230/61: 'Long-Term Economic Survey 1948–51'.

25 PRO T229/47: E. A. G. Robinson, 'Draft Economic Plan 1948– 51', 23 June 1947.

26 PRO T229/29: EPB(47) 3rd Conclusions, 7 Aug. 1947.

27 PRO T230/144: 'Long-Term Economic Survey 1948–52'.

28 PRO CAB 134/216: EPC(48) 29th Conclusions, 16 July 1948.

29 PRO CAB 134/191: ED(48) 4th Conclusions, 12 July 1948, and CAB 134/216: EPC(48) 22nd Conclusions, 14 Sept. 1948.

30 PRO CAB 134/210: EPB(48) 8th Conclusions, 1 Aug. 1948.

31 *European Co-operation: Memoranda Submitted to the OEEC Relating to Economic Affairs in the Period 1949 to 1953*, Cmnd. 7572, 1948.

32 J. Mitchell, 'Economic Planning and the Long-Term Programme', (unpublished Ph.D. thesis, University of Nottingham, 1955).

Chapter 6

1   For a fuller discussion of the wartime debate, see Alec Cairncross, *Years of Recovery: British Economic Policy, 1945–51* (London: Methuen, 1985), pp. 165–6.

2   Details of these discussions are contained in PRO T236/2398: 'Sterling-Dollar Exchange Rate – Future Policy'.

3   PRO T236/2398: R. L. Hall to E. N. Plowden, 'Sterling-Dollar Rate', 28 Mar. 1949.

4   *ibid.*

5   See PRO T232/82: 'European Exchange Rates'; and Alan S. Milward, *The Reconstruction of Western Europe, 1945–51* (London: Methuen, 1984), ch. 9.

6   J. C. R. Dow, *The Management of the British Economy, 1945–60* (Cambridge: Cambridge University Press, 1964), p. 41.

7   PRO CAB 134/222: EPC(49)63, H. Wilson-Smith and R. L. Hall, 'Report on a Visit to the United States in June 1949', Annex, 6 June 1949. Also information from Lord Roberthall.

8   B. Pimlott, *Hugh Dalton* (London: Jonathan Cape, 1985), p. 570.

9   PRO CAB 134/222: EPC(49)72, Chancellor of the Exchequer, 'The Dollar Situation', 28 June 1949.

10   Pimlott, *op. cit.*, p. 570.

11   PRO CAB 134/222: EPC(49)72, *op. cit.*

12   B. Donoughue and G. W. Jones, *Herbert Morrison: Portrait of a Politician* (London: Weidenfeld & Nicolson, 1973), p. 438.

13   PRO T269/1: R. L. Hall, 'Caliban', 16 June 1949.

14   See PRO T269/1: Cobbold to Bridges, 23 June 1949 and 14 July 1949; Cobbold to Prime Minister, 3 Aug. 1949.

15   PRO CAB 134/220: EPC(49) 27th Meeting, 7 July 1949.

16   *FRUS 1949. Vol. 4.* (Washington, DC: State Dept, 1975), pp. 799–801: Snyder to Secretary of State, 9 July 1949 and 10 July 1949.

17   Douglas Jay, *Change and Fortune. A Political Record* (London: Hutchinson, 1980), pp. 186–7.

18   *ibid.*, p. 197.

19   *ibid.*, pp. 186–7.

20   P. M. Williams, *Hugh Gaitskell* (Oxford: Oxford University Press, 1979), pp. 197–9.

21 Kenneth Harris, *Attlee* (London: Weidenfeld & Nicolson, 1982), pp. 436–8.

22 PRO PREM 8/1178 Part 1: E. E. Bridges, 'Economic Situation', 26 July 1949.

23 PRO T269/2: CM(44)53, 29 Aug. 1949.

24 PRO PREM 8/1178 Part 1: Attlee to Cripps, 5 Aug. 1949. Most of this letter is also printed in Jay, *Change and Fortune*.

25 PRO PREM 8/1178 Part 1: Wilson to Attlee, 8 Aug. 1949.

26 PRO T269/1: 'Minutes of Meeting of Ministers Held at Chequers at 5.30 p.m. on Friday 19th August 1949'.

27 PRO T269/3: CP(49)185, Chancellor of the Exchequer, 'The Economic Situation – Washington Talks', 29 Aug. 1949.

28 See PRO T230/254: 'Devaluation of Sterling'.

29 PRO T269/1: Cobbold to Bridges, 23 June 1949; Cobbold to Chancellor, 26 Aug. 1949, and G. Bolton, 'Variable Rates', 18 Aug. 1949.

30 PRO PREM 8/973: E. N. Plowden to B. Gilbert, 'De Dip 4267', 8 Sept. 1949; and B. Gilbert to E. N. Plowden, 'De Dip Rose 8,663', 12 Sept. 1949.

31 For a full report on the Washington discussions from the British point of view see PRO T230/254: ER(L) (49)274, 'Tripartite Economic Discussions, Washington, 1949', 25 Oct. 1949.

32 *FRUS 1949, op. cit.* at note 16, p. 822: Policy Planning Staff, 'Position Paper for the Discussions with the British and Canadians on Pound-Dollar Problems', 3 Sept. 1949.

33 *ibid.*, p. 847: Memorandum by Secretary of State, 19 Oct. 1949.

34 Dow, *op. cit.*, p. 43.

35 PRO T236/2777: Paris Embassy to Foreign Office, Telegram no. 978, 20 Sept. 1949.

36 Pimlott, *op. cit.*, pp. 571–3.

37 PRO CAB 129/36 Part 1: CP(49)170, Prime Minister, 'Government Expenditure', 4 Aug. 1949.

38 PRO T230/259(254): Economic Section, 'The Internal Financial Situation September 1949', 30 Sept. 1949, subsequently circulated to the Economic Policy Committee as EPC(49)102, in CAB 134/222.

39 PRO T269/4: R. L. Hall to E. N. Plowden, 13 Oct. 1949.

40 Diary of Hugh Dalton, entry for 10 Oct. 1949, British Library of

Political and Economic Science.

41 See PRO CAB 134/220: EPC(49) 32nd Meeting, 10 Oct. 1949 and EPC(49) 33rd Meeting 12(?) 1949.

42 Diary of Hugh Dalton, entry for 12 Oct. 1949; and information from Lord Roberthall.

43 See Cairncross, *Years of Recovery*, pp. 193–5 for further details.

44 *House of Commons Debates* (Hansard), 5th series, vol. 468, 26 Oct. 1949.

45 *FRUS 1949, op. cit.* at note 16, p. 850: US Ambassador in London to Secretary of State.

46 PRO T229/213: 'Draft Report of Working Party on Wages Policy and Devaluation', 6 Oct. 1949.

47 PRO CAB 128/16: CM(49)64 and 66, 7 Nov. 1949.

Chapter 7

1 PRO FO 371/77741: Ellis Rees to Berthoud, 2 Feb. 1949.

2 PRO T229/207: E. N. Plowden, 'Note of a Meeting with Monsieur Monnet', 17 Feb. 1949.

3 PRO FO 371/77933: E. N. Plowden, 'Note of Four Conversations with Monsieur Monnet between March 3rd and March 7th, 1949, at one of which was present the Chancellor of the Exchequer'.

4 *ibid.*: Briefing for E. N. Plowden, 2 Apr. 1949.

5 Richard Mayne, *The Recovery of Europe* (London: Weidenfeld & Nicolson, 1970).

6 Quoted in Jean Monnet, *Memoirs* (London: Collins, 1978), p. 280.

Chapter 8

1 Douglas Jay, *Change and Fortune. A Political Record* (London: Hutchinson, 1980), pp. 192–3.

2 *House of Commons Debates* (Hansard), 5th series, 4 Apr. 1950, cols. 1018–21.

3 *House of Commons Debates* (Hansard), 5th series, 18 Apr. 1950, col. 79.

4 Alec Cairncross, *Years of Recovery: British Economic Policy, 1945–51*

(London: Methuen, 1985), p. 421.

5   PRO PREM 8/1186: CP(50)35, Chancellor of the Exchequer, 'Budget Policy', 15 Mar. 1950.

6   PRO CAB 128/17: CM(50)12, 17 Mar. 1950.

7   PRO T232/199: Rowan to Hitchman, 14 Feb. 1950.

8   *ibid.*: Hitchman to Rowan, 21 Feb. 1950.

9   PRO CAB 134/255: EPC(50)44, Chancellor of the Exchequer, 'Fundamental Discussions with the United States', 27 Apr. 1950; Annex B, letter from J. W. Snyder, 11 Apr. 1950; and Annex C, letter from Cripps to Snyder.

10 *ibid.*: Annex A.

11 PRO T232/199: 'Fundamental Discussions with the United States'.

12 *ibid.*: Washington to Foreign Office telegram Remac No. 74, 23 June 1950 (Rowan to Wilson-Smith and Hitchman).

13 PRO CAB 134/225: EPC(50)28, Chancellor of the Exchequer, 'Proceedings at the Meetings of OEEC Ministers in Paris', 10 Feb. 1950; Annex, 'European Payments Union', 27 Jan. 1950.

14 OEEC, *A Decade of Co-operation* (Paris, OEEC, 1958), pp. 79–80.

15 PRO CAB 134/225: EPC(50)28, *op. cit.*

16 *ibid.*: EPC(50)10, Chancellor of the Exchequer, 'A New Scheme for Intra-European Payments', 7 Jan. 1950, para. 5.

17 *ibid.*, para. 4.

18 *ibid.*, para. 7.

19 For an example of Gaitskell's adaptability see P. M. Williams (ed.), *The Diary of Hugh Gaitskell 1945–1956* (London: Jonathan Cape, 1983), pp. 178–82.

20 Robert Triffin, *Europe and the Money Muddle: From Bilateralism to Near Convertibility 1947–56* (New Haven, Conn.: Yale University Press, 1957), p. 208.

Chapter 9

1   Jean Monnet, *Memoirs* (London: Collins, 1978) p. 293.

2   *ibid.*, p. 293

3   *ibid.*, pp. 294–301.

4   Quoted in Alan S. Milward, *The Reconstruction of Western Europe*

1945–51 (London: Methuen, 1984), p. 397.

5   Michael Charlton, *The Price of Victory* (London: BBC, 1983), p.92.

6   PRO T229/749: E. N. Plowden to Chancellor, 11 May 1950.

7   PRO PREM 8/1428: R. L. Hall, 'Franco-German Steel and Coal Authority', 11 May 1950.

8   *House of Commons Debates* (Hansard), 5th series, 11 May 1950, cols. 589–90.

9   PRO CAB 134/293: Meeting of Committee on Proposed Franco-German Coal and Steel Authority, 15 May 1950.

10   Record of conversation between Sir Stafford Cripps and Monsieur Monnet, 15 May 1950 [CE 2338/2141/181]; and extract from minutes of Economic Policy Committee meeting held on 16 May 1950, EPC (50) meeting.

11   Monnet, *op. cit.*, p. 306.

12   PRO T229/749: E. N. Plowden, 'Notes of a Meeting Held at the Hyde Park Hotel S.W.1 on 16th May 1950 with M. Jean Monnet, Commissioner-General of Planning for the French Government', 16 May 1950.

13   PRO CAB 134/293: Report by Plowden to Committee on Franco-German Coal and Steel Authority, 17 May 1950.

14   PRO T229/749: FG(50)2 also EPC(50)55, 'Interim Report by Officials on Proposed Franco-German Steel and Coal Authority', 19 May 1950.

15   The British note is contained in *Anglo-French Discussions Regarding French Proposals for the Western European Coal, Iron and Steel Industries, May–June 1950*, Cmnd. 7970.

16   A. Bullock, *Ernest Bevin, Foreign Secretary 1945–51* (London: Heinemann, 1984) p.779. See also Cmnd. 7970.

17   Cmnd. 7970.

18   *ibid*.

19   A translation of this is contained in PRO T229/749.

20   *ibid.*: 'Notes of Telephone Conversation between Sir Edwin Plowden and M. Monnet on 29th May 1950'.

21   See Cmnd. 7970.

22   PRO CAB 128/40: CP(50)120, 'Integration of French and German Coal and Steel Industries', 2 June 1950.

23   PRO CAB 129/17; CM(50)34, 2 June 1950.

24   PRO PREM 8/1428: Note by Prime Minister, 7 June 1950.

25 See PRO CAB 129/40; CP(50)128 covering FG(WP)(50)38, 'Integration of Western European Coal and Steel Industries', 16 June 1950; and CP(50)149, 'Integration of the European Coal and Steel Industries. Report by a Committee of Ministers', 1 July 1950.

26 Dean Acheson, *Present at the Creation* (London: Macmillan, 1970), p.385.

27 PRO FO 371/77933: Briefing for E. N. Plowden, 2 Apr. 1949.

28 PRO FO 371/77933: Briefing for E. N. Plowden, 2 Apr. 1949.

29 Information from the late Earl of Stockton and Lord Roberthall.

30 Letter from Lord Home to the author dated 11 Dec. 1985.

Chapter 10

1 PRO T237/82: 'Note of Meeting between the Prime Minister and American Ambassador on 24th July 1950', 25 July 1950.

2 PRO CAB 129/41: CP(50)181, Chancellor of the Exchequer, Defence Requirements and United States Assistance', 31 July 1950.

3 PRO CAB 128/18: CM(50)52, 1 Aug. 1950.

4 *ibid.*: CM(50)55, 4 Sept. 1950.

5 *ibid.*: CM(50)52, 1 Aug. 1950.

6 P.M. Williams, *Hugh Gaitskell* (London: Jonathan Cape, 1979), p.227; and John Campbell, *Nye Bevan* (London: Weidenfeld & Nicolson, 1987), p.193.

7 *FRUS 1950. Vol. 3* (Washington DC: State Dept., 1977), p.1673: Ambassador Douglas to Secretary of State, 9 Aug. 1950.

8 Information from Dr Lincoln Gordon.

9 PRO T237/82: W. Strath (to E. N. Plowden), 'United States Assistance for United Kingdom Defence Programme', 6 Sept. 1950.

10 PRO CAB 130/63; GEN.333/1, E. E. Bridges, 'The Economic Impact of Increased Defence Expenditure', 7 Sept. 1950.

11 *ibid.*: GEN.333, 1st Meeting, 8 Sept. 1950.

12 PRO T237/82: Sir H. Brittain to E. E. Bridges, 13 Sept. 1950; and R. W. B. Clarke to Sir H. Brittain, 13 Sept. 1950.

13 *ibid.*: Untitled memorandum by Sir Oliver Franks, 27 Sept. 1950.

14 *ibid.*: H. Gaitskell to C. R. Attlee, 3 Oct. 1950.

15 PRO T232/198: 'Record of Meeting Held in the State Department at 4.15 p.m. on 10th October 1950'.

16 P. M. Williams (ed.)., *The Diary of Hugh Gaitskell 1945–1956* (London: Jonathan Cape, 1983), 'Personal Memorandum by Gaitskell on His Visit to Washington 8–12 October 1950', p. 209.

17 PRO T232/198: 'Note of a Meeting with Harriman', 10th Oct. 1950; and 'Record of Meeting held in the State Department at 4.15 p.m. on 10th October 1950'. See also Williams *The Diary of Hugh Gaitskell*, pp.203–11.

18 PRO T232/198: Telegram BOUND 2648, Washington Embassy to Foreign Office, 2 Oct. 1950.

19 Williams, *The Diary of Hugh Gaitskell*, p. 192.

20 B. Donoughue and G. W. Jones, *Herbert Morrison: Portrait of a Politician* (London: Weidenfeld & Nicolson, 1973), p. 466.

21 B. Pimlott, *Hugh Dalton* (London Jonathan Cape, 1985), p.585; and Williams *Hugh Gaitskell*, p. 163.

22 Kenneth Harris, *Attlee* (London: Weidenfeld & Nicolson, 1982), p. 460.

23 PRO PREM 8/1200: Working Party on PM's visit to Washington, December 1950, 'General Survey of World Situation', 2 Dec. 1950.

24 *ibid.*: N. A. Robertson, 'Note of a Meeting of the Cabinet on Saturday December 9th, 1950 in the Privy Council Chamber, Ottawa, at which the Prime Minister of the United Kingdom was present', undated.

25 *ibid.*: Foreign Office, 'Present Strategic Situation. Economic Considerations', 2 Dec. 1950; also 'The Prime Minister's Visit to Washington, New York and Ottawa, December 1950', especially 'Annex on Working Party on Raw Materials'.

26 *FRUS 1950, op. cit.* at note 7, Chargé in London (Holmes) to Secretary of State, 3 Dec. 1950, p.170.

27 Williams, *The Diary of Hugh Gaitskell*, p. 224.

28 PRO PREM 8/1200: Robertson, *op. cit.* at note 24.

29 *ibid.*: 'The Prime Minister's Visit', *op. cit.*

30 PRO CAB 128/18: CM(50)85, 12 Dec. 1950.

31 *ibid.*: CM(50)87, 18 Dec. 1950.

32 *House of Commons Debates* (Hansard), 5th series, cols. 1168–70, 13 Dec. 1950.

33 PRO CAB 128/18: CM (50)87, 18 Dec. 1950.

Chapter 11

1   PRO CAB 129/44: CP(51)20, Chancellor of the Exchequer, 'Economic Implications of Defence Proposals', 19 Jan. 1951.

2   *ibid.*

3   P. M. Williams, *Hugh Gaitskell* (London: Jonathan Cape, 1979), p. 245.

4   *House of Commons Debates* (Hansard), 5th Series, 29 Jan. 1951, cols. 581, *et seq. The Prime Minister's Statement on Rearmament* was also published as Cmnd. 8146 (1951).

5   *FRUS 1951. Vol.4, Pt.1.* (Washington DC: State Dept, 1985), Ambassador in UK (Gifford) to Secretary of State, 4 Jan. 1951.

6   *ibid.*: Gifford to Secretary of State, 31 Jan. 1951.

7   *ibid.*

8   *ibid.*: Chief of ECA Mission in London (Batt) to ECA Administrator (Foster), 21 Mar. 1951; and Memorandum of Conversation by Alexander Rosenson of State Department Monetary Affairs Staff, 6 Apr. 1951.

9   PRO CAB 128/19: CM(51) 23rd Conclusions, 2 Apr. 1951.

10 PRO CAB 229/290: Economic Section, 'World Prices and Inflation', 3 Sept. 1951.

11 See above, Chapter 10.

12 PRO CAB 134/264: ES(51) 11th Meeting, 5 Apr. 1951.

13 *ibid.*: ES(51) 15th Meeting, 24 May 1951.

14 PRO T172/2033: TUC, 'Wages Policy – Draft Statement for Circulation to Affiliated Unions', 19 June 1950.

15 PRO T229/323: Synopsis of a White Paper on Full Employment, Prices and Incomes', unsigned, undated.

16 PRO T172/2033: E. E. Bridges, 'Wages Policy', 28 Apr. 1950.

17 Information from Lord Roberthall.

18 PRO T172/2033: 'Report by Chancellor on his discussions with TUC Representatives on 6 Feb. 1951'.

19 PRO CAB 134/230: EPC(51)65, Chancellor of the Exchequer,

'Economic Policy', 22 June 1951.

20 Information from Lord Roberthall.

21 PRO T171/403: Economic Section, 'The General Budgetary Problem in 1951'. 2 Feb. 1951; and BC(51) 4th Meeting, 2 Feb. 1951.

22 *House of Commons Debates* (Hansard) 5th series, cols 826 ff., 10 Apr. 1951.

23 Williams, *Hugh Gaitskell*, pp. 152–5.

24 PRO CAB 128/19: CM(51)25, 9 Apr. 1951.

25 *ibid.* and Kenneth Harris, *Attlee* (London: Weidenfeld & Nicolson, 1982), p. 477.

26 *ibid.*

27 Williams, *Hugh Gaitskell*, p.173.

28 PRO CAB 128/19: CM(51)26, 9 Apr. 1951.

29 Williams *Hugh Gaitskell*, p. 173.

30 Harris, *op. cit.*, ch. 26.

31 *Economic Survey for 1952*, Cmnd. 8509.

32 Lord Croham, interview with P. Hennessey in *The Times*, 9 Jan. 1978.

33 Alec Cairncross, *Years of Recovery: British Economic Policy, 1945–51* (London: Methuen, 1985), pp. 232–3.

34 Compare the June forecast for the balance of payments in EPC(51)65, 'Economic Policy' by the Chancellor (PRO CAB 134/230), with the September situation report by Gaitskell in CP(51)242, 'The Balance of Payments Position' (PRO CAB 129/47).

35 PRO CAB 128/20: CM (51) 58th Conclusions, 4 Sept. 1951.

36 *ibid.*; and Cairncross, *op. cit.*, p. 238.

37 PRO CAB 134/265: ES(51)43, Chief Planning Officer, 'The Balance of Payments for 1951/2', 19 June 1951.

38 Williams, *Hugh Gaitskell*, p. 188.

39 PRO CAB 128/20: CM(51) 58th Conclusions, 4 Sept. 1951.

40 PRO CAB 129/47: CP(51)251, Chancellor of the Exchequer, 'Report on Discussions in Washington and Ottawa on Balance of Payments and Defence Questions', 25 Sept. 1951, Annex 1, 'United Kingdom Balance of Payments Position' (Memorandum submitted to US Ministers).

41 *FRUS, op. cit.* at note 5, Chargé in London (Holmes) to Secretary

of State, 17 Aug. 1951 and 27th Aug. 1951 and Ambassador in UK (Gifford) to Acting Secretary of State, 4 Sept. 1951. See also PRO CAB 129/47: CP(51)251, *op. cit.*

42 P. M. Williams (ed.), *The Diary of Hugh Gaitskell 1945–1956* (London: Jonathan Cape, 1983), pp. 267 and 274 ff.

43 PRO CAB 128/20: CM(51) 60th Conclusions, 27 Sept. 1951.

44 Williams, *The Diary of Hugh Gaitskell*, p. 277; and PRO CAB 129/47: CP(51)251, *op.cit.*, Annex 2, 'Measures to Combat UK Balance of Payments Difficulties'.

45 Williams, *The Diary of Hugh Gaitskell*, pp. 282–3.

Chapter 12

1 P. M. Williams (ed.), *The Diary of Hugh Gaitskell 1945-1956* (London: Jonathan Cape, 1983), pp. 255–6.

2 PRO CAB 134/489: MAC(51)146, Note by Chairman, '"Committee of Twelve" – United Kingdom Organisation', 4 Oct. 1951.

3 Quoted in PRO CAB 134/492: MAC(51)143, Note by Chairman, 'Operation "Wise Men"', 27 Sept. 1951.

4 See *Manchester Guardian* and *Daily Herald* of 7 July 1952.

5 Eric Roll, *Crowded Hours* (London: Faber & Faber, 1985), p. 87.

6 PRO PREM 11/138: Plowden to Foreign Office, 7 Dec. 1951. Telegram No. 43321.

7 Jean Monnet, *Memoirs* (London: Collins, 1978), pp. 361–2.

8 *The Financial Relations of the United States, op.cit.*, Supreme Allied Commander Europe (Eisenhower) to RC Chairman, 14 Dec. 1951.

9 PRO CAB 134/489: MAC(51)185 (Revise), 'Brief for the Prime Minister's American Visit – The Report of the Temporary Council Committee', 22 Dec. 1951.

10 *ibid.*

11 *ibid.*

12 PRO CAB 129/49: C(52)49, Secretary of State for Foreign Affairs, 'The Report of the Temporary Council Committee of the North Atlantic Council', 19 Feb. 1952.

Chapter 13

1   A. Seldon, *Churchill's Indian Summer: The Conservative Government 1951–55* (London: Hodder & Stoughton, 1981), ch. 5, p. 154.
2   R. A. Butler, *The Art of the Possible* (London: Hamish Hamilton, 1971), p. 156.
3   Anthony Howard, *RAB. The Life of R. A. Butler* (London: Jonathan Cape, 1987), pp. 198, 199.
4   *ibid.*, pp.199 and 386 note 69.
5   Butler, *op. cit.*, p. 157.
6   PRO PREM 11/132: C(51)1, Chancellor of the Exchequer, 'The Economic Position: Analysis and Remedies', 31 Oct. 1951.
7   PRO T229/399: E. N. Plowden to W. Strath, 3 Sept. 1951.
8   Butler, *op. cit.*, p. 158.
9   *House of Commons Debates* (Hansard), 5th series, vol. 486, cols. 1128–1573.
10 See PRO PREM 11/132: 'Financial Policy 1951 and 52' and T229/402: 'Urgent Economic Problems in 1952 and 53'.
11 *ibid.*
12 J. C. R. Dow, *The Management of the British Economy, 1945–60* (Cambridge: Cambridge University Press, 1964), pp. 71–3 and Butler, *op. cit.*, pp. 157–9.
13 Russell Jones, *Wages and Employment Policy 1936–85* (London: Allen & Unwin, 1987).

Chapter 14

1   PRO T236/3240: R. W. B. Clarke, 'Convertibility', 25 Jan. 1952.
2   PRO T236/2944: G. Bolton, 'Floating Sterling', 22 Mar. 1951.
3   *ibid.*: R. W. B. Clarke, Notes ref. R.W.B.C.4276, 4280 and 4281, 21 Mar. 1951.
4   PRO T236/3245: R. L. Hall, 'Note for the Record', 4 Mar. 1952.
5   *ibid.*
6   *ibid.*
7   *ibid.*: 'A draft Memorandum by the Chancellor of the Exchequer', 21 Feb. 1952.
8   PRO T236/3240: E. E. Bridges to Sir E. Plowden, 22 Feb. 1952.

9   *ibid.*

10   *ibid.*: R. L. Hall to Sir E. Plowden, 22 Feb. 1952.

11   PRO PREM 11/138: Churchill to Eden, 22 Feb. 1962.

12   *ibid.*: Eden to Churchill, 23 Feb. 1952.

13   PRO T236/3245: R. L. Hall, *op. cit.*

14   Letter from the late Lord Robbins to the author dated 15 Dec. 1981.

15   PRO T236/3240: Cherwell to Chancellor, 25 Feb. 1952.

16   PRO T236/3242: CC(52) 23rd, 24th, 25th Conclusions, 28 and 29 Feb. 1952.

17   *ibid.*

18   *ibid.*

19   *ibid.*; Donald MacDougall, *Don and Mandarin. Memoirs of an Economist* (London: John Murray, 1987), pp. 98 and 99.

20   Alec Cairncross, *Years of Recovery: British Economic Policy 1945–51* (London: Methuen, 1985), p. 265. Also information from Lord Roberthall.

21   PRO T236/3242: CC(52) 25th Conclusions, 29 Feb. 1952.

22   PRO PREM 11/137: Cherwell to Prime Minister, 18 Mar. 1952.

23   PRO T236/3243: Treasury Overseas Finance Division, 'External Sterling Plan', 4 Apr. 1952.

24   PRO T236/3242: R. L. Hall, 'The Future of Sterling', 25 Mar. 1952.

25   PRO T236/3243: Treasury Overseas Finance Division, *op. cit.*

26   Information from Lord Roberthall.

27   PRO CAB 129/53: C(52)217, Chancellor of the Exchequer, 'External Financial Policy', 28 June 1952.

28   *ibid.*: C(52)221, Paymaster General, 'External Financial Policy', 30 June 1952.

29   PRO CAB 129/(52)196, Minister for Housing and Local Government, 'Economic Policy', 17 June 1952; and CAB 129/53: C(52)226, Minister for Housing and Local Government, 'The Great Debate: Financial and Economic Policy', 4 July 1952. See also MacDougall. *op. cit.*, p. 104.

30   PRO CAB 129/56: C(52)376, Secretary of State for Foreign Affairs, 'Commonwealth Economic Conference', 31 Sept. 1952, Annex.

31   *ibid.*: C(52)377, Paymaster-General, 'The Collective Approach to

Convertibility', 31 Oct. 1952.

32 Information from Lord Roberthall.

33 US National Archives, Department of State Decimal Files, UK
1953: British Ambassador in US (Makins) to Secretary of State
13 Feb. 1953, enclosing copy of 'A Collective Approach to Freer
Trade and Currencies', dated 10 Feb. 1953.

34 Information from Dr Lincoln Gordon.

35 PRO T171/413: BC(52)27, R. L. Hall, 'Economic Prospects for
1953', 4 Dec. 1952.

36 *ibid.*: BC(53)15, R. L. Hall, 'The Economic and Budgetary Problem in 1953', 9 Feb. 1953.

37 *ibid.*: Governor of Bank of England to E. E. Bridges and Chancellor, 25 Mar. 1953.

38 *ibid.*: Chancellor to Prime Minister, 20 Mar. 1953.

39 *Employment Policy*, Cmnd. 6527 (1944).

40 J. C. R. Dow *The Management of the British Economy, 1945–60*
(Cambridge: Cambridge University Press, 1964), p.75.

41 PRO T171/413: BC(53)15, *op. cit.*

Chapter 15

1 Royal Commission Schools Inquiry. Evidence of Edward Huth,
June 1867.

2 James Callaghan, *Times and Chance* (London: Collins, 1987),
pp. 107, 108.

3 P. M. Williams, *Hugh Gaitskell* (London: Jonathan Cape, 1979),
p. 227.

4 Alec Cairncross, *Years of Recovery. British Economic Policy 1945–51*
(London: Methuen, 1985), p. 53.

5 *Control of Public Expenditure*, Cmnd. 1432, July 1961.

6 Information from Dr Lincoln Gordon.

Dramatis Personae

Abbot, Douglas (1899–1986) war service 1915–18; elected Canadian House of Commons 1940; Minister of Defence 1945; Minister of Finance 1946–54; Justice of Supreme Court, Canada 1954–73.

Acheson, Dean (1893–1971) lawyer; Democrat; Under-Secretary of US Treasury 1933; Under-Secretary of State 1947–9; Secretary of State 1949–53.

Adenauer, Konrad (1876–1967) Lord Mayor of Cologne 1917–33 and 1945; President of Federal Republic of Germany 1950–64; Federal Chancellor 1949–63; Foreign Minister 1951–5.

Alexander, A. V. (later Lord) (1885–1965) First Lord of the Admiralty 1929–31, 1940–5 and 1945–6; Minister of Defence 1947–50; Chancellor of the Duchy of Lancaster 1950–1; Labour Leader in the House of Lords 1955–65.

Allen, Douglas (later Lord Croham) (b.1917) Board of Trade 1939; Royal Artillery 1940–5; Cabinet Office 1947; Treasury 1948–58; Ministry of Health 1958–60; Treasury 1960–4; Department of Economic Affairs; 1964–8 Permanent Secretary, Treasury 1968–74; Head of Home Civil Service and Permanent Secretary, Civil Service Department 1974–7; Chairman, BNOC 1982–5 and Guinness Peat

Group 1983–7; President, Institute for Fiscal Studies since 1979.

Alphand, Hervé (b.1907) Inspector of Finance, Ministry of Commerce 1937–8; Financial Attaché, Washington Embassy 1940–1; Director of Economic Affairs, French National Committee, London 1941–4; Ambassador to OEEC, to UN 1955–6 and to USA 1956–65; Secretary-General, Ministry of Foreign Affairs, France 1965–73.

Anderson, Sir John (later Viscount Waverley) (1882–1958) Nationalist MP, Scottish Universities 1938–50; civil servant 1917–37; Governor of Bengal 1932–7; Lord Privy Seal 1938–9; Home Secretary and Minister of Home Security 1939–40; Lord President of the Council 1940–3; Chancellor of the Exchequer 1943–5.

Armstrong, William (Lord) (1915–80) Principal Private Secretary to successive chancellors of the exchequer 1949–53; Joint Permanent Secretary, Treasury 1962–8; Head of Home Civil Service 1968–74; Chairman, Midland Bank 1976–80.

Attlee, Clement R. (Earl) (1883–1967) war service 1914–18; Labour MP, Stepney (Limehouse) 1922–50 and Walthamstow West 1950–5; Deputy Leader of the Labour Party 1931–5; Under-Secretary of State for War 1924; Chancellor of the Duchy of Lancaster 1930–1; Postmaster-General 1931; Leader of the Labour Party 1935–40; Lord Privy Seal 1940–2; Secretary of State for the Dominions 1942–4; Lord President of the Council 1943–5; Deputy Prime Minister 1942–5 Minister of Defence 1945–6; Prime Minister 1945–51; Leader of the Opposition 1951–5.

Avon, Earl of – see **Eden, Sir Anthony**

Beaverbrook, Max (later Lord) (1879–1964) born Ontario, Canada; MP in UK 1910–16; Chancellor of the Duchy of Lancaster and Minister of Information 1918; Minister of of Aircraft Production 1940–1; Minister of Supply 1941–2; Lord Privy Seal 1943–5; owner of *Daily Express*.

Berrill, Sir Kenneth (b.1920) economist; CEPS 1947–8; Lecturer in

Economics, University of Cambridge 1949–69; Fellow and Bursar of St Catherine's College, Cambridge 1949–62; Fellow and Bursar of King's College, Cambridge 1962–9; Special Adviser to Treasury 1967–9; Chairman, University Grants Committee 1969–73; Head of Government Economic Service and Chief Economic Adviser to Treasury 1973–4; head of Central Policy Review Staff 1974–80; Chairman, Securities and Investment Board 1985–8.

Berthoud, Sir Eric (b.1900) Anglo-American Oil Co. 1929–39 member, British Economic and Military Mission to Soviet Union 1941–2; Assistant Secretary 1942–4 and Under-Secretary, Ministry of Fuel and Power 1946–8; Assistant Under-Secretary, Foreign Office, 1948–52; Ambassador to Denmark 1952–6 and to Poland 1956–60.

Bevan, Aneurin (1897–1960) Labour MP, Ebbw Vale 1929–60; Minister of Health 1945–51; Minister of Labour January–April 1951; Labour Parliamentary Spokesman on the Colonies January–November 1956 and on Foreign Affairs 1956; Deputy Leader of the Labour Party 1959–60.

Bevin, Ernest (1881–1951) General Secretary, Transport and General Workers' Union 1921–40; on TUC General Council 1925–40; Labour MP, Wandsworth Central 1940–50 and Woolwich East 1950–1; Minister of Labour 1940–5; Foreign Secretary 1945–51; Lord Privy Seal for a month, 1951.

Bidault, Georges (1899–1983) history teacher and journalist; Chairman, Resistance Council France 1943; Minister for Foreign Affairs 1944–8; President of Provisional Government 1945; Premier 1958; President of Council 1950, 1951; President of Rassemblement pour l'Algérie française 1959.

Bolton, George (later Sir) (b.1900) Adviser to Bank of England 1941–8 and Executive Director Bank of England 1948–57; British Executive Director 1945–52 and alternate Governor, IMF 1952–67; Director, Bank for International Settlements 1949–57; Chairman, Bank of London & South America 1957–70.

Bridges, Sir Edward (later Lord) (1892–1969) war service 1914–18; Fellow of All Souls College, Oxford 1920; Treasury 1919–38; Secretary of the Cabinet 1938–46; Permanent Secretary, Treasury and head of Home Civil Service 1945–56.

Brittain, Herbert (later Sir) (1894–1961) war service 1915–19; entered Treasury 1919 where Third Secretary 1942–53 and Second Secretary 1953–7.

Brown, Patricia (b.1927) CEPS 1947; Treasury 1948–54; US Embassy, London 1956–9; Under-Secretary, Treasury 1959–85.

Butler, Richard Austen 'Rab' (later Lord) (1902–82) Conservative MP, Saffron Walden 1929–65; Under-Secretary of State for Foreign Affairs 1938–41; Minister of Education 1941–5; Minister of Labour 1945; Chancellor of the Exchequer 1951–5; Lord Privy Seal and Leader of the House of Commons 1955–61; Home Secretary 1957–62; First Secretary (Central Africa) 1962–3; Foreign Secretary 1963–4; Master of Trinity College, Cambridge 1965–78.

Cairncross, Alec (later Sir) (b.1911) Lecturer in Economics from 1935 and Professor of Applied Economics, University of Glasgow 1951–61; member, Central Economic Information Service 1940; member, Economic Section, War Cabinet Secretariat 1941–2; Adviser to Ministry of Aircraft Production 1942–5; Economic Adviser to Board of Trade 1946–9; Economic Adviser to HM Government 1961–4; head of Government Economic Service 1964–9; Master of St Peter's College, Oxford 1969–78; Chancellor of University of Glasgow since 1972.

Carli, Guido (b.1914) Governor of Bank of Italy 1960; Senator 1983; member, Board of Directors of Committee of Confindustria (General Confederation of Italian Industry).

Chandos, Viscount – see **Lyttleton, Oliver**

Cherwell, Lord (1886–1957) Personal Assistant to Prime Minister 1940; Paymaster-General 1942–5 and 1951–3; Professor of Experimental Philosophy, University of Oxford 1919 and 1953–6.

Churchill, Winston (later Sir) (1874–1965) Conservative MP 1900–4, Liberal MP 1904–22; President of the Board of Trade 1908–10; Home Secretary 1910–11; First Lord of the Admiralty 1911–15; Chancellor of the Duchy of Lancaster 1915; Minister of Munitions 1917; Secretary of State for War and Air 1919–21; Secretary of State for the Colonies 1922; Chancellor of the Exchequer 1924–9; First Lord of the Admiralty 1939–40; Prime Minister and Minister of Defence 1940–5 and 1951–5.

Clarke, R. W. B. 'Otto' (later Sir) (1910–75) journalist at *Financial News* in 1930s; Assistant Secretary 1945, Under-Secretary 1947, Third Secretary 1955 and Second Secretary, Treasury 1962; Permanent Secretary, Ministry of Aviation 1966; Permanent Secretary, Ministry of Technology 1966–70.

Cobbold, Cameron F. (later Lord) (1904–1987) Executive Director 1938, Deputy Governor 1945, and Governor 1949–61 of the Bank of England; Lord Chamberlain of Her Majesty's Household 1963–71.

Compton, Sir Edmund (b.1906) Assistant Secretary, Under-Secretary and Third Secretary, Treasury 1942–58; Comptroller and Auditor-General 1958–66.

Cripps, Sir Stafford (1889–1952) lawyer and King's Counsel; Labour MP Bristol East 1931–50 and South-East 1950–2; Solicitor-General 1930–1; Ambassador to USSR 1940–2; Lord Privy Seal and Leader of the House of Commons 1942; Minister of Aircraft Production 1942–5; President of the Board of Trade 1945–7; Minister of Economic Affairs 1947; Chancellor of the Exchequer 1947–50.

Croham, Lord – see **Allen, Douglas**

Crookshank, Harry (later Viscount) (1893–1961) Secretary for Mines 1935–9; Financial Secretary to the Treasury 1939–43; Postmaster-General 1943–5; Minister of Health 1951–2; Lord Privy Seal and Leader of the House of Commons 1952–5.

Cunliffe, Geoffrey (1903–78) Aluminium Controller, Ministry of Supply and Ministry of Aircraft Production 1939–41; Managing Director, British Aluminium Co. 1947–59.

Dalton, Hugh (later Lord) (1887–1962) Labour MP, Camberwell (Peckham) 1924–9 and Bishop Auckland 1929–31, 1935-59; Reader in Economics, London School of Economics 1925–36; Minister of Economic Warfare 1940–2; President of the Board of Trade 1942–5; Chancellor of the Exchequer 1945–7; Chancellor of the Duchy of Lancaster 1948–50; Minister of Planning and Local Government 1950–1.

Douglas, Lewis (1895–1974) Lecturer in History, Amherst College; Director of the Budget 1933–4; Principal and Vice-Chancellor of McGill University 1938–40; President, Mutual Life Assurance Co. 1940–7; US Ambassador, London 1947–50.

du Parcq, Lord (1880–1949) High Court Judge and Lord of Appeal in Ordinary 1946–9.

Eady, Sir Wilfred (1890–1962) Deputy Chairman 1940–1 and Chairman, Board of Customs and Excise 1941–2; Joint Second Secretary, Treasury 1942–52.

Eden, Sir Anthony (later Earl of Avon) (1897–1977) Conservative MP, Warwick and Leamington 1923–57; Under-Secretary of State for Foreign Affairs 1931–3; Lord Privy Seal 1934–5; Foreign Secretary 1935–8, 1940–5 and 1951–5; Secretary of State for the Dominions 1939–40; Secretary of State for War 1940; Leader of the House of Commons 1942–5; Deputy Prime Minister 1951–5; Prime Minister 1955–7.

Eisenhower, Dwight D. (1890–1969) US general; Commander-in-Chief, North Africa 1942 and Europe 1943–5; Army Chief of Staff 1945–8; NATO Supreme Commander 1950–2; President of the USA 1953–61.

Engledow, Sir Frank (1890–1983) war service 1914–18; Professor of

Agriculture, University of Cambridge 1930–57.

Fleming, J. Marcus (1911–76) economist; Deputy Director of Economic Section, Cabinet Office 1947–51; Visiting Professor, Columbia University, New York 1951–4; IMF 1954–76.

Franks, Sir Oliver (later Lord) (b.1905) Professor of Moral Philosophy, University of Glasgow 1937–45; civil servant, Ministry of Supply 1939–46; Permanent Secretary Ministry of Supply and MAP 1945–6; Provost of Queen's College, Oxford 1946–8; British Ambassador, Washington 1948–52; Chairman, Lloyds Bank 1954–62; Provost of Worcester College, Oxford 1962–72.

Gaitskell, Hugh (1906–63) Reader in Political Economy, University of London 1938; wartime civil servant, Ministry of Economic Warfare and Board of Trade; Labour MP, Leeds South 1945–63; Minister of Fuel and Power 1947–50; Minister of State for Economic Affairs 1950; Chancellor of the Exchequer 1950–1; Leader of the Labour Party and of the Opposition 1955–63.

Gifford, Walter (1885–1966) US Ambassador, London 1950–3.

Gilbert, Sir Bernard (1891–1957) war service 1917–18; joined Treasury 1918, where Second Secretary 1944–56.

Glenconner, Lord (1899–1983) war service 1914–18; Chairman, C. Tennant Sons & Co. 1930–67; director of many public companies.

Gordon, Lincoln (b.1913) educated Harvard and Oxford, Rhodes Scholar; government service with National Resources Planning Board and other agencies, Washington 1939–45; Consultant to State Department, ERP 1947–8; Director of Programme Division and Economic Adviser, ECA European Office 1947–51; Minister of Economic Affairs to UK 1952–5; Professor of International Economic Relations, Harvard Business School 1955–61; Ambassador to Brazil 1961–6; President of The Johns Hopkins University 1961–71; Fellow of Woodrow Wilson Center for Scholars since 1972.

Hall, Robert (later Lord Roberthall) (1901–88) educated University of Queensland and Oxford Rhodes Scholar; Fellow of Trinity College, Oxford 1927–50; Ministry of Supply 1939–46; Adviser to Board of Trade 1946–7; Director of Economic Section, Cabinet Office 1947–53; Economic Adviser to HM Government 1953–61; Advisory Director, Unilever 1961–71; Adviser to Tube Investments 1961–76; Principal of Hertford College, Oxford 1964–7; Hon. Sec. 1948–58, President 1958–60 and Vice-President of Royal Economic Society 1960–86.

Hall-Patch, Sir Edmund (1896–1975) born in Russia; sometime musician and novelist; served with Reparations Commission after First World War; Financial Adviser to Government of Siam 1920s; served in China and Japan on behalf of Treasury 1930s; seconded to Foreign Office 1944; Deputy Under-Secretary of State and leader of British Delegation to OEEC 1948; UK Executive Director, IMF and Bank for Reconstruction and Development 1952–4.

Harriman, W. Averell (1891–1986) US railway company director and merchant banker; served in Office of Production Management 1940–1; Special Representative of the US President, UK 1941; Ambassador to USSR 1943–6; Ambassador for ERP 1948–50; Special Assistant to President 1950–1; Director, Mutual Security Agency 1951–2; Chairman, Temporary Council Committee of NATO 1951–2; Governor of New York 1955–8; Assistant Secretary of State 1961–3; Under-Secretary of State 1963–5; Personal Representative of the US President in Vietnam negotiations, Paris 1968–9.

Hennessy, Patrick (later Sir) (1898–1981) war service 1914–18; member, Advisory Council, Ministry of Aircraft Production 1940–1; Chairman and Chief Executive, Ford Motor Co. 1956–68.

Hirsch, Etienne (b.1901) joined Free French forces 1940; broadcast from London to France as Commandant Bernard; Assistant Director, Free French Forces (Armaments) in, Algiers from 1943; President of French Supply Council, London 1945; head of Technical Division 1946–9, Assistant Director General 1949–52 and Director General of Commissariat Général du Plan 1952–9; member and President, Euratom 1959.

Hitchman, Sir Alan (1903–80) Private Secretary to Ernest Bevin 1940; Ministry of Labour 1926–47; Treasury 1947–51, where Deputy Chief Planning Officer 1948–9; Permanent Secretary, Ministry of Materials 1951–2; Permanent Secretary, Ministry of Agriculture 1952–9; member 1959–66 and deputy-chairman of UK Atomic Energy Authority 1964–6.

Hoffman, Paul (1891–1974) President, Studebaker Car Corporation 1935–48; Administrator, ERP 1948–50; President, Ford Foundation 1950–3; Chairman, Studebaker Car Corporation 1953–6; head of UN Special Fund 1959–65; Administrator, UN Development Programme.

Holmes, Julius (1899–1968) US Minister, US Embassy, London 1948–53.

Home of the Hirsel (formerly Earl of Home, disclaimed for life 1963) **(b.1903)** Conservative MP, South Lanark 1931–45 and Lanark 1950–1; Joint Parliamentary Under-Secretary, Foreign Office 1945; Minister of State, Scottish Office 1951–5; Secretary of State for Commonwealth Relations 1955–60; Lord President of the Council 1959–60; Secretary of State for Foreign Affairs 1960–3; Prime Minister 1963–4; Secretary of State for Foreign and Commonwealth Affairs 1970–4.

Ismay, Lord (1887–1965) Regular Army 1905–45; Chief of Staff to Minister of Defence (Winston Churchill) and Deputy Secretary, War Cabinet 1940–5; Secretary of State for Commonwealth Relations 1951–2; Secretary-General of NATO 1952–7.

Jay, Douglas (later Lord) (b.1907) Fellow of All Souls College, Oxford 1930–7 and since 1968; City Editor, *Daily Herald* 1937–41; Ministry of Supply 1941–3; Board of Trade 1943–5; Personal Assistant to the Prime Minister 1945–6; Labour MP, Battersea North 1946–74 and Wandsworth Battersea North 1974–83; Economic Secretary to the Treasury 1947–50; Financial Secretary to the Treasury 1950–1; President of the Board of Trade 1964–7.

Keynes, J. Maynard (later Lord) (1883–1946) economist; Fellow of King's College, Cambridge 1909–46; member, Committee on Finance and Industry 1929–31; member, Economic Advisory Council 1930; member, Economic Advisory Council, Committee on Economic Information 1930–9; Treasury 1914–9 and 1940–6; Editor, *Economic Journal*, 1911– 44.

Kipping, Norman (later Sir) (1901–79) Standard Telephones & Cables Ltd 1926–42; Ministry of Production 1942–5; Board of Trade 1945; Director General of Federation of British Industries 1946–65.

Knollys, Viscount (1895–1966) UK Representative, International Materials Conference and Minister, British Embassy, Washington 1951–2; Chairman, Vickers Ltd and other companies.

Lee, Sir Frank (1903–71) Colonial Office 1926–40; Treasury 1940; Ministry of Supply 1946; Permanent Secretary, Ministry of Food 1949–51; Permanent Secretary, Board of Trade 1951–9; Permanent Secretary, Treasury 1960–2; Master of Corpus Christi College, Cambridge 1962–71.

Leslie, S. C. 'Clem' (1898–1980) Australian; wartime Public Relations Officer, Home Office; head of Information Division, Treasury 1947–59.

Lyttleton, Oliver (later Viscount Chandos) (1893–1972) war service 1914–18; Conservative MP 1940–54; War Cabinet 1941–5; Colonial Secretary 1951–4; Chairman, Associated Electrical Industries 1945–51 and 1954–63; President, Institute of Directors 1954–63.

MacDougall, Sir Donald (b.1912) economist; member, Prime Minister's Statistical Branch 1940–5; Fellow of Wadham College, Oxford 1945–50; Economic Director, OEEC, Paris 1948–9; Chief Adviser, Prime Minister's Statistical Branch 1951–3; head of Government Economic Service 1969–73; Chief Economic Adviser, CBI 1973–84; President, Royal Economic Society 1972–4.

Macmillan, Harold (later Earl of Stockton) (1894–1986) war service 1914–18; Conservative MP, Stockton 1924–9 and 1931–45,

Bromley 1945–64; Parliamentary Secretary, Ministry of Supply 1940–2; Parliamentary Under-Secretary of State for the Colonies 1942; Minister Resident at Allied HQ, North-West Africa 1942–5; Secretary for Air 1945, Minister of Housing and Local Government 1951–4, Minister of Defence 1954–5; Secretary of State for Foreign Affairs 1955; Chancellor of the Exchequer 1955–7; Prime Minister 1957–63; Chancellor of University of Oxford 1960–86.

Makins, Sir Roger (later Lord Sherfield) (b.1904) Fellow of All Souls College, Oxford; joined Foreign Office 1928; Minister in Washington 1945–7; Assistant Under-Secretary 1947–8 and Deputy Under-Secretary of State, Foreign Office 1948–52; British Ambassador, Washington 1953–6; Joint Permanent Secretary, Treasury 1956–9; Chairman, UK Atomic Energy Authority 1960–4.

Marjolin, Robert (1911–86) joined de Gaulle in London 1941; head of French Supply Mission, USA 1944; Secretary-General of OEEC 1948–55; Vice-President, Commission for European Economic Community (CEEC) 1958–67; Professor of Economics, University of Paris 1967–9; director of many companies.

Marris, R. L. (b.1924), economist; CEPS 1947–50; UN, Geneva 1950–2; Fellow of King's College, Cambridge 1951–76; Lecturer in Economics 1951–72 and Reader in Economics 1972–6, University of Cambridge; Professor of Economics, University of Maryland 1976–81; Professor of Economics, Birkbeck College, London since 1981.

Maudling, Reginald (1917–79) Conservative MP, Barnet 1950–79; Economic Secretary to the Treasury 1952–5; Minister of Supply 1955–7; Paymaster-General 1957–9; President of the Board of Trade 1959–61 Colonial Secretary 1961–2; Chancellor of the Exchequer 1962–4; Home Secretary 1970–2.

Mayne Richard (b.1926) writer; Personal Assistant to Jean Monnet 1963–6; head, UK Office of EEC 1973–9.

Meade, James (b.1907) economist and Nobel Laureate; Economic

Section, Cabinet Office 1940–7, of which Director 1945–7; Professor of Economics, London School of Economics 1947–57; Professor of Economics, University of Cambridge 1957–68.

Monnet, Jean (1888–1979) French Civil Supplies Service, London 1914; French representative on Inter-Allied Maritime Commission, London during First World War; Deputy Secretary-General of League of Nations 1919–1921; returned to family brandy business, J. G. Monnet, 1921; merchant banker 1926–39; Chairman, Franco-British Economic Co-ordination Committee 1939; member, British Supply Council, Washington 1940–3; Commissioner for Armament Supplies and Reconstruction, Algiers 1943–4; General Commissioner for French Modernisation Plan 1946–52; President, High Authority of Coal and Steel Community 1952–5; Chairman, Action Committee for United States of Europe 1956–75.

Morrison, Herbert (later Lord) (1888–1965) Labour MP, Hackney South 1923–4, 1929–31 and 1935–45, Lewisham East 1945–51 and Lewisham South 1951–9; Leader of the London County Council 1934–40; Minister of Transport 1929–31; Minister of Supply 1940; Home Secretary 1940–5; Deputy Prime Minister, Lord President of the Council and Leader of the House of Commons 1945–51; Foreign Secretary 1951; Deputy Leader of the Labour Party 1945–55.

Morton, Sir Desmond (1893–1979) war service 1914–18; ADC to Field Marshal Earl Haig 1917; Director of Industrial Intelligence Centre 1930–9; Principal Assistant Secretary, Ministry of Economic Warfare 1939; Personal Assistant to the Prime Minister 1940–6.

Nicholson, Max (b.1904) head of Allocation of Tonnage Division, Ministry of War Transport 1942–5; Secretary of Office of Lord President of the Council 1945–52; member, Advisory Council on Scientific Policy 1949–64; Director General of Nature Conservancy 1952–66.

Nitze, Paul (b.1907) US businessman and diplomat; Director of Policy Planning Staff, Department of State 1950–3; Secretary of the Navy 1963–7; Deputy Secretary of Defence 1967–9; member of US delegation, Strategic Arms Limitation Talks, 1969–74; Head of US negotiating team, Arms Control Talks, Geneva 1981–4; Special Adviser to President on Arms Control Matters 1984.

Padmore, Sir Thomas (b.1909) Principal Private Secretary to Chancellor of the Exchequer 1943–5; Second Secretary, Treasury 1952–62; Permanent Secretary, Ministry of Transport 1962–8.

Petsche, Maurice (1895–1951) teacher; civil servant; Minister of Finance 1948–51.

Rickett, Sir Denis (b.1907) Principal Private Secretary to Attlee when Prime Minister 1950–1; Economic Minister and head of UK Treasury and Supply Mission, Washington 1951–4; Third Secretary, 1955–60 and Second Secretary, Treasury 1960–8; Vice-President, World Bank 1968–74.

Robbins, Lionel (later Lord) (1898–1984) War service 1916–19; member, Economic Advisory Council 1930; Professor of Economics, London School of Economics 1929–61; Director of Economic Section, War Cabinet Secretariat 1941–5; President, Royal Economic Society 1954–5; Chairman, Committee on Higher Education 1961–4; *Financial Times* 1961–70; Court of Governors, London School of Economics 1968–74.

Roberthall – see **Hall, Robert**

Robinson, Sir Austin (b.1899) war service 1917–19; economist; Fellow of Sidney Sussex College, Cambridge since 1922; Professor of Economics Cambridge 1950–65; member, Economic Section, War Cabinet Secretariat 1939–42; Economic Adviser and head of Programmes Division, Ministry of Production 1942–5; Economic Adviser to Board of Trade 1945–6; member, Central Economic Planning Staff 1947–8; Director of Economics, Ministry of Power 1967–8.

Roll, Eric (later Lord) (b.1907) Professor of Economics, University of Hull 1935–46; Deputy Head of British Food Mission to North America 1941–6; Assistant Secretary, Ministry of Food 1946–7; Under-Secretary, Treasury (member, CEPS) 1948–9; Minister, UK

Delegation to OEEC 1949; Deputy Head UK Delegation to NATO, Paris 1952; Under-Secretary, Ministry of Agriculture and Food 1953–7; Deputy Secretary 1959–61; Economic Minister, Washington 1963–4; Permanent Under-Secretary of State, Department of Economic Affairs 1964–6; Director of *The Times* 1967–80, of Bank of England 1968–77; Joint Chairman, Warburg & Co. Ltd. since 1983 (Chmn. 1974–83).

Rosenstein-Rodan, Paul (1902–85); economist; Professor of Political Economy, University College, London 1934–47; Economic Adviser to World Bank 1947–62; Professor of Economics, Massachusetts Institute of Technology, 1952–68.

Rowan, Leslie (later Sir) (1908–72) Treasury 1933; Assistant, later Principal Private Secretary to Prime Minister 1941–7; Permanent Secretary, Office of Minister for Economic Affairs 1947; Second Secretary, Treasury 1947–9 and 1951–8 when head of Overseas Finance Division; Economic Minister, British Embassy, Washington 1949–51; Managing Director 1962–7 and Chairman, Vickers Ltd. 1967–71.

Salisbury, Marquess of (1893–1972) war service 1914–18; Parliamentary Under-Secretary of State for Foreign Affairs 1935–8; Secretary of State for the Colonies 1942; Lord Privy Seal 1942–3 and 1951–2; Secretary of State for Dominion Affairs 1943–5; Lord President of the Council 1952–7.

Salter, Arthur (later Lord) (1881–1975) economist; Director of Ship Requisitioning 1917; Chairman, Allied Maritime Transport Council Executive 1918; Parlimentary Secretary to Ministry of Shipping 1939–41; Joint Parliamentary Secretary to Ministry of War Transport 1941; head of British Merchant Shipping Mission, Washington 1941–3; Minister of State for Economic Affairs 1951–2; Minister of Materials 1952–3.

Schuman, Robert (1886–1963) born in Germany, fought in German army in First World War; became a French citizen and elected a Deputy 1919; fought in the Resistance in Second World War; founder of

Mouvement Radical Populaire; Minister of Finance 1946; Prime Minister November 1947–July 1948; Foreign Minister 1948–52; Minister of Justice 1955.

Sherfield, Lord – see Makins, Sir Roger

Shinwell, Emmanuel (later Lord) (1884–1986) Labour MP, Linlithgow 1922–4 and 1928–31, Durham 1935–70; Minister of Fuel and Power 1945–7; Secretary of State for War 1947–50; Minister of Defence 1950–1; Chairman of Parliamentary Labour Party 1964–7.

Snyder, John Wesley (b. 1895) banker, Arkansas and Missouri; Director of Office of War Mobilisation and Reconversion 1945–6; Secretary of US Treasury 1946–53.

Spaak, Paul-Henri (1899–1972) Prime Minister of Belgium 1938–9; Minister of Foreign Affairs 1939–46 and 1954–7; Secretary-General of NATO 1957–61.

Spofford, Charles (b.1902) US lawyer; Deputy US Representative, North Atlantic Council and Chairman, North Atlantic Council of Deputies 1950–2; member, European Co-ordinating Committee (US) 1952.

Stanley, Oliver (1896–1950) war service 1914–18; Minister of Transport 1933–4; Minister of Labour 1934–5; President of the Board of Education 1935–7; President of the Board of Trade 1937–40; Secretary of State for War 1940; Secretary of State for the Colonies 1942–5.

Stockton, Earl of – see Macmillan, Harold

Stokes, Richard R. (1897–1957) businessman; Labour MP, Ipswich 1938–57; Minister of Works 1950–1; Minister of Materials and Lord Privy Seal 1951; Labour Spokesman on Defence 1955–6.

Strath, William (later Sir) (1906–75) Inland Revenue 1929–38; Air Ministry and Ministry of Aircraft Production 1938–45; Ministry of Supply 1945–7; Treasury 1947–55, where Deputy Chief Planning

Officer 1949–55; member, UK Atomic Energy Authority 1955–9; Permanent Secretary, Ministry of Supply 1959; Permanent Secretary, Ministry of Aviation 1959–60; Director and Deputy Chairman, Tube Investments 1972–4.

Swinton, Philip Cuncliffe-Lister (later Earl of Swinton) (1884–1972) President of the Board of Trade 1922–3, 1924–9 and 1931; Secretary of State for Air 1935–9; Minister Resident in West Africa 1942–4; Minister for Civil Aviation 1944–5; Minister of Materials 1951–2; Secretary of State for Commonwealth Relations 1952–5.

Tewson, Sir Vincent (1898–1981) Assistant General Secretary 1931–46 and General Secretary, TUC 1946–60.

Thorneycroft, Peter (later Lord) (b.1909) President of the Board of Trade 1951–7; Chancellor of the Exchequer 1957–8; Minister of Aviation 1960–2; Minister of Defence 1962–4; Chairman of the Conservative Party 1975–81.

Trend, Burke (later Lord) (1914–1987) Treasury 1937; Deputy Secretary of the Cabinet 1956–9; Third Secretary 1959–60 and Second Secretary, Treasury, 1960–2; Secretary of the Cabinet 1963–73; Rector of Lincoln College, Oxford 1973–83.

Triffin, Robert (b.1911) economist; Director of Exchange Control Division, IMF 1946-8; US Observer to Intra-European Payments, OEEC 1948–9; Adviser on Policy, Trade and Finance to ECA, Paris; US Alternate Representative on the Board of EPU 1950–1.

Truman, Harry S. (1884–1972) Democratic Senator from Missouri 1934–44; Vice-President of the USA 1945; President of the USA 1945–53.

Turner, George (later Sir) (1896–1974) war service 1914–18; War Office 1911–39; Ministry of Supply 1939–48 where Second Secretary 1942–8; Permanent Under-Secretary of State for War 1949–56.

Uri, Pierre (b.1911) economist; Economic and Financial Adviser to Commissariat Général du Plan 1947–52; Director, European Coal and Steel Community 1952–9; has subsequently held numerous academic posts.

Waverley, Lord – see **Anderson, Sir John**

Weaver, Sir Tobias (b.1911) bank clerk, Toronto 1932; teacher 1935–6; Assistant Director Education, Wilts and Essex 1936–9; Admiralty 1941; War Office 1942; Department of Education and Science 1946–73, where Deputy Secretary 1962.

Weeks, Hugh (later Sir) (b.1904) Director of Statistics, Ministry of Supply 1939–42; Director General of Statistics and Programmes and Member of Supply Council 1942–3; Head of Programmes and Planning Division, Ministry of Production 1943–5; Member CEPS and of Economic Planning Board 1947–8.

Wilson, Harold (later Lord) (b.1916) economist; Labour MP, Ormskirk 1945–50 and Huyton 1950–83; Director of Economics and Statistics, Ministry of Fuel and Power 1943–4; President of the Board of Trade 1947–51; Shadow Chancellor 1955–61; Shadow Foreign Secretary 1961–3; Leader of the Opposition 1963–4 and 1970–4; Prime Minister 1964–70 and 1974–6.

Wilson-Smith, Henry (later Sir) (1904–78) Treasury 1930–46; Permanent Secretary, Ministry of Defence 1947–8; Second Secretary, in charge of Overseas Finance Division, Treasury 1948–51; Director, Bank of England, 1964–70.

Woods, John Henry (later Sir) (1895–1962) war service 1914–18; Treasury 1920–43; Permanent Secretary, Ministry of Production 1943–5; Permanent Secretary, Board of Trade 1945–51.

Woolton, Earl (1883–1964) Minister of Food 1940–3; Minister of Reconstruction and member of War Cabinet 1943–5; Lord President of the Council 1951–2; Chancellor of the Duchy of Lancaster 1952–5; Chairman of Conservative Central Office 1946–55.

Wrangham, Cuthbert Edward (Denis) (1907–82) Air Ministry and Ministry of Aircraft Production 1939–45; Chairman, Monopolies Commission 1954–6, Power Gas Corporation 1960–1, Short Bros & Harland 1961–7, C. Tennant Sons & Co. 1967–72 and of other companies.

Zuckerman, Sir Solly (later Lord) (b.1904) educated University of Cape Town and University College Hospital, London; Professor of Anatomy, University of Birmingham 1943–68; Scientific Adviser to Combined Operations HQ 1939–46; chairman and member of many Advisory Committees including Chief Scientific Adviser to Secretary of State for Defence and to HM Government 1946–71.

Select Bibliography

UK Public Records

Cabinet Office
CAB 21 (Prime Minister's Briefs).
CAB 124 (Lord President's Files).
CAB 128 (Cabinet Conclusions).
CAB 129 (Cabinet Papers).
CAB 130 (Cabinet Committees: Minutes and Memoranda).
CAB 132 (Lord President's Committee and Sub-Committees:
       Minutes and Memoranda).
CAB 134 (Cabinet Committees: Minutes and Memoranda).
Foreign Office
FO 371.
Prime Minister's Office
PREM 8 (1945–51).
PREM 11 (1952–).
Treasury
T171 (Budget and Finance Bill Papers).
T222 (Organisation and Methods).
T228 (Trade and Industry Division).
T229 (CEPS).
T230 (Economic Section Papers).
T232 (European Economic Co-operation Committee Files).
T233 (Home Finance Files).
T234 (Home and Overseas Planning Division).

T236 (Overseas Finance Division).
T238 (Overseas Negotiations Committee).
T247 (Keynes Papers).
T267 (Treasury, Historical Memoranda).
T269 (Papers on Devaluation 1949 and Consequent Measures).

US National Archives

Decimal File 840.50 (Marshall Plan).
Decimal File 841.50 (Internal Financial Affairs of Great Britain).
Decimal File 841.51 (Internal Financial Affairs of Great Britain).

Offical Reports and Papers

United Kingdom
All published by HMSO, London.
Central Statistical Office, *Annual Abstract of Statistics.*
————, *Economic Trends.*
————, *Economic Trends Annual Supplement.*
————, *Monthly Digest of Statistics.*
————, *National Income and Expenditure (annual from 1957).*
Department of Employment, *British Labour Statistics Historical Abstract 1886–1968* (1971).
Foreign Office, *European Co-operation: Memoranda Submitted to the OEEC relating to Economic Affairs in the Period 1949–53 (Including the Long-Term Programme,* Cmnd.7572 (1948).
House of Commons, *Parliamentary Debates* (Hansard, 5th series, 1909–).
Ministry of Reconstruction, *Employment Policy,* Cmnd.6527 (1944).
Prime Minister, *Statement on the Economic Considerations affecting Relations between Employers and Employed,* Cmnd.7018 (1947).
————, *Statement on Personal Incomes, Costs and Prices* Cmnd.7321 (1948).
Treasury, *Capital Investment in 1947,* Cmnd.7268.
————, *Economic Survey* (annual 1947–53).
————, *National Income and Expenditure of the United Kingdom* (annual 1946–51).

———, *United Kingdom Balance of Payments* (annual or biennial from 1948).

International and United States

Committee of European Economic Co-operation, *Vol.1: General Report* (London: HMSO, 1947).

US Department of State, *The Foreign Relations of the United States [FRUS] 1947–53* (Washington DC: State Dept, 1973–82).

Organisation for European Economic Co-operation, *A Decade of Co-operation* (Paris: OEEC, 1958). *Europe. Third Report of the OEEC* (Paris: OEEC, 1951).

———, *European Recovery Programme. Second Report of the OEEC* (Paris: OEEC, 1950).

———, *Interim Report on the European Recovery Programme*, 3 vols. (Paris: OEEC, 1948).

———, *Report to the Economic Co-operation Administration on the First Annual Programme* (Paris: OEEC, 1949).

United Nations, *Economic Survey of Europe* (Geneva: ECE, annual from 1949).

———, *Economic Survey of Europe since the War* (Geneva: ECE, 1953).

Newspapers and Periodicals

Financial Times
The Times

Unpublished Works

Jones, Russell, 'The Wages Problem in Employment Policy 1936–48' (M.Sc. thesis, Bristol University, 1984).

Mitchell, J. 'Economic Planning and the Long-Term Programme' (unpublished Ph. D. thesis, University of Nottingham, 1955).

Peden, G. C., 'Economic Aspects of British Perceptions of Power on the Eve of the Cold War' (MS. 1984).

Rollings, N. 'The Control of Inflation 1945–53' (MS. 1984).

Sherfield, Lord, 'Clement Attlee and Foreign Policy' (The Attlee Foundation Lecture, 1986).

Other MSS.

Dalton Papers (British Library of Political and Economic Science).
Meade Papers (British Library of Political and Economic Science).

Published Works

Acheson, Dean, *Present at the Creation* (London: Macmillan, 1970).
Barnett, Correlli, *The Audit of War. The Illusion and Reality of Britain as a Great Nation* (London: Macmillan, 1986).
Beveridge, Lord (Sir William), *Full Employment in a Free Society* (London: Allen & Unwin, 1944.
Birkenhead, Lord, *The Prof. in Two World Wars: The Official Life of Professor F.A. Lindemann, Viscount Cherwell* (London: Collins, 1961).
Boyle, Lord (Sir Edward Boyle), 'The Economist in Government', in Bowers, J.K. (ed.), *Inflation, Development and Integration* (Leeds: University Press, 1979).
Brittan, S., *Steering the Economy* (Harmondsworth: Penguin, 1971).
Bullock, A. (Lord Bullock), *Ernest Bevin: Foreign Secretary 1945–51* (London: Heinemann, 1984).
Butler, R.A. (Lord Butler). *The Art of the Possible* (London: Hamish Hamilton, 1971).
Cairncross, Sir Alec (with B. Eichengreen), *Sterling in Decline* (Oxford: Black Wells, 1983).
Cairncross, Sir Alec, *Years of Recovery: British Economic Policy, 1945–51* (London: Methuen, 1985).
Callaghan, James, *Time and Chance* (London: Collins, 1987).
Campbell, John, *Nye Bevan* (London: Weidenfeld & Nicholson, 1987).
Charlton, Michael, *The Price of Victory* (London: BBC, 1983).
Clark, Colin, 'The Value of the Pound', in *Economic Journal* (1949).
Clarke, R. W. B., *Anglo-American Collaboration in War and Peace 1942–49* ed., A. K. Cairncross (Oxford: Oxford University Press, 1982).
Cooke, Colin, *The Life of Richard Stafford Cripps* (London: Hodder & Stoughton, 1957).
Dalton, Hugh (Lord Dalton), *High Tide and After: Memoirs 1945–60* (London: Frederick Muller, 1962).
Donoughue, B., and Jones, G. W., *Herbert Morrison: Portrait of a Poli-*

tician (London: Weidenfeld & Nicholson, 1973).

Dow, J. C. R., *The Management of the British Economy, 1945–60* (Cambridge: Cambridge University Press, 1964).

Feinstein. C. H., *National Income Expenditure and Output of the United Kingdom 1855–1965* (Cambridge: University Press, 1972).

Gardner, Richard N., *Sterling-Dollar Diplomacy* (Oxford: Oxford University Press, 1956).

Hancock, W. K., and Gowing, M. M., *The British War Economy*, History of the Second World War, UK Civil Series (London: HMSO, 1949).

Harris, Kenneth, *Attlee* (London: Weidenfeld & Nicolson, 1982).

Howard, Anthony, *RAB. The Life of R. A. Butler* (London: Jonathan Cape, 1987).

Jay, Douglas, *Change and Fortune. A Political Record* (London: Hutchinson, 1980).

Jay, Douglas, *Sterling. Its Use and Misuse. A Plea for Moderation* (Oxford: University Press, 1986).

Jones, Russell, *Wages and Employment Policy 1936–85* (London: Allen & Unwin, 1987).

MacDougall, Donald, *Don and Mandarin. Memoirs of an Economist* (London: John Murray, 1987).

Mayne, Richard, *The Recovery of Europe* (London: 1970).

Milward, Alan S., *The Reconstruction of Western Europe 1945–51* (London: Methuen, 1984).

Monnet, Jean, *Memoirs* (London: Collins, 1978).

Morgan, Kenneth O., *Labour in Power 1945–51* (Oxford: Oxford University Press, 1984).

Peden, G. C., 'Keynes, The Treasury and Unemployment in the Later 1930s', in *Oxford Economic Papers*, vol. 32 (March 1980).

Peden, G. C., *British Economic and Social Policy. Lloyd George to Margaret Thatcher* (Oxford: Philip Allan, 1985).

Pelling, Henry, *The Labour Governments 1945–51* (London: Macmillan, 1984).

Pimlott, B., *Hugh Dalton* (London: Jonathan Cape, 1985).

Robbins, Lord (Lionel Robbins), *The Economic Problem in Peace and War* (London: Macmillan, 1947).

Robinson, Sir Austin, 'The Economic Problems of the Transition from War to Peace: 1945–49' in *Cambridge Journal of Economics* (1986).

Roll, Eric, *Crowded Hours* (London: Faber & Faber, 1985).

Salter, Lord (Sir Arthur Salter), *Slave of the Lamp* (London: Weidenfeld & Nicholson, 1967).

Sayers, R. S., *Financial Policy 1939–45*, History of the Second World War, UK Civil Series (London: HMSO and Longmans, 1956).

Seldon, A. *Churchill's Indian Summer: The Conservative Government 1951–55* (London: Hodder & Stoughton, 1981).

Trades Union Congress, *A Policy for Real Wages* (London: TUC, 1948).

Triffin, Robert, *Europe and the Money Muddle: From Bilateralism to Near Convertibility 1947–56* (New Haven, Conn.: Yale University Press, 1957).

Williams, P. M., *Hugh Gaitskell* (London: Jonathan Cape, 1979).

Williams, P. M., (ed.) *The Diary of Hugh Gaitskell 1945–1956* (London: Jonathan Cape, 1983).

Worswick, G. D. N., and Ady , P. (eds.), *The British Economy 1945–50* (Oxford: University Press, 1952).

Worswick, G. D. N., and Ady , P. (eds.), *The British Economy in the 1950s* (Oxford: University Press, 1982).

Index